NAPOLEON III : THE MODERN EMPEROR

THE EMPEROR
From the miniature by Pommayrac.

" That he is a VERY extraordinary man with great qualities there can be NO doubt wrote Queen Victoria."

NAPOLEON III: THE MODERN EMPEROR

By

ROBERT SENCOURT

The First Empire, as compared with the Second is an episode. Both its victories and its defeats were by the side of its successors, sterile ; and colossal as were its commotions, they were, as a whole, singularly barren of proportionate and permanent result. For in general, they evoked reactions strong enough, but only strong enough, to overwhelm them. Hence the whole affair ended at Vienna in an order which was as nearly a successful " As you were " as any which has ever been issued in history. Wholly different were the consequences of the Second Empire. Its triumphs too were transitory : but its transit left both the map and the moral order of Europe revolutionized.

F. A. SIMPSON

BOOKS FOR LIBRARIES PRESS
FREEPORT, NEW YORK

First Published 1933
Reprinted 1972

INTERNATIONAL STANDARD BOOK NUMBER:
0-8369-6783-6

LIBRARY OF CONGRESS CATALOG CARD NUMBER:
71-38366

PRINTED IN THE UNITED STATES OF AMERICA
BY
NEW WORLD BOOK MANUFACTURING CO., INC.
HALLANDALE, FLORIDA 33009

PREFACE

OF all the brilliant volumes which have recently renewed the life of the Second Empire, hardly one, except in England, has dealt with the Emperor himself. Even Mr. Guedalla's famous volume—so dazzling in its display of the gifts which have made its author one of the most coveted guests at the dinner-parties of London and of Buenos Ayres, and now enriched by the best series of portraits of Napoleon III yet published—neither attempts to solve the riddle of the Emperor's policy nor to explain the qualities which led first to his success and at the last to his ruin.

The truth was that the necessary materials were not yet at Mr. Guedalla's disposal. The magisterial work of Mr. Simpson had not yet advanced as far as the second volume. And so painstaking are his methods that I, also, have been compelled to work without using his final researches, though he has most kindly placed at my disposal his criticism and his advice, even to the generosity of reading my MS. To this debt I must add my personal obligations to his colleagues, Dr. Gooch and Professor Temperley; and in France to historians equally distinguished, M. Emile Bourgeois of the Institut, M. Gabriel Hanotaux of the Académie Française, M. A. Pingaud, M. Henri Salomon, M. Jean Bourguignon. Under the guidance of these masters, I have been favoured with opportunities to make use of enormous masses of new material in the Record Office, in the Archives of the Quai d'Orsay, in which I was aided again by the extreme graciousness of the archivists, M. de Noyelle, M. Rigault, and M. de la Roche, and in the National Archives of Vienna where again the personal kindness of the officials, Professor

PREFACE

Dr. Bittner, Professor Dr. Lothar Gross, and Dr. Fritz von Rheinöhl, placed me under an immense debt and made my work a delight. In addition to these precious opportunities in National Archives, I must mention an even greater obligation, that which I owe to Evelyn, Duchess of Wellington and Sir Victor Wellesley in placing at my disposal the private correspondence of the first Earl Cowley. And next to these comes Lady Burghclere who handed over to me the correspondence of Mary, Countess of Derby (afterwards Marchioness of Salisbury) which she is arranging to publish. And yet again I am indebted to the Duke of Alba and the Duc de Morny whose archives enable me to clear up the relation of Napoleon III to two of his most intimate advisers.

Indeed, we cannot understand the Emperor till we understand both the Empress, Morny, and Morny's mother, Queen Hortense. It is only very lately that Her Imperial and Royal Highness Princess Napoleon has allowed the story of Hortense (or at least most of it) to appear, and at the same time the Italian Government have opened an enormous amount of new material in their four new volumes of the correspondence of Cavour and Nigra. I am indebted not only to Princess Napoleon and to Her Royal Highness Princess Beatrice, who has allowed me to quote from two unpublished letters of Queen Victoria, and to Her Majesty the Queen of Holland for a like graciousness in connection with the letters of Queen Sophia ; but to a large and cosmopolitan company for further help and information :—Princess Oettingen, Princess Murat, Princess de la Moskowa, Prince Poniatowski, Prince Johann zu Schwarzenberg, M. Paléologue, Ambassadeur de France ; the Marquise d'Espeuielles, Mary, Countess of Lovelace, Count Walewski, the Earl of Clarendon, the Earl

PREFACE vii

of Malmesbury, the Earl of Lytton, Earl Russell, Count Corti alle Catene, Count A. Mayendorff, Count Giovanni Pellegrini, Viscount Halifax, Baron Jean de Bourgoing, Dom Fernand Cabrol, O.S.B., and Dom Bernard du Boisrouvray, Abbots of Farnborough; Sir Eric Phipps and the staff of his Legation in Vienna, M. Philippe Roy and the staff of his Legation in Paris, Herr Werner von Schnitzler and Herr Joachim Kuhn of the German Embassy in Paris, Sir Buckston Browne, M. André Maurois, Dr. M. Parturier, Professor Fiedler, Professor de Arteaga, Dr. Engels-Janosi, M. Pierre Josserand, the late M. Quatrelles d'Epine, Major Oakley, and Miss M. D. Evans. For my illustrations I am indebted to Princess Oettingen, the Duke of Alba, M. Jean Bourguignon, Mr. Julian Sampson, M. Philippe Ninnin, and Dr. Mercier des Rochettes.

I feel bound also to make special mention of my debt to the distinguished work, left in MS. and unfortunately still unpublished, of the Benedictine monk, Dom Elie Herment, so kindly placed at my disposal by the Abbots of Farnborough.

It is a painful task to discredit the work of a predecessor. But on further study of the archives in the capitals I have visited, I feel obliged to repeat the warnings I gave in my *Empress Eugénie*, that Professor Oncken, in his book *Die Rheinpolitik von Napoleon III*, is misleading not only in his argument but in his omissions from the archives on which he was working. My own impression has been endorsed by that of two leading historians in Vienna. I am indebted to Herr Kühn for showing me that in the case of Egbert von Durckheim one finds a German historian who can treat of the Franco-Prussian question without suppressing essential evidence when found.

I feel that this is the more important because, while I have, in the course of this book, to be precise as to the unscrupulousness of Bismarck, and the great scandals of his career, I have not found in my many visits to Germany (and I know Prussia well) that he is typical of his country, for which I have always had a great affection, and the greatness of which one has so many reasons to admire. And I do not suggest that because Bismarck engineered the War of 1870 that it was wanted by any Prince in Germany, nor by the people as a whole ; nor do I forget that it was the excitement of the French that gave Bismarck his opportunity.

With great masses of new material added to the old, I have attempted, so far as one can do so before the classic work of Mr. Simpson is completed, and in the compass of one volume, to solve the secret of Napoleon III. It is not only scholars, friends, and national collections who have done so much for me. Time itself has set to work to explain this important and mysterious man in bringing into the world of fact so many of the things which he left merely as schemes. In fact, he is, I suggest, the man not of his own age so much as of ours. And whether we look at our own social problems, at the complexity of European politics to-day, or back to the years when he was called the Emperor of Europe, Napoleon III with his success and his failure, with his mysteries and his expansiveness, is, in the extraordinary complexity of his character, his adventures, his dreams, and his plots, a deeper, a more intriguing, a more significant man than we have so far conceded, or in fact than it was possible to concede with the material placed in front of me when I wrote the *Empress Eugénie*, or in contrast with her vigorous and her consistent Austrian policy. His importance rises on the horizon of our own decade. He is in every sense the modern man.   R. S.

CONTENTS

		PAGE
PREFACE	. . . .	v

I. PREPARATION

CHAP.		
I.	THE TEMPERAMENT OF QUEEN HORTENSE	13
II.	SWITZERLAND AND ITALY	27
III.	THE GROWTH OF DOGGEDNESS . . .	54
IV.	THE IMPRISONMENT AND ESCAPE . . .	78

II. POWER

V.	THE PRESIDENCY	94
VI.	THE INAUGURATION OF THE EMPIRE . .	120
VII.	THE CRIMEAN WAR	145
VIII.	APPARENT TRIUMPH	171
IX.	PLOTTING ON THE GRAND SCALE . . .	186
X.	THE WAR IN ITALY	209
XI.	THE CHURCH AND THE POPE . . .	230
XII.	THE QUESTION OF THE MAP	249
XIII.	THE NEW WORLD	268
XIV.	THE MENACE OF DISASTER	279
XV.	THE CONFIDENCE OF MILLIONS . . .	296

III. TRAGEDY

XVI.	DOWN THE ROAD TO RUIN	312
XVII.	THE EMPEROR A PRISONER	344
XVIII.	DEATH WAYLAYS	362
	LIST OF SOURCES	374
	INDEX	378

LIST OF ILLUSTRATIONS

The Emperor, from the miniature by Pommayrac.
frontispiece

	FACING PAGE
La Reine Hortense. From the bust by Bosio at Malmaison.	20
Doña Eugénia de Guzmán with her sister. From the water-colour drawing by Joseph West	66
Prince Louis Napoleon. From a photograph in the Duke of Alba's collection	84
Napoleon III. From the bust by Carpeaux at Malmaison	128
The Empress Eugénie. From an engraving by Delafosse in the possession of Mr. Julian Sampson	138
Princess Richard Metternich. From a portrait in the possession of Princess Oettingen	182
The Emperor in his bedroom at the Tuileries. From a painting in the Duke of Alba's collection	184
The Imperial Tombs at Farnborough. Photographed from the air	238
The Emperor in his last exile. From a photograph in the Duke of Alba's collection	252
The Empress Eugénie. From the bust by Carpeaux at Malmaison	266
Napoleon III. From a portrait in the possession of Dr. Mercier des Rochettes	270
The Prince Imperial. From the bust by Carpeaux at Malmaison	328
The Château de M. Amour—Bellevue, near Sedan	346
Facsimile of a letter from the Emperor to the Countess of Montijo. (Two sheets)	356

TO
MADELEINE DU BOS

Le Souvenir est l'intérêt composé
d'un capital qui se nomme amitié.   NAPOLEON III.
(An inscription at Malmaison).

PART I
PREPARATION

I

THE TEMPERAMENT OF HORTENSE

> Al hayle, my swete freende,
> Foly, and childhood wole thee sheende
> Which thee hav put in gret affray;
> Thou hast bought deere the tyme of May
> That made thyn herte merry to be,
> In yvell tyme thou wentest to see
> The jardyne whereof Ydilnesse
> Bare the keye and was maistresse.
> — CHAUCER.

I

"YOUR story," wrote the Empress Josephine to her only daughter, "is bound to mine."[1]

Hortense de Beauharnais had most of the temperament and more than the talents of her mother. She always made a deep impression on Napoleon. "Her thought is so logical," he said once, "that you might believe she had no feeling, but when you really know her, you see that it is her feelings which make her reasoning so true." For such a gifted member of the family, a great position must be found: and it appealed to both Napoleon and Josephine to marry her to his young brother Louis. Hortense did not want this marriage; Louis wanted it still less; but what did personal antipathy count in such a matter against Napoleon's decision as to what was

[1] *Mémoires Historiques de l'Impératrice Joséphine*, i, 24.

fitting? Louis's resistance was stormed like the walls of a beleaguered city. "An attack as fierce as it was surprising tore from him his consent." Such was Napoleon's own account of what happened [1]; he had failed to notice that the tactics of the battlefield are not equally apt to matters of the heart.

Louis and Hortense were in no way suited to each other. In early youth he had made a fatal mistake which left its inevitable mark upon his temper, a temper which was always rough in the grain.

"*L'esprit de Louis*," said Napoleon, "*est naturellement porté au travers, et à la bizarrerie.*" And Hortense herself was not quite a normal type. She had the impressionableness of an artistic temperament which in spite of its intuitions sometimes led her astray, and could hardly have been saved from doing so even if she had not had to play her part in an unforgettable fate.

When quite a young girl she had fallen under the mastery of Napoleon. She always remembered how, when she had first met him at a dinner in 1796, he had made her back ache as he leaned across her to talk to her mother. She remembered how he used to tease her and call her a bigot as she was preparing for her first communion till finally she met him with the retort: "You have done it yourself." And yet this insistent imperative man was he to whom she owed everything. When her royalist father, Alexandre de Beauharnais, had been guillotined in 1794, when her brother Eugène was striving to regain their property, when her widowed mother had been released from prison, it was Napoleon whose interest suddenly changed their whole position. And though he may have married her to a man she did not like, he gave that brother the crown of Holland.

[1] *Mémorial de St. Hélène.*

In 1806, therefore, young Hortense found herself a Queen : her brother had been married to a daughter of the King of Bavaria : and three of her brothers-in-law were Kings. Her two baby sons had become princes, heirs to the throne of Holland, perhaps to that of France itself.

And yet Hortense was sick and depressed in her palace at The Hague. Talented, capricious, and indulged, she was one of those women who pine for lack of sympathy, and whose nerves never allow them to charm except when they have their own way. And never was this sensitive plant in a bleaker climate than in the society of her husband. Though Queen, she lived almost as a prisoner, doting on her eldest boy. Sometimes the King would try and win him away from her by spoiling him ; sometimes he would terrify the boy with an outbreak of anger ; and the boy clung the more to the mother who always loved and never frightened him. King Louis was not pleased : the child had been born nine months, almost to a day, after his parents' wedding, and the father made it clear that he doubted whether he should expect a child so soon. The Queen had never been able to free herself from his suspicion. Men were found (such men always are to be found in courts) who for hire undertook to watch her and report her every action. The letters she wrote were opened lest they might contain any allusion to events in her husband's dominions. More than once she found her desk open and her papers upset, and if she had chosen she might have surprised the King's spies in the very act. And then she found herself forsaken even by her own courtiers who found that consideration for her did not improve their prospects. Anyone who addressed her, even though to ask a favour, would fall under suspicion : no Minister dared converse with her on even the most trifling matter. The damp air of Holland depressed her still more, and the King's only mercy was to beg her to admit an infidelity of which she proclaimed herself innocent, or to surrender his will to hers on conditions she felt intolerable. "Ah!" he seemed to say, "how I would love you if you would only admit that you have committed adultery." [1] All his protestations of affection came back to that. He was in fact both insistent and insulting; and Hortense did not know which mood grated on her most. At last her life was so hard, and seemed so hopeless that often, as she gazed out at the sea from one of her houses on the shore, and saw the English vessels blockading the harbours, she wished that they might transport invaders to make her a prisoner.[2]

In these hard days her baby fell ill, and died, and deep in sadness she escaped in 1807 to the valley of Cauterets where the stream flashes white beneath the wild gloom of the Pyrenees. "The image of desolation," she wrote, "is pleasing to one whose only hope is death and, indeed, I never felt at ease except when sitting beside those ghastly chasms," [3] for danger suggested death, and death seemed her only way of escape; her attendants were anxious at finding how often she evaded them to wander in places that seemed odd for her to choose.

Then letters came: they came among others from her husband. He, too, it appears, was in the depths of melancholy, mourning the child; he, too, was anxious about her, and yet after all he had said to her he dared not return. But her heart softened towards him: she accepted his explanation that it

[1] *Mémoires de la Reine Hortense*, i, 286.
[2] Madame de Rémusat. *Mémoires*, ch. xviii.
[3] *Mémoires de la Reine Hortense*, i, 298.

was his love which had made him cruel to her, and his plea that only her company could renew his interest in his work. So she invited him to join her at Cauterets ; yet, when he arrived, she felt, as she had always felt with him, restless and uncomfortable ; she began to doubt whether she had the strength to make the sacrifice she had so long promised, and he left without saying more to her than that he shared her sorrow for their dead child. He had arrived at Cauterets on 3rd June, 1807 ; he left Hortense there on 6th July.[1]

A little later she received a letter from the Emperor : " They tell me," he wrote, " that you no longer care for anything : that you are indifferent every way ; and I notice that you are silent. That isn't right, Hortense ; it isn't what you promised. Your boy was everything to you : so your mother and I are nothing ! If I had been at Malmaison, I would have shared your suffering, but I would have wished also that you would give something of yourself to those who love you best.

" Good-bye, my child, pluck up your spirits : one must cultivate resignation. Keep well so as to fulfil all your duties. My wife is quite sad to think about you ; don't make her more sorrowful still.

Your affectionate father,
Napoleon." [2]

Such was the Emperor's counsel : and yet Hortense still hesitated. They gave her *Corinne* to read—it had just appeared—but she could not be bothered with *Corinne*.[3] She made a trip over the Pyrenees to Spain ;

---

[1] *Mémoires de la Reine Hortense*, i, 299.
[2] *Lettres de Napoléon à Joséphine*, pp. 118, 130.
[3] Cochelet : *Napoléon et la Reine Hortense*, p. 80.

she quite shocked the Marquis de Castellane by the fatiguing expedition she made by mountain tracks to Gavarnie [1]; she went hunting, and then one day the sound of the horn loosened the restraint of her stifled grief, and she burst into tears, and so her heart began to cure of its long paralysis.[2] But she did not meet King Louis till 12th August at Toulouse. "I was not sufficiently mistress of myself," wrote Hortense, "to hide from my husband the sort of repugnance, and even the fear which our reunion aroused in me. But he wanted it so keenly, and seemed in fact to be so happy with it, that our reconciliation took place at Toulouse." "On 12th August," wrote Louis to Hortense, "I met you again at Toulouse, and threw myself into your arms."[3] The date is of the greatest interest, because it was on 20th April, 1808, that in Paris, in the Rue Cerutti, Hortense gave birth to her third son, Louis Napoleon, who in course of time became the heir of the Emperor. A very little calculation shows that there is a space not of nine months, but of eight months and eight days, between the dates. Nine months before the birth of this child, Hortense, often escaping from her suite to soothe her melancholy, was still at Cauterets.

The prince, it is to be supposed, was born before his time. He was so weak at his birth that they washed him in wine, and wrapped him in cotton wool, and the accoucheur, according to Hortense, said to one of the attendants: "It is the right of Queens to bring forth their children before the time: they never count like other women."[4] King Louis accepted his paternity, but not without reawakening his old

---

[1] L. Perez: *Figures du Temps Passé*, p. 396.
[2] *Revue des Deux Mondes*, 1st August, 1914.
[3] A. Duboscq: *Louis Bonaparte en Hollande*, p. 228.
[4] *Mémoires de la Reine Hortense*, ii, 3.

suspicions of Hortense. On what they were founded we shall see.

Napoleon, then preparing to invade Spain, ordered a salute for the child's birth, and cannons boomed far along the Pyrenees. In spite of this, relations between the King and Queen of Holland were certainly not improved. "You treat a young wife," Napoleon had written to Louis the year before, "as if you were drilling a regiment"[1]; but as we have seen, this was not quite true. Louis seemed to love her, although he doubted her. And no wonder he was in a quandary. Hortense had been brought up by a mother whose conduct gave good cause for scandal, and certainly she herself was not a woman without temperament; without being beautiful (for even apart from her false teeth, her nose was too long, her mouth too large, and her lips too thick for beauty) she had in her rather Jewish face, and about her whole person, at once a distinction and a languor that immediately tempted men to think that she was among the most amorous of women. She was full of kindness, full of affection; and, although there was something impressive in her bearing, the alluring grace of her movements, the friendly ease of her manner, the soft fire in her eyes, and in fact the sweetness of her whole expression invited men to gallantry, and some to dalliance.[2] The very tone of her voice—it was sweet, clear, tremulous—announced that there was something luscious in her temperament. Her husband, therefore, was not unreasonable if he thought that a heart, which never thrilled to his own, must have had an exchange of tenderness with others;

---

[1] Blanchard Jerrold: *Napoleon III*, i, 431.
[2] Tascher de la Pagerie: *Mon Séjour aux Tuileries*, i, 8, 9. V. Masuyer: *Revue des Deux Mondes*, 1st August, 1914.

in fact, the time of October, 1811, was not so far off; and in that month Hortense gave birth to a child who, beyond any possibility of doubt, had a father other than her husband. And soon after her third son Louis was born, the intimacy of Hortense at Fontainebleau with Decazes set everyone gossiping afresh. In after days, a rumour ran through Paris that Napoleon had insisted on his brother keeping quiet and that never again would he be asked to accept a child that was not his.[1] There is, of course, no evidence that another man was intimate with her [2] before her reconciliation with Louis Bonaparte at Toulouse. Napoleon, whose own name was mentioned, was nowhere in the neighbourhood. There was much talk about the Dutch Admiral Verhuell: but the Maréchal de Castellane makes it clear that, at that time, she hardly knew the Admiral. There was, it is true, the other Verhuell, the diplomat, but no one has suggested that this brother was intimate with the Queen. As for M. Decazes, the secretary to the Emperor's mother, who paid her so much court at Fontainebleau, what he suggested in a talk years afterwards with Thiers evidently disposes of this question; in all cases where there is no evidence, gossip, especially about a woman so temperamental as Hortense, cannot count as history. Louis Napoleon takes his place among the Bonapartes as the Emperor's nephew, Hortense's husband's son.[3]

But even when one has disposed of that question, one must remember that it is not easy for children to grow up when they know that, even if their own

[1] F. H. Wellesley: *The Paris Embassy*, p. 208.
[2] A. Lebey: *Strasbourg et Boulogne*.
[3] Lebey: *Strasbourg et Boulogne*, pp. 2-14. F. A. Simpson: *Rise of Louis Napoleon*, Appendix B.

LA REINE HORTENSE BY BOSCO
From the bust at Malmaison.

"There was something luscious in her temperament."

birth is regular, their mother has often stooped to folly. Napoleon blamed Hortense for making Louis unsatisfactory as a King, so unsatisfactory that in fact Napoleon soon ordered him to abdicate. " However contrary and unbearable Louis was, he loved her," said the Emperor, " and in such a case, with such great interests at stake, every woman should be enough mistress of herself to overcome her feelings and should know how in her turn to give love. If she had been able to control herself, she would have been spared the sorrow of her recent lawsuits, she would have lived a happier life, she would have followed her husband to Holland ; Louis would not have run away from Holland : I should not have found myself compelled to bring his kingdom back into the French Empire, which contributed to my ruin in Europe : and many things would have turned out differently." [1]

But Hortense suffered misfortunes for which Napoleon should be the last to blame her. She not only saw her husband dethroned : she saw her mother divorced ; she was induced to act as a maid of honour to Marie Louise, and it was Marie Louise who was godmother to her third son, when at last, on 5th November, 1810, he was ceremonially baptized at Fontainebleau with the eldest son of the Duc de Bassano and over twenty children of the Imperial nobility.[2] For Hortense, like her brother Eugène, had fallen in with the Emperor's suggestion that, in staying at his side, they would shield their mother from scandal, and persuade Europe that Josephine had freely sacrificed her great position in the interests of France, and of posterity.

But meanwhile King Louis, who, like his brother

---

[1] Jerrold : op. cit., i, 65.
[2] *Moniteur*, 5th November, 1810.

Joseph, identified himself with the cause of his subjects, had found his capital invaded by French troops. On 1st July, 1810, therefore, he abdicated and fled, and Hortense found herself regent of his kingdom. Leaving her baby son in Paris, she hurried to The Hague ; there she heard that her husband was taking the waters at Toeplitz in Bohemia ; but with her repugnance for his person as acute as ever, she decided not to join him, and before long she was back in Paris at the Imperial court. She was present in the Tuileries on 20th March, 1811, when the King of Rome was born, and was a witness of Napoleon's discomfiture at the sight of his young wife's torture in bringing the child to birth. She took the baby for Josephine to see.

And yet, at that very time, although she had not seen her husband since 1807, men noticed that her figure was already suggesting another pregnancy. An A.D.C. of the Emperor's, Charles de Flahault, himself an illegitimate son of Talleyrand, had passed the winter at Bourbonne, while Hortense took the waters a few miles up the Paris road at Aix-les-Bains. There she again repaired after the birth of Marie Louise's son. Flahault danced beautifully, he was an accomplished musician, he sat his horse to perfection ; he had, like Hortense, a rich sweet voice, and a personal charm. His good looks, his distinguished manners, a peculiar attraction in the way he moved, made Hortense feel that in this young man she found her ideal ; and what a delightful change he seemed from these Corsican Bonapartes who were so rude and hostile to her ! When in October she hurried back to Paris, she was announced to be in a critical condition, and during her journey she felt extremely ill. She had had lung trouble ; but perhaps her attendants guessed why the trouble seemed suddenly to move from her chest to her abdomen. And she screamed aloud. " But one does not die of lumbago," said her friend, Madame de Souza. On 22nd October, 1811, the registrar noted the birth of a boy who was credited with a certain Monsieur Demorny for his father who had married Louise Fleury and lived at Villetaneuse.

But Hortense did not allow her life to be disturbed by events of this kind : she was still firm in the Emperor's favour. Endowed by him with the domain of St. Leu, and an income of two million francs, she still lived in the Court with the style and title of Queen. Her brother was still the Viceroy of Italy, though his royal wife could no longer think that her seed would be kings ; and her young cousin Stéphanie was living happily in Baden as Grand Duchess. And there was always something about Hortense which enabled her to make great play with her advantages. " You are the only woman I fear," Caroline Murat said to her. " I can't tell you how you do it ; but you have the secret of attracting and rousing interest . . . everyone is drawn to you." [1]

Napoleon had always paid a great attention to her sons, even after the birth of the King of Rome. They were brought up in all the strictness of imperial etiquette : often they went to breakfast with the Emperor : sometimes they were allowed to visit at Malmaison a grandmother who always spoiled them, though she flattered herself that she did not. As for Louis, he was a witty and an expansive child. " How I love beautiful nature," he would say in a walk, or to his French tutor, " I should like to be able to change myself into a bird : then I would fly away when you come." He once wrote a letter to his

---

[1] *Mémoires de la Reine Hortense*, ii, 10.

mother which she always treasured. " Little Mummy," it began, " Oui-oui has tumbled on his gee-gee : Oui-oui not hurt himself : he is very fond of Mummy. Oui-oui." And if we were to seek a motto for the striking career the boy grew up to have, this letter shows that as a young child, he was the father of his manhood. He often tumbled from his hobby-horse, he admitted it and was frank ; but he never allowed that he was hurt ; and a good-natured affection seemed always melting from his heart : how much of his story is there : " *Oui-oui a fait pouf dans le dada : Oui-oui n'a pas bobo : il aime Maman beaucoup à cœur.*" [1]

2

It was during the exile at Elba that Louis, then seven years old, saw his mother accept from Louis XVIII the title of Duchess, and he listened to her shriek as she stood beside Josephine's vault in the ugly little church at Rueil. It was to the quiet château at Malmaison that the King William of Prussia and the Czar Alexander came and each kissed the little boys while they talked to Hortense. It was at Malmaison that little Louis took a ring, crept on tip-toe up to the Czar, put the ring on an imperial finger and rushed away. His mother called him back, and insisted on him telling what he had done : what ring it was. " Uncle Eugène gave it me," the child answered ; " It's the only thing I have, and I wanted to give it to the Emperor Alexander who is good to Mamma." And the Czar put the ring on his watch-chain. " The most attractive thing about him," wrote Hortense of her new admirer,

[1] Jerrold : *Napoleon III*, i, 93, 94.

"is that his character craves for affection."[1] Indeed, being an impressionable man, the Emperor Alexander was by no means irresponsive to the subtle charms of Queen Hortense, who soon exchanged the reserve with which she had at first greeted him[2] for the *abandon familier rempli de séduction* by which she played upon the hearts of men. He did not care for the King whom he regarded as "the most fatuous of *émigrés*".[3] Very often, therefore, he left the Bourbon court at the Tuileries for the society of the mistress of St. Leu who could put such ardour into affection, such unreserve into intimacy, such sweetness into both.[4] And on one of these occasions Hortense added to her claims on him by actually saving his life. Taking young Louis by the hand, he was looking at the waterworks at Marly and strayed so near to one of the great wheels that, in another moment, he would have been caught by it and dashed to pieces,[5] if Hortense had not rushed forward with a scream and rescued him.

In the intervals of entertaining King and Emperor, she had other things with which to busy herself. First there was the estate of Josephine to settle and the pensions to pay to her dependents. And then her mind was occupied with something which touched her even more closely. Her husband, now no longer King of Holland but mere Count of St. Leu, had settled finally at Florence, and demanded possession of the children whom at one time he had been so shy of claiming as his own. Hortense refused to give them up. He then brought a lawsuit against her,

[1] *Mémoires de la Reine Hortense*, ii, 221.
[2] "*Je me laissai aller à plus d'abandon*," ii, 222.
[3] A. Sorel : *L'Europe et la Révolution Française*, viii, 343.
[4] V. Masuyer : *Revue des Deux Mondes*, 1st August, 1914.
[5] Cochelet : *Napoléon et la Reine Hortense*.

a lawsuit which dragged on until March of 1815.[1] The Court decided that she must give up her elder son. Two days before the decree was announced, she heard that the Emperor and King of Elba had left his island realm and landed at Golfe Juan. In Paris, there was a preliminary yell of execration, but before many days the Bourbon King had fled. The Emperor was back, had received his nephews at the Tuileries, greeted them with an affection which was none the less warm for the absence of Marie Louise and her son, started for Waterloo, and returned in dismay. And a legend survived that, as Napoleon patted the head of Louis, he prophesied that the boy would grow up to have a good heart, and a lofty soul, and be perhaps the hope of the imperial race.[2] Could the Emperor, in those critical days have divined that within twenty years his own son Napoleon, and Hortense's son Napoleon, and even Eugene de Beauharnais—once his heir—would all be dead, and leave Louis as his lineal claimant?

[1] Jerrold : op. cit., i, 89.
[2] Renault : *Histoire du Prince Louis Napoléon*. This is denied categorically by Froehner, *Revue des Deux Mondes*. 1st April, 1931.

II
FROM SWITZERLAND TO ITALY

> a glorious time,
> A happy time it was ; triumphant looks
> Were then the common language of all eyes ;
> As if awaked from sleep, the nations hailed
> Their great expectancy : the pipe of war
> Was then a spirit-stirring sound indeed,
> A blackbird's whistling in a budding grove,
> We left the Swiss exulting in the fate
> Of their near neighbours.
> WORDSWORTH : *The Prelude*, vi, 756–766.

> There go the pale blue shadows so light and showery,
> Over sharp Apuan peaks rathe mists unwreathe,
> Almond trees wake, and the paven yards grow flowery,
> Crocuses cry from the earth at the joy to breathe ;
> There through the deep-caved gateways of haughty turreted
> Arno—house-laden bridges of strutted stalls—
> Mighty white oxen drag in the jars rich-spirited,
> Grazing the narrow walls.
> TRENCH : *The Vine*.

I

AFTER the Hundred Days, Queen Hortense (for the Duchess of St. Leu never forgot that an international treaty confirmed her in the royal title) was not allowed to stay anywhere near Paris. She went first to Dijon where, as her carriage drove through the street, she was greeted with the cry "*Dehors la Bonaparte*".[1] It was an Austrian officer, Gerbner, who saved her, alike from royalists at Dijon and Imperialists at Dôle,[2] and she had no sooner arrived at a hotel in Geneva than she received

[1] Jerrold : *Napoleon III*, i, 104.
[2] *Mémoires de la Reine Hortense*.

orders to leave Switzerland ; she dared not return to France for she had been ordered away from there by a Prussian general. " But I can't throw myself into the lake," [1] said Hortense, and the Austrians again pleaded for her protection while she consulted with Madame Mère who, also under an Austrian guard, was on her way to Rome. And at last she obtained permission to take the waters at Aix-les-Bains. She was not long at Aix before a message arrived from Louis to claim her eldest son.

The boy was torn from his mother's arms : and the younger child was left alone in tears. " I did not know how to calm the grief of my dear Prince Louis," said his nurse. " He grieved so much at the departure of his brother that he fell ill of jaundice." [2] Hortense, too, reeled from the blow. Her strength left her ; two or three times a day she fainted, and then she fell into a sort of stupor. At last they gave her orders to move on, and at the beginning of December of that fateful year—it was still 1815—she was on her way to Constance. She was insulted at Geneva : near Fribourg she was actually arrested : at Prégny, they told her they thought King Joseph was with her in woman's disguise and searched her bedroom ; and even when she arrived at Constance, she found a letter from her cousin Stéphanie telling her that the Grand Duke dared not allow her to tarry within his frontiers. But at this point Hortense defied her hunters, refused to budge from the inn, looked for a house and found one where the Rhine issues from the Untersee. "At last I have a little home," she said[3] : but just a year later, finding that the Swiss were

---

[1] Jerrold : i, 105. [2] Cochelet : *Mémoires*.
[3] Jerrold : op. cit., i, 107–110.

feeling kinder to her, she bought a country house, Arenenberg, a few miles away on the Swiss side, and there looking down over delightful scenery on to the Untersee she made her home until her death.

2

The boy who found a home at Arenenberg could hardly have been the same as the one who left St. Leu. At the age when instinct is giving place to reason, all his habits had been changed, and his confidence had been shaken in everything around him. Up to that time, he had longed only to escape from etiquette, and even to have to flee from palaces had been a welcome change ; but now he was uprooted ; one adventure had followed another ; the restrained regular life was exchanged for movement and danger, then solitude had descended upon his house. He was at eight years old his mother's only darling, and with the bad tutor engaged for him, he had every inclination to keep the brain of a namby-pamby.

Temperamentally, he was a sensitive and quiet child : while his brother was full of spirits and energy he hung back in wonder. If his brother said he wanted to be a soldier, Louis's fancy was taken by the boy who sold violets at the gate of the Tuileries ; he was shy, moody, highly strung. At times, after those strange adventures, he would wake from a nightmare with a scream, and remain in panic at the thought of being left alone with the night. And yet, like most quiet children, he saw everything, and brought out his shrewd remarks, which were treasured by his nurse, as at an earlier age they had been repeated by Josephine. But for the most part, he remained dreamy, perhaps in his mild way he even seemed a little sulky. The tutor his mother engaged for him, the Abbé Bertrand, did not make him learn, and all we know of his rule was that his pupil hung up in his bedroom two pictures, one of a boy kneeling, while he listened to a reprimand before the birch descended, another which showed a schoolboy stealing the instrument of pain while his preceptor's back was turned.[1] King Louis heard that this old Abbé was a scandal of incompetence, and then Hortense engaged a young man, Philippe Le Bas. "All they have been able to teach him," said Le Bas of his pupil, " is to detest his work, and about a great many things he knows almost nothing." [2] But the new tutor knew just how to manage the boy. The day was mapped out from dawn to dusk. Hours for walking, in his tutor's company, and a swimming lesson made the only break in a régime of Latin, Greek, German, grammar, geography, and history. The change effected by this regular discipline was immense. Le Bas soon won his pupil's heart; he saw that the boy had a temperament at once warm and tractable, that he hung on his tutor's good opinion, that he had a good brain and above all an excellent heart. There was energy, too, for the Prince was keen on his games. Le Bas demanded this energy not only for play but for work. Conscientious, methodical, and sympathetic, he effected in five months an immense change. His pupil was still rather lazy, and would often be lost in a dream. But, changing discipline for comradeship at the same time as he maintained his firm pressure, Le Bas made Louis Napoleon into a scholar.

[1] Jerrold, i, 112, 113.
[2] Le Bas : *Jeunesse de Napoléon III*, p. 42.

Hortense had heard that there was an excellent school at Augsburg : Augsburg was near enough to Munich and, therefore, to her brother Eugène to have a special appeal to her, and while she settled the endless international formalities of her stay at Arenenberg, she spent at Augsburg the greater part of her time. Young Louis made great progress there and in a short time was fourth in his class. By the end of 1821, he had become a model of diligence and, wrote the tutor, "*j'ai toujours à me louer de son aimable et bon caractère.*" [1] He had taste, he had imagination, and at fourteen and a half he had got on so well as to be reading Homer, Plutarch, and Virgil.

The tutor had come at an opportune moment. It was not only that the boy, in the most thorough sense, had been spoilt. It was not only that his instincts were like unbaked dough. Although Hortense believed that she never spoilt her children, nothing could in fact have been worse for a boy than her impulsive, temperamental influence, the influence of a woman romantic enough to capture a boy's imagination and enlist his loyalties till his admiration and his instincts were turned aside into a highly coloured realm where wrongs and memories and caprice seemed so important that everything else —and especially work—tasted insipid and was inevitably rejected as contemptible. She was, as her name implied, an artificial flower, and any boy who was removed from the strong and sickly scents of the garden of Hortense to the open field and mountain side would have been happier and healthier. But the change in the young Prince was more than ever necessary because in him there were unusual qualities.

There are two types of nervous sensitiveness in

[1] Le Bas : op. cit.

boys; in one, the romantic temperament is diffuse and always remains so; but in another, the change into virility wholly transforms the physical nature and with it the character. The new tonic in the blood hardens the mind, the muscles, and even the bones. The whole youth, both in his energy and in his susceptibilities, assumes the temperament of strongly marked sex. It was just as this change was about to develop that the firm discipline, the youthful energy, and the methodical normality of Le Bas transformed the nervous child into a vigorous and capable youth. The boy had inherited the warm blood, the romantic dash, and the abnormal impressionability of his mother, but with it were the qualities Le Bas brought out : a sustained energy, a cool daring, and a taciturn reserve. These at times revived the old story of a Dutch origin and kept turning his eyes back to the cool efficiency peculiar to the organizing genius of the portentous Emperor whom the Prince had on one side of his family as the brother of his father Louis, and on the other as the husband of his grandmother Josephine. It was as a boy at Augsburg that he heard of the Emperor's death. His tutor gave him three days' holiday, and invited him to dinner, and soon the spirits of youth revived as they always do when the demands of mourning allow a reaction.[1] " *Mais cela n'empêche pas*," wrote the boy, " *que je n'aie une haine éternelle contre les Anglais.*" And if he was tempted to do wrong, turned the devil to flight with the name of Bonaparte.

The last years of the great man's life were not the least important for his nephew. The meteor, kindling in its flight, had hastened across the astonished earth,

[1] Le Bas : *Jeunesse de Napoléon III*, p. 95.

a power at once of revolution and of settlement, of war and order. Behind the flashing suddenness of decision was his instinct for organization, behind the fierce ambition the sense of noble human principles founded on justice. And from the cloud of his tragic exile, the life, which seemed lost in waste or hid behind despair, spoke once again, and words of greater power; the meteor was lost in a lightning flash, but it was made one with thunder. And men, who could not resist the magnetism of his sudden glory, learnt to associate it with a noble dream of good fortune for France and Europe.

Such was the task which in those hard years the fallen Emperor set himself—and perhaps it was the most important of his tasks. For of all the changes he had made in Europe, already none remained. His dynasties had been swept away; the ancient frontiers were renewed and at the end he saw France with more constricted frontiers than she had before his advent. He had left her indeed a centralized administration, a code of law, a compromise between nationalism and fraternity, with a new emphasis on the native aristocracy of gifted men, and a saving assertion of the prestige of power, because he fully recognized the need of both religion and authority. But he himself, and all his family, like his plans for Europe, were lost in the gathered blackness of his last defeat, until the thunders that came forth from it gathered strength, and spoke to human hearts with a human voice of promises yet to be fulfilled. The one secret of his government, he said, had been " endlessly to kindle ambition, curiosity, and hope ". " Yes," he said again, " I have stolen fire from heaven as a gift to France." He alone, wrote Hortense, " understood then all the good he had wanted to do." [1]

[1] *Reine Hortense en* 1831, p. 3.

Therefore he hung, a cloud—now rimmed with flame from fire beyond, now dissolving in the radiance of light—over the ripening organism of Hortense's son, inspiring him with the power to conjure evil with the name of Bonaparte. Was not young Louis also a child of renown, one with the days when the giant was on the earth and had come in unto the daughters of men? His mother taught him so as she talked to him and sang. There was a thrill in those songs of hers, which echoed Mozart and Cimarosa in tunes which were at once sprightly and languorous, courtly and popular.

Mon fils, she sang in one of them,

> Mon fils, objet de nobles vœux,
> Prends de ta mère
> Cette bannière
> Qu'illustrèrent tous tes aïeux,
> Qu'illustrèrent tous tes aïeux.
> Et fidèle à la roi promise,
> Dans les revers
> Dans les revers
> Redis, l'honneur est ma devise,
> Autre ne sers,
> Autre ne sers.
>
> Pour l'honneur ne redoute rien !
> Que l'indigence
> Que l'innocence
> Trouvent en toi leur vrai soutien,
> Trouvent en toi leur vrai soutien.
> Et jusqu'au terme de ta vie,
> Je t'en requiers
> Je t'en requiers,
> Ton Dieu, ta belle, ta patrie
> Autre ne sers
> Autre ne sers.

Whether she was encouraged by an astrologer, or by the sybil's voice of her own genius, Hortense gave her son her own assurance that he, too, was to see his eagles soar above the lightning. The hours of trained exercise and drilled mind would be interrupted by—

> The song and the silence in the heart
> Which in part are prophecies and in part
> Are longings wild and vain.

He also was to be in some way the agent of this vast beneficence. Already he felt his heart glow to sympathy with suffering, and his nerves quickened his hardening muscles to knightly impulses. He was once seen to come in from a walk in his shirt sleeves because, like St. Martin, he had given away his coat; at another time he gave a tramp his boots and waistcoat; he had made friends with all the poor about; yet another time he dived into the Rhine from the bridge at Mannheim to gratify the whim of a cousin for a floating flower. Parquin, an old fire-eater of the Empire who had married Louise Cochelet, took the Prince aside, and with endless recollections of the great campaigns breathed fire into him. Yet young Louis still talked little, and seemed always in a dream: a dream that may have been of greatness, but which some thought was a preoccupation with the thoughts and memories of his amours: for at Arenenberg there was always a fresh story about his love affairs, and there was a general idea that he was like Youth in the *Romance of the Rose* [1] " of herte wylde and thought volage ". The rumour was supported by his thick lips and the coarse virility of the Beauharnais nose; and by the fact that though short and by no means handsome,

---

[1] Tascher de la Pagerie, *Mon Séjour aux Tuileries*, i, 10. "*Il avait un cœur aussi volage que tendre.*"

he did attract. In his curious eyes there was nothing precise or definite. They were at times foxy, at others fishy in their dullness, the most penetrating observer could surprise neither an emotion nor a hope in them. Then with their awakening came a captivating change ; for though they were of a pale blue, and the lids hung heavy over them, as though they were occupied with an inward vision rather than with the scene before them, they would suddenly light up with a light so warm, and an expression of such affectionate friendliness, that they focussed the magnetic power which quietly emanated from his whole figure. Both in their impenetrability and in their radiance they were a power.[1]

And at other times, his sentimental, melancholy mood would be exchanged for the shock of a dive or a hard swim, or for the balanced steadiness of eye and nerve with his gun. For, though a swim generally puts an expert marksman out, he more than once carried off the prize in the shooting competitions of the Canton. He excelled no less as a rider than a shot : in fact, he looked always quite at his best on horseback ; so in his interchange of moodiness with goodwill, of silence with expansiveness, of voluptuous intrigue with hard exercise, the youth showed that his temperament was one of those —well known to nerve specialists—in which emotional sensibility sways between extremes like a swing. He was now up, now down. At one moment he conceived himself the man chosen by Providence to recreate Europe ; at another he was paralysed by his melancholy languor. His parentage weighed heavy on him. His father was, as Napoleon said, an eccentric and unstable type, whose capricious

---

[1] Beaumont-Vassy : *Mémoires Secrets*, p. 348.

moods were made the more extreme by contracting syphilis in one of the earliest adventures of his youth. Such was the doubtful inheritance he offered to his sons; and Hortense exaggerated it, first by her own innate impressionability of nerves, which was, as we have seen, at its worst in the months before Louis was born; and secondly, by the influence of her presence which Louis loved. And yet his overbalanced figure, with the big head and the short legs, was already marked as that of one who was growing up to be a man to reckon with. The tendency to idleness had gone, and with it all traces of the milksop; we have seen what took their place: the thick hooked nose, the pulsing heart, the studious mind, the stiffened sinews. And amorous excess, though it does not breed sacrifice, goes often with more generous impulses than uprightness.

Hortense dismissed Le Bas in 1827, and Louis spent a year doing an artillery course at Thun. It was a virile training, and he found himself quite able to share the strenuous life of the young Swiss, to climb up, comrade of the antelope and eagle,

"To the side of the icy fountain,
Where the gentians blue-bell'd blow,"

and to cover thirty or forty miles in a day of mountain air.[1] Above him the white peaks of the Oberland lifted the solid earth into the blue of heaven, and over darkening gulfs held the evening glow against appearing stars. Here was indeed joy for one who loved the beauty of nature [2]: but what more distinctly marked the trend of his mind at this time was his essay on the defence of Switzerland. Although not

[1] *Reine Hortense en* 1831, p. 21.
[2] Jerrold, i, 135-8.

published until 1833, it was prepared at Thun. It shows first a thorough grasp of strategical principles, a great talent for organization, a power to incorporate detail, and above all the Prince's strong sense of a unified command as the only means of attaining success in war. His views, although strongly in sympathy with Swiss republicanism, were naturally dominated by the sense of authority inherent in his position, and dominant in every consideration of the great genius to whom he owed the cloud of glory which trailed from his name, and was the spring within him of both ardour and ambition. In July, 1830, the fall of Charles X gave him new hopes for both his family and for France.

Louis Philippe, in founding the July monarchy, effected a compromise with the principles which Napoleon had preached from St. Helena; and naturally the hopes of all the Bonapartes rose high. Might there not be again a home for them in France? That was the thought which was uppermost in the minds of all of them, and which kept the heart and nerves of Louis restless with great surmise through the whole summer at the Thunersee. By the beginning of September, however, they knew that Louis Philippe had in turn enforced the old proscription against them. " Renewed by those we held to be our friends," wrote Hortense, " it strikes us to the heart."

She did, indeed, receive a message through the Grand Duchess Stéphanie, that she could return to France herself, if without her family. Scorning such an offer, she started for Italy with her son in November, 1830. She had engaged a new companion, Valérie Masuyer, and set out on an adventure which proved to be not only the strangest and saddest in her romantic life, but which in time to come was actually to lead to one of the great changes which make the Europe of to-day so different from that Europe that conquered Napoleon.

It was still before the days of trains, and Hortense's road to Italy was through the Tyrol, over the Reschen Pass and down the Etschthal to Meran, Bozen, and Trent, and so to Venice. There she had many friends. Passing Padua and Bologna, she at last arrived at Florence, where she was happy to find herself dispensed from the society of her husband. He was away in Rome conferring with his mother and his family, while his elder son stayed at Florence to entertain Hortense and Louis.

The young Napoleon, who had just married his cousin Charlotte, King Joseph's daughter, had grown up into a striking and a handsome youth. Although the pipe he smoked in the street, the tobacco pouch from which he filled it, and above all the gold rings he wore in his ears gave him rather the air of a Corsican brigand as he drove about Florence, he had a lively and well-balanced mind ; he was logical and eloquent ; and his fine features shone with health and intelligence. " *C'est l'Empereur en prince et en beau* " wrote Valérie Masuyer, and she was in fact quite in love with him.[1] What an admirable king, she thought, he would make for the empty throne of Belgium. But the mind of this young Napoleon was seething with other ideas : he called himself a Republican, and he had given his heart to the agitators in the Papal States. His father's temper was still so cantankerous that his endorsement of the Pope's authority only made it more distasteful to a high-spirited son. Who, therefore, could be surprised if the son entertained inclinations and sympathies, that seemed less old-fashioned than

[1] *Revue des Deux Mondes*, 1st August, 1914.

such a father's? There was something in the very features of the Count of St. Leu, the combination of the hooked nose and prominent chin above the tight mouth which invited the spirit of rebellion from the warm character expressed in the handsome and mobile features of his son. Young Napoleon, in fact, was sworn a *carbonaro*, bound by secret oath to combine against the civil authority of the Pope's government in the States of the Church. To his brother, Louis, he had always been, as we saw, a hero to admire and follow ; Louis, who also called himself a Republican, and who hated the Holy Alliance which regarded him always as a danger, and which tried to keep him like a ticket-of-leave man in a penal settlement, was soon singing Republican songs as he went about Florence. The rumour was that he also had become a *carbonaro*, a member of the secret society of rebels in the Papal States who planned to save the world from religion and authority and who wrote in their own blood the curses they invoked upon themselves if ever they betrayed their lurid cause.

Just at that time the Pope died, and in the time of uncertainty which followed, Rome might have seemed to some as though it were a dead body and a heap of ruins. But to the Bonapartes it was still the Eternal City from which they, the Bonapartes, might pluck the secret of how to last for ever. Madame Mère was still living there, almost blind now. She had moved from the Villa Borghese to the Palazzo Rinuccini in the Piazza Venezia, accumulating in her memory every word she could gather about the life of her immortal son, and amazed always at the magnitude of the power which had come forth from her into the world, and vanished from it in enigma, while she still lived on. When she drove out in the streets, the people greeted her with the cry of " *La Madre di Napoleone* ! " And now around her were gathered her sons, Louis from Florence, Lucien, Joseph, and Jérome from Westphalia with his wife, the daughter of the King of Württemberg, and his two children, Mathilde and Napoleon Jérome. A little time after Louis left, Hortense arrived. Wife and husband had met in the narrow streets of Montefiascone and exchanged talk without either descending from the carriage. Hortense had then driven on, but not cheerfully.[1] For where is the woman who can regard with equanimity the fact that her marriage has been a failure ?

In Rome she had a sumptuous apartment in the Palazzo Borghese ; yet so primitive were the manners of the time that the ladies as they came up the grand staircase had to hold in their skirts, for fear they should soil the dresses on the unpleasant marks of human passage which had been left upon the stairs.[2] How she and Louis passed their time we hardly know, but it is plain that his study was but little on the Papacy. Indeed, even when at Mass, he ignored the sacred ceremonies to play with his little cousins, Mathilde and Napoleon.[3]

For it is a not uncommon result of dissipation that it kills the life of the spirit. Louis not only played little pranks in Church : he gave up belief in a future life. He fell out of sympathy with both Rome and Catholicism, intrigued with agitators, and sheltered in his rooms men sought by the police. This was soon known in a place where everyone suspected was subject to careful watching. On 13th December,

[1] Masuyer : *Revue des Deux Mondes*, 1st August, 1914.
[2] " Mémoires de la Princesse Mathilde " : *Revue des Deux Mondes*, 15th December, 1927.
[3] Ibid.

1830, armed officers appeared, therefore, at the Palazzo Borghese, told Louis he must leave Rome within an hour and watched him while he packed. He was then driven out of Papal territory under an escort of dragoons ; but the only result was that he returned to his brother in Florence [1] to engage in fresh conspiracies against the priests who governed Rome.

In February Hortense herself decided to leave, and it was thought that again the Papal authorities had influenced the decision. But no : it was her sons who had asked her to leave Rome and for this reason : that the elder being a sworn *carbonaro*, and the younger having been won over to join the insurgents, they dared not set out from Florence, while Hortense was in Rome, and could be imprisoned as a hostage. Hortense did not take their news with the docility that their solicitude expected. Always rather hysterical, and now also overtired, she felt that she herself had been made their victim. She implored her husband to bring them back, but, imperturbable, he told her that that was her duty. " *Il y a une caisse vide dans certains cerveaux* " she said.[2]

She wrote letters to her sons : tore them up, began again ; tried to influence her husband. His only answer was that if they did not return at once, he would send them his curse ; and why, he asked, had not Hortense set out to bring them back, taking with her a force of Tuscany *sbirri* to entrap them, and bring them home as prisoners ?

Meanwhile the two brothers had joined the insurgents ; they had been received with enthusiasm at Spoleto and at Terni. From there they had gone down the Tiber valley, and had engaged the Papal

[1] Masuyer : op. cit.
[2] *Revue des Deux Mondes*, 1st October, 1914.

troops at Città Castellana. But this time it was the new masters who distrusted them, and the leader of the insurgents had recalled them to Ancona.

At Ancona, therefore, Hortense decided to join them. She had spent the days of uncertainty yawning, because—as her lady thought—she was bored. But night after night she had walked up and down in her bedroom, the prey to a thousand nameless fears. Day after day, she argued with her husband,[1] then she announced that she would start for Smyrna, and wait her last hours amidst the sun and blossom. She soon saw, however, that she must do something more arduous if she would save her sons and win them back to her. She made another plan to go to Ancona, pass in disguise through Piedmont, enter France, make a surprise entry into the Tuileries, and throw herself at the feet of Louis Philippe.[2] But how was she to do it?

No one would help her. The Ministers of the Foreign Powers made difficulties in the usual way ("Soon they will have to hold a congress before we can move", Louis had written to his father years before from Augsburg)[3]; but Hortense found an unexpected ally in Mr. Seymour, the British Minister. At the risk of losing his post, he faked a passport for her as a Mrs. Hamilton travelling with two sick sons, and even obtained diplomatic visas for Piedmont and France. In addition to this she obtained a visa for her own passport given in her own name, and, intending to return by another road as Mrs. Hamilton, she left Tuscany near Siena as the Duchess de St. Leu, in the company of Carlo Zappi, a *carbonaro*, and Valérie Masuyer, her companion. She then started

[1] *Queen Hortense en* 1831, pp. 83, 4.
[2] *Revue des Deux Mondes*, 1st October, 1914.
[3] Jerrold : op. cit., i, 118.

for Foligno. And so anxious was her husband to see her start, that he had even lent her a carriage.

On the 12th March, Hortense, with her two companions, drove up Val d'Arno to Arezzo. They saw—

> Cortona raise to heaven
> Her diadem of towers.

At Camoscia, they noted the road on the right leading to Chiusi (the Clusium of Lars Porsena), and Siena. It was by that route that in a few days time Hortense hoped to pass with her two sons as Mrs. Hamilton. She did not know what was to happen in those days. She did not know that her sons were in the North while she was hurrying southward. She passed on the right the reedy borders of Lake Trasimeno, and from Perugia she saw the houses of Assisi, a lilac patch upon the violet hills of Umbria. On the 14th she had reached Foligno and slept in the same room where her sons had slept. " I was like a condemned felon awaiting his sentence," she wrote, " every moment, every noise drew me to the window." [1] There she received news that there was an epidemic of measles among the insurgents. Setting out at once for Forli where they were, she heard at Ponte Centesimo that her son, Napoleon, was very ill with it.

"Napoleon isn't dead, is he, Mlle Masuyer?" said Hortense. " If he were dead, we should know."

" Yes, Madame, we would know." As she answered these words, Mlle Masuyer saw the messenger reel back and burst into tears, and move off, his face covered by his hands; she did not need to question why. But she said nothing to Hortense who hurried on

[1] *Queen Hortense en* 1831.

over the Apennines to Pesaro.[1] There, lodging in the palace of her nephew, the Duke of Leuchtenberg, she met Louis and heard his story.

Recalled from Cività Castellana by the Carbonaro commander, they had gone back to Forli. On their way Louis had been almost captured by the Austrians at Spoleto. There he had flung himself at the feet of the Archbishop, Count Mastai-Ferretti, who had given him five thousand francs and driven him out of Spoleto in his own carriage. Such was the only encounter of Louis Napoleon with the man who is known to history as Pius IX.[2] At Forli, on the 10th, Napoleon had fallen ill. He had inflammation of the lungs and, after being bled, fainted from the pain. He was racked by his cough: and when it was seen that he had measles, he insisted that his brother should leave him for fear of infection. On the 17th, alone with Roccaserra, he died.[3]

Louis had come to meet his mother, but they dared not return to Forli, for the avenging Austrians were expected at any moment. Hortense therefore took him southward with her through Senigallia to Ancona where she had been again promised a lodging in the palace of the Duke of Leuchtenberg. There she learnt from the newspapers that Vienna had promised to put down the insurrection, and a force of twenty thousand Austrian troops had already entered the Papal States. Their commander had declared that, if Louis were captured, he would be shot out of hand. She had hardly grasped the news, when Louis announced that he had a violent headache

[1] *Revue des Deux Mondes*, 1st October, 1914.
[2] Paléologue : *Cavour*, p. 79.
[3] *Revue des Deux Mondes*, 1st October, 1914, p. 321. Such is Masuyer's account, though Hortense said that Louis was present at the end.

and felt extremely ill. The Queen decided that he had better come into her own rooms, and in fact there was an inner room inside her own bedroom. When the doctor came next morning, he declared at once that Louis, in his turn, had caught measles. It was now the Passion Week of 1831. And no sooner had Louis's illness settled upon him than the Austrian troops occupied Ancona.

Hortense no longer yawned : no longer talked of escaping to a flowery retreat on the outskirts of Smyrna. Her inventive genius came to the aid of the need for action. She saw boats in the little harbour, which flew the tricolour and learnt that they were leaving for Corfu. She secured a visa for her son from the authorities of Ancona before the Austrian troops arrived. Then she announced he had gone on board. Processions of porters travelled between the palace and the little ship with boxes : and quickly the ship sailed. Naturally, it was taken for granted in Ancona—and soon all over Europe— that Louis was on the Adriatic. Hortense now announced that she was very ill, and that no one could enter her room. And there for a week she nursed her son until the worst of the measles had passed over, and she felt that he was fit to travel.

The Austrian commander (it was the very officer, Baron Gerbner, who sixteen years before had saved her from the mob at Dijon) had not the slightest suspicion that Prince Louis was in her rooms, although, if the Prince had raised his voice, the commander could have heard him through the thin partition that separated them. When she asked Gerbner for permission to leave Ancona for Florence, he at once gave it. The moment she chose for her departure was the dawn of Easter Day.

Guards slept at the very door of her room, and she

could not get her son past them, for they knew each of her attendants. She rose therefore while they were still asleep. Louis, now disguised as her footman, climbed into the box-seat of her carriage, and she passed the Austrian guards before daylight, announcing that she would hear, as she did hear, her Easter Mass in the hut encased in inlaid marble which is known to Catholic piety as the Santa Casa of Our Lady of Loreto. " Who," she asked, " after losing what is dear, has not felt a deep emotion on entering a church ? " [1]

From there she drove over the Apennines to Foligno, and so back through Assisi and Perugia to Camoscia. Again and again, and yet again, on the road, her son had been recognized : and at Camoscia the party had once more to run the gauntlet of the frontier officers of the Grand Duke of Florence. In fact, as crowds of fugitives from Forli were passing through Tuscany, to this post had been sent a special commissioner who was responsible for everyone passing by. Hortense judged it safer to arrive at the frontier by night : but the men on duty could not let her pass. She then sent on her own courier with her passport to the commissioner who was in bed some miles further on. Receiving the most solemn promises that Hortense was alone, and believing, like the rest, that Louis was at Corfu, he allowed Hortense to come on to Camoscia where he was to visit her next morning. By next morning, Hortense hoped with a change of horses to be far on her road to Siena.[2]

Yet when she came into the village, she found that there had been so many fugitives before her that

[1] *La Reine Hortense en* 1831, p. 151.
[2] This account follows Valérie Masuyer (*Revue des Deux Mondes*, 1st October, 1914), and Queen Hortense's own early memoir, published 1834 (*La Reine Hortense en* 1831).

a change of horses was not to be obtained. Her own team could go no further. As she dared not enter the inn, where either she or Louis might be recognized, all she could do was to stay and rest in her carriage. But her son could not rest with her, for in no circumstances could a footman share a carriage with his mistress! And yet except as a footman Prince Louis's case was desperate. He was therefore obliged to rest on a bench. After a few hours halt, the horses could again be flogged on, and, before the commissioner awoke, Hortense was once more on her way to Siena. She was still travelling on her own passport as the Duchess de St. Leu.

What was she to do at Siena? both she and her son were well known there. The danger at Camoscia she had escaped by driving away from there as soon as she could along by-roads, and changing horses and drivers as often as possible. So she had managed to pass the night in a small village in the Val di Chiana in comparative calm. "If it were not for that night's sleep," she said, "I would have died." But at Siena she could not hope to pass unrecognized, and she dare not have Louis with her. He therefore left her party at the gate, and planned to meet her on the other side of the town on the road to Poggibonsi. But again she was held up for a change of horses, and he had almost decided that she had been detained in the city, when she and Valérie Masuyer, having driven out of the gates, found him on the road, eating some apples. She now was really on her way to Paris, and decided that the time had come for her to make use of the faked passport given her by Mr. Seymour. Carlo Zappi impersonated her older son, and Louis was able to exchange the footman's place for the master's. So as Mrs. Hamilton, she arrived at the gates of Pisa before the dawn, but not without arousing suspicion from the police, who wanted to know why she had been travelling by night. The Grand Duke, she said, had taken their horses to Siena, and only at the last moment could they get their pairs. This answer was taken as satisfactory : for Continental police knew that it was seldom worth their while to look askance at an English passport, and before two days Hortense and Louis, skirting the mountains " which shut off Lucca from the Pisan eye," had passed over the frontiers of Tuscany, and found themselves in the Duchy of Modena.

Her road led her to Seravezza near Carrara where her son Napoleon had worked marble quarries and set up a paper-mill ; and now Hortense for the first time had leisure to indulge her grief.

There are few places more beautiful even in Italy than the region they were now traversing in the loveliest week in spring. Behind them the Apuan Alps rose blue into the air's intenser blue ; from them fresh streams foamed down and filled the valley with the voice of living water ; forests of green oak and pine replaced the olive, and fruit blossom rose above the vineyards and the soft blue which gave a bloom to the distances, and softened the brilliance of the sparkling sea. In such a scene Hortense felt that she must walk, and, as Seravezza was on a valley off the main road, walking was more than usually attractive. But the lady was not a walker. She sat down at the foot of a tree, and Louis fetched a peasant's cart. Seravezza was so near that it seemed a pity not to see the paper-mill which Napoleon had built : the man who showed them over it mentioned that the young proprietor had died, that he had been very good to the poor, and deeply loved ; but as no name was spoken, no hint given that the Prince had fought with the insurgents, the man did not guess why his story brought tears to his listeners' eyes.

Hortense had intended to drive back to her stage. A peasant woman, with one baby in her arms and another unborn, begged her to give up the cart, and Hortense, hearing from the driver that if the woman did not get her cart back her husband would beat her, saw that she had no right to keep it. " I managed, although fainting with fatigue," wrote Hortense, " to finish our little journey on foot." But exhausted as she felt, she had at once to face a new danger : when she came back to the inn, she heard that the Court jeweller of Florence had just arrived there. Of course, he knew her, and she dare not risk an encounter with him ; so the weary woman had to leave the village on foot and wait till the carriage overtook her.

The road before her was fascinating, now leading up the cliff to a distant view of the sunny waters, now passing beside the field of maize, now bordered by the aloe or the vine. It was enough to console for the dream of Smyrna : in spite of mourning, in spite of danger, she could say, " we loved it."

> Nor knew we well what pleased us most,
> Not the clipt palm, of which they boast,
> But distant colour, happy hamlet,
> A moulder'd citadel on the coast,
>
> Or tower, or high hill-convent, seen
> A light amidst its olives green,
> Or olive-hoary cape in ocean
> Or rosy blossom in hot ravine,
>
> Where oleanders flushed the bed
> Of silent torrents, gravel spread
> And crossing oft we saw the glisten
> Of ice, far up on a mountain head.

And so they travelled on in the blue unclouded weather. The effect of measles passed off ; the travellers' spirits rose ; the adventure seemed enjoyable. Although Louis alone could speak English—and his English had always a very strong foreign accent—they managed with their English passport to pass the Consul at Genoa. They were recognized several times more, but never by enemies. And Louis and his friend were now in a mood to embark on fresh adventures, to force a kiss from a peasant girl after she had jumped for shelter behind a rock, and to count the miles along the coast road which his uncle had built above the beautiful Italian Riviera : Rapallo, Santa Margarita, Alassio, Bordighera, San Remo, Mentone, Monaco, Nice, and after Nice, over the stony valley of the Var across the frontier to Antibes and Golfe Juan—for once again the proscribed exiles, under the foreign names they had assumed, had, after sixteen years, set foot on their native France, and almost at the very spot where in the year before their exile the great man had landed from Elba to claim the Empire he regarded as his own. The nephew's claim was a humbler one : it was merely for a right to serve in the French army.

For as yet he barely realized that he was virtually the claimant to the Imperial throne. Yet he knew that the Duke of Reichstadt was dying a prisoner in Vienna, that in his own family he, born the youngest, was now the eldest surviving son. He, in fact, reversed the order of his names, and signed, as his brother had signed, Napoleon Louis.

The Italian adventure of that winter which had glided from 1830 into 1831 had not only made him the virtual heir of the Bonapartes. It had turned him from a Catholic into almost a *Carbonaro*. The stimulus of movement, of command, of danger had been given to the cause that he held sacred, the cause of the people against privilege and authority. The idea of tradition faded from his mind, and with it religion ; that of the rights of man took its place—of the nature with which man had been endowed, of the freedom of the individual, of the emancipation from the rules of priests so that men should have comfort and well-being among earth's rich sun and flowers, of earth's green fields and groves, and so that the senses should expand their life unfettered in a glow of geniality in which men should embrace one another with the enthusiasm of brothers, though not, in Prince Louis's own words, so fervently as to strangle one another. And why not link in the brotherly embrace ? What prevented it ? Tyranny, privilege, vested interest, which made the forfeit of independence, the deference to rank almost a sacred duty, because courts and cathedrals supported one another. The whole system of the Church was irksome, because it insisted on the idea of sacrifice, on the exchange of the immediate good for a lasting good, a good of another kind, which it needed a super-human faculty to appreciate. Men were beginning to refuse that sacrifice ; for the fires of charity, growing cold, had left faith itself a charred log. And in any case, no men could be prepared to have their civil life administered by priests. Such was the idea of the Italian insurgents : such were the ideas that, in the excitement of exchanging worthy, strenuous, republican Switzerland for the warm blue Italian day, Louis Napoleon had made his own. He had given them the spirits of his youth. He had risked his life for them.

For ardent spirits, who have embraced the cause of freedom, there are two alternatives : to react against them after disillusion, or to see them solidify into maturer patience, after compromise. The spirit of Louis Napoleon was a spirit of compromise. All his hopes went back to a man who had made revolution his step to an imperial throne. Hortense saw that her sons could never have been accepted as republicans : for their name involved the singularity of power. The son who was left combined his generous sympathies with personal ambition ; he was the embodiment of the people's cause, but with that cause were the eagles who made Napoleon's crown. Italy showed him how to combine the two : for Italy had made him a conspirator. A conspirator does not breathe in openness the spirit's Alpine air. Conspiracy, with its long silence, its tenacious cunning, its excited hopes, its slowly maturing plan bursting out through ruthless pressure in violent occasions exactly suited the temperament of Prince Louis Napoleon. " His silence and calm hide a passionate temperament," wrote Valérie Masuyer, " although he is both cautious and inclined to gloom. His heart is ingenuous, and yet like his mind it is tortuous. Though he never fell in love for the sake of being in love, his heart is inclined to be captured by an adventure for the joy of being in a conspiracy.[1]

Italy made conspiracy a sacred cause. And as the habit and mood of the conspirator wormed their inevitable way through all the convolutions and crevices of Louis Napoleon's weighted brain, the generous blood by which that brain was nourished beat with enthusiasm at every memory of his adventure for freedom on the wooded mountains and the purple hillsides, in the verdant valleys and beside the tideless seas, where men spoke the language of Boccaccio ; the very idea of conspiracy became sacred to the cause of what he conceived as Italy. This was to lead to pregnant results which at a later date involved his doom.

[1] *Revue des Deux Mondes*, 1915, iii, 867.

III

THE GROWTH OF DOGGEDNESS

> If to despise
> The barren optimistic sophistries
> Of comfortable moles, whom what they do
> Teaches the limits of the just and true
> (And for such doing, they require not eyes),
> If sadness at the long heart-wasting show
> Wherein earth's great ones are disquieted,
> If thoughts, not idle, while before me flow
> The armies of the homeless and unfed—
> If these are yours, if this is what you are
> Then am I yours, and what you feel I share.
>
> MATTHEW ARNOLD.

> "I am the child of destiny," said Prince Floristan. "That destiny will again place me on the throne of my fathers. That is as certain as I am now speaking to you. But destiny for its fulfilment ordains action. Its decrees are inexorable, but they are obscure, and the being whose career it directs is as a man travelling in a dark night; he reaches his goal even without the aid of stars or moon.
>
> DISRAELI (*Endymion*).

I

As Louis drove back into France his eyes were filled with tears at the thought that his brother was not with him. The little party slept at Cannes, and then drove over the Estérel to Fréjus, on their way towards Aix and Avignon. At Montélimar in the Rhone valley, after a good dinner, the Prince went round the town with Zappi. Stopping at a café to look at the newspapers, they found that the officers there had stopped their billiards to ask if the newcomers had not come from Italy, and if they could not give some news of what had happened to the Bonaparte Princes. The officers had felt some satisfaction, so they said, in thinking that Louis had escaped the Austrians, and was safe in the Adriatic. So when for the first time the Prince found himself among French army men, he found that their great preoccupation was himself! Again his eyes filled with tears, he hurried back to Hortense, and prepared his letter for Louis Philippe asking for leave to serve in the French army.[1]

At Fontainebleau, which was full of poignant memories for Hortense, the heart of her son was again all fire and flame. They entered Paris by the Porte d'Italie, but Hortense, instead of taking the shortest road to her hotel, ordered the postilion to drive through the Jardin des Plantes and the Grands Boulevards. The enthusiasm of Louis rose as the city of Paris unfolded on him, until he thrilled with admiration and at last became so excited that he actually stood up in his place in the carriage to drink it in with all his eyes.

It was six in the evening when they reached their resting-place, the Hotel de Hollande, in the Rue de la Paix ; and when Holland's dethroned Queen arrived there with her English passport, the Parisians, only a few yards away in the Place Vendôme, were preparing to erect on the great column in its centre a statue of the Emperor.

The plan of Hortense was to appeal to Louis Philippe through the Count d'Houdetot, whose cousin, Mrs. Lindsay, was her friend and neighbour

[1] V. Masuyer : *Revue des Deux Mondes*, 1914, vi, 249.

at Arenenberg. The evening after her arrival d'Houdetot was announced, and Valérie Masuyer received him. She took a candle in her hand and led him into an inner room. As the rays of candlelight fell on the features of Hortense, he leapt back with a yell of amazement. He had thought she was at Malta. But Hortense had made her plan : she had claims on Louis Philippe because it was she who in the days of her power had obtained pensions for his mother and his sister. Louis Philippe presented his courtesies to her through Casimir Périer, his Prime Minister, and shortly afterwards she was secretly received at the Palais Royal by the King himself.[1]

Although Louis Philippe had not welcomed the news of Hortense's arrival in Paris, he greeted her with a sympathy which came from the heart of a man and of a king. " I know all the sufferings of exile," he said, " and if yours had not ceased already it is not my fault." Hortense answered that she did not wish to embarrass him by her presence : but that to exile the Bonapartes was impolitic as well as unjust. He knew that she had claims for property, which so far had been made in vain. " I understand affairs and offer myself as your man of business," he said. He referred with the greatest cordiality to Hortense's father, whom he remembered, and to the Grand Duchess Stéphanie, her cousin. In fact Hortense thought he was as kind a monarch as the old King of Bavaria. Before she left him, he had brought in both his wife and his sister, who were so sympathetic that she felt that they were receiving her as one of their own family.[2]

[1] V. Masuyer : *Revue des Deux Mondes*, December, 1914. *La Reine Hortense en* 1831. Jerrold : op. cit., i, 185, 6.
[2] *La Reine Hortense en* 1831. Guizot : *Mémoires*.

But none the less, she was hurried out of Paris after the 5th May, and although Louis had another illness which kept him in bed on the great anniversary, they were forced to hurry on to England. These very facts persuaded him that they dare not let him remain and he was profoundly convinced that the heart, not only of the Army but of the people, was with the Imperial cause.[1] And when they arrived at their hotel in George St., they were already arranging portfolios in a future cabinet to be presided over by Napoleon II. In London they were joined by his cousin, Achille Murat, who had once been Crown Prince of Naples. They met the Princess Lieven and Lord Holland, who, when he heard from Hortense that the Bonapartes were the victims of injustice, changed the subject. They were entertained by the Duchess of Bedford at a breakfast and paid several visits to Woburn. They made friends with the Duchess of St. Albans, who, having come to London as a country girl, attracted the attention of the old banker, Thomas Coutts, who left her the richest widow in London. She thus became the wife of the Duke who traced his descent to Charles II. A rumour spread that Louis was a candidate for the throne of Belgium: but that was soon known to be absurd.

One evening, however, he went to Covent Garden to see some tableaux of the Life of Napoleon: it had been judged wiser not to bring in St. Helena. But even so, when the Prince came back to his hotel, they were afraid he was going to be ill. His eyes were red with tears, his features were twisted with emotion, and his face was colourless. For Louis had in every way the most impressionable emotions. When it had been suggested in Paris that Louis

[1] *Revue des Deux Mondes*, 1915, iii, 849.

Philippe might allow him to enter the French army and even become a peer of France, he had asked at what price. "If you would give up the name of Bonaparte," was the answer.

"I would rather," he cried back, "be lying dead in my brother's coffin." [1]

2

On the 7th of August, Hortense, now under the name of Madame Arenenberg, made her way home through France. Though she felt it would be too great a strain to see St. Leu, she tried to enter Malmaison, and was turned back as a stranger at the gates. But no one could refuse her the right to enter the church at Rueil; and she and Louis knelt at the right of the altar beside the marble tomb of Josephine.

And so when, as summer mellowed into autumn, the little party came back to Arenenberg, Louis's whole position and outlook were changed. The one Napoleon had died of measles, the other of consumption. A single day, said his foster sister, had changed his character from that of a mild, unambitious, and impressionable youth: he had suddenly become a man of purpose.[2] He was now the heir of the Bonapartes. An eventful year had thrilled his mind with the idea of what that meant. Italy in her convulsive struggle against authority had been a lute to the name of Napoleon. He had found his own exploits the thing uppermost in the minds of French

[1] *Revue des Deux Mondes*, 1915, iii, 864.
[2] N. W. Senior: *Conversations*, ii, 114.

officers. He had thrilled at the sight of Paris. He had lain in bed in the Rue de la Paix on the very day that his uncle's statue was placed at the head of the Vendôme column. He had been received as a personage in England, and had his name associated already with a waiting crown. And finally he had looked at Rueil on the tomb of Josephine. Henceforth he was a spirit dedicated to one end, and to that every thought must be gradually turned. It was after all not for nothing that he had been hunted in his youth, and that he had not even as a boy been able to move without the sanction of five ambassadors.

He began to think out his position. He put together the essay on Switzerland which he had been writing before he left Thun. He received a deputation from patriots in Poland which told him that the effect of the name of Bonaparte was incalculable. He wrote a pamphlet called *Revues Politiques*.

Did the word *Republic*, he asked, necessarily mean liberty? Did not the history of Switzerland show that a republic was not incompatible with anarchy. It was to the great Emperor of the French, wrote Louis Napoleon, that Switzerland owed popular government. For, making a transition from old to new ideas, making a compromise between a powerful authority and the people's will, he crowned his republican laurels with an imperial diadem. He wanted to ensure both progress and stability. Then, with Russia and England out of the way, he would have seen Poland, Italy, Westphalia, complete and independent kingdoms.

Such were already the ideals of Louis Napoleon : such were the ideas he was to restate in his little book, *Des Idées Napoléoniennes* in 1839. He saw his uncle, we cannot doubt that he saw himself, as the guardian angel, who was designed by providence to guide a time of transition. The spirit of an institution is good, he wrote, because it is based on the wants of the time. But wants change : nature is not stationary : institutions grow old. It is the Heavenly Spirit, the Spirit of Perfection which bears us onward. Changes are inevitable, are welcome, to put the laws in harmony with the age.

But who is to decide what changes are necessary : who is to erect new institutions ? " The people ! who have always an instinct that leads them to choose what is best for them. But can the people exercise their power without limit ? Ought they not to recognize a limit for themselves by choosing schemes submitted to them by intellectual leaders ? The great masses of them cannot deliberate. Therefore, in order to conciliate popular sovereignty with the principle of order, the enlightened bodies should unify purpose, and the people should be content to accept or reject their proposals."

This is the idea which Louis Napoleon united with the idea of a central command : thus it was that he would secure his political ends which were independence, freedom, stability, the aristocracy of merit, and the diffusion of material comfort. For though he wanted people to be free, he saw that they could only be free if there was a strong central principle of order : and that there could only be material comfort if a future were sufficiently assured for commerce to develop freely : and that the only means of either order or advancement was the aristocracy of merit.

Here, already stated, by this young man of twenty-five, are the principles on which he acted when he had risen to be the absolute ruler of France, and when he dictated to Europe. And what is still more interesting to us to-day : they are the very ideas which Europe, after its last convulsion, has accepted as the last word in principles succeeding parliamentary government. Plebiscites, dictatorship founded on direct national choice without the intermediary of parliaments, self-determination for peoples, the guarantee of order against anarchy and confusion, the defence of commerce against an uncertain future : these are governing ideas of 1933, exactly a hundred years after Louis Napoleon wrote them down and published them in his little yellow pamphlets. And as we go further into the history of his life, we shall see with what uncanny fullness he foresaw other developments of our time. For we shall see him busy in turn with the extinction of pauperism, with the separation of Poland from Russia as a separate state, with the question of order in Mexico as a nucleus of Latin culture in America to modify the dangerous domination of purely republican and materialistic order in the United States of the North, and—not least amazing—with the actual settlement of the Roman question in giving the Pope a small independent territory in a united Italy, so that he shall be politically independent without being encumbered by political government. He was the first ruler of modern times to inspire great schemes of town-planning. He surrounded himself with men of talent and made his court a model for those that survive to-day. All these things we shall see in turn develop from the pamphlets of Louis Napoleon at twenty-five. He in fact, more than any man of the nineteenth century, is the man of the present hour.

And we shall see these innovations, in which we take pride as those of our own time, worked out in his flashing career. For his magnetic hold over men ran even with what he felt from that time on to be the government of his star. Nor is it less interesting to find the seed of his thoughts growing up in a climate like Catholicism which is present to the modern world as then, nor that the compost in which they sprouted forth was a temperament which, like the relaxed tempers of the present hour, was influenced in its depths by the fact that it did not allow moral principles or tradition to curb the voluptuous outpouring in which it found its favourite distraction. He resembled our political system in his temperamental unrestraint in spending money. For when as a young man he travelled with his mother, she felt bound to make him dependent for his cash on her companion. And, like the men of to-day, this modern Napoleon did not in his heart believe in anything more spiritual than comfort and kindness. There were immense ranges of heights in moral and metaphysical science to which his eye was blind, or if at times he caught a glimpse of them, as of the distant Alps which he could in clear twilights descry from the hills around his home, it was as though they were, in Ruskin's words, " infinitely beyond all that we had ever thought or dreamed—the seen walls of lost Eden " [1] : something in which he did not believe, but which he vaguely longed for, and of which those around him whispered as something at last to be scaled with the walls of sacred death. For Hortense, having abandoned faith at one time, had once again become a woman who opened her heart to the presences of the soul.[2]

3

When he had written his pamphlets, the time had come for him to think of a bride. On the 4th April,

[1] *Preterita.*
[2] V. Masuyer : *Revue des Deux Mondes*, 1st June, 1913.

1836, his uncle Jérome—who had been King of Westphalia, who had married Princess Catharine of Württemburg, and who was then known as the Prince de Montfort—arrived at Arenenberg with his daughter, Mathilde, and his son, Napoleon. Mathilde was still only fifteen (her brother two years younger) and perhaps it was not surprising if at the first glance her cousin did not seem intensely interested. But she had very beautiful shoulders : and that evening she came down to dinner so *décolletée* that her father protested. Prince Louis, however, did not protest : his eyes feasted on her : his manner became exuberant. Mlle Masuyer looked amused but slightly cynical. " *Chez lui*," she wrote, " *la chair est faible.*" [1] When Queen Hortense was asked whether all was finally arranged between the cousins, she did not know what to answer. Sometimes her husband said yes, sometimes no : and he gave no hint of what allowance he might make to his son. As for Jérome, he spent his money lavishly ; he flung it away : and then he complained that he was penniless. And where were the young couple to live ? Princess Mathilde would think only of Florence, and the very mention of Florence made Hortense ill. So nothing was settled when the family of Jérome left Arenenberg in May.

Louis, to tell the truth, was more occupied with the throne of France than with the affection of his young cousin.

4

For that summer there came other visitors to Arenenberg. A young man, Fialin de Persigny—he was of the Prince's own age—came with letters from

[1] *Revue des Deux Mondes*, 1915, iii, 867.

Joseph, for he worshipped the Emperor and everything to do with him. He brought also a Colonel Vaudrey, who commanded a regiment at Strasbourg. Old Parquin conspired with them.

"According to a maxim of the Emperor's," said Louis, "anything may happen, and we must be ready for anything." "Louis," answered Queen Hortense, "*prends garde aux échauffourées.*" Nevertheless, at dawn one morning in October, when Louis went to say good-bye to Hortense, she gave him for luck a ring which had been the Emperor's.

Four days later he was at Strasbourg. He had long been convinced that the sympathies not only of the army but even of the people were with the Bonapartes as against the Bourbons. On the morning of the 30th October, his heart beat fast and high as the clock struck six. In a few minutes he was to appear at the barracks of the 4th Artillery and summon them to rally to his eagle. Colonel Vaudrey had already gathered his regiment in the barrack yard and, when Louis Napoleon appeared, he turned to his regiment and said: "Soldiers, a great revolution begins to-day under the auspices of the nephew of the Emperor Napoleon. He is before you and comes to lead you." There was a cry of *Vive l'Empereur*! the Prince made an harangue, the men drew their swords and held their shakos aloft. They formed up and marched through the city to the headquarters of the garrison. But the general in command was not to be won over. The rebels therefore placed him under arrest.

The Prince then went on to other barracks, where again he expected a regiment to be drawn up to receive him. But this time the plan had failed and the men were still in their quarters preparing for inspection. At the cry of *Vive l'Empereur*! they hurried to the windows: they began to form up, and in a few moments he was expecting another ally with a corps of engineers and the third artillery. But at this critical moment, disaster appeared in the form of the commanding officer, Taillandier. He told the men they had been taken in. " It is not the Emperor's nephew: it is Colonel Vaudrey's. I recognize him." The men now turned with equal suddenness against the man who, as they thought, had fooled them. Taillandier soon had his men formed. The Prince could not form his. Soldiers of the line and artillerymen were tangled together in an unmanageable mob. The men loaded their muskets, fixed their bayonets, drew their swords. The gunners arrested the infantry, the infantry the gunners. The Prince, convinced that he had won the new regiment, dashed among them: they dug at him with their bayonets. He tried to rally his own men: but it was too late. They were in confusion. He was separated from his officers: and while trying to mount a restive horse, among a few supporters, he was forced against a wall, and arrested. And there his adventure ended. For though the Fourth Artillery made another attempt in his favour, their commanding officer was captured, and they could obtain no ammunition. Meanwhile, Fialin de Persigny had joined Colonel Vaudrey's mistress, Madame Gordon, and was destroying the proclamation which had been prepared. Louis Napoleon, under a strict guard, was taken to Paris where he was confined in the Conciergerie under Gabriel Delessert. M. Delessert, when the Prince arrived, was entertaining a Spanish child, his daughter's friend, Doña Eugénia de Guzman. And as the young Bonaparte arrived, the little girl looked down at him from an upper window.

The government of Louis Philippe thought it more

discreet not to draw too much attention to a Bonaparte, either as conspirator or martyr. Instead of giving him a trial, they spread a report that he was contemptible : " I was told this morning," wrote, for example, Lord Granville to Lord Palmerston on 4th November, " that the young Louis Bonaparte fainted at the moment of his arrest, that he has since been continually shedding tears and writing letters imploring the mercy of the Government ; and that these letters were ill-written and misspelt." [1] They judged that the Prince would look more contemptible if he was pardoned unconditionally, and so he was shipped off to the United States without even having to give his promise to stay there. After a day or two in the Citadel de Port Louis in Brittany, he was given back 15,000 francs of the 200,000 which was in his possession when he was captured, placed on board the *Andromède* which sailed under sealed orders for the Equator, allowed a glimpse of the Corcovado from the beautiful harbour of Rio de Janeiro, and then taken on to Norfolk in Virginia.

On the 9th April he wrote to his mother from New York that he had received the most charming letters from all his cousins except Mathilde [2] ; and from the moment of his capture she had never addressed him a single word. " I shall never marry," he wrote, " a woman who has so little heart."

As for the Comte de St. Leu, he marked his disapproval of his son's adventure by withdrawing his allowance.

When he arrived at New York, Louis Napoleon settled at the Washington Hotel in Broadway, and was received at once by the best people. Although

[1] F. A. Simpson : *Rise of Louis Napoleon*, p. 122.
[2] Jerrold : ii, 20–4.

THE DOÑA EUGÉNIA DE GUZMAN
In a white collar, with her sister, afterwards Duchess of Alba: from a water-colour drawing by Joseph West, 1840. The original in the possession of the Duke of Alba.

" A Spanish child, his daughter's friend."

a wild young Corsican, Antoine Bonaparte arrived directly after with an undue inclination towards the oyster saloon and the bar, Prince Louis, in spite of his extreme susceptibility in the society of women, made and maintained a reputation for being dignified, serious, and good. The Schuylers and the Bayards set an example of entertaining him. He dined, he danced, he made excursions. He was introduced into the Grand Order of Owls by the Grand Sachem and attended their " esoteric sittings in select council ". He seized every occasion to talk politics, and he kept his eyes open. One day he saw at a money changer's the notice : " SOVEREIGNS CHANGED FOR NAPOLEONS." " That," he said to his companion, the Marquis de Gricourt, " would suit me perfectly." [1]

His impressions of the young American republic were not very favourable. He saw that the standards were narrow : men were free to make money but not to cultivate the arts of leisure : they were allowed to live active lives, but not to have many ideas. Business was already all in all, and great fortunes had upset the balance of society : and so, for the first time, men were no longer exclusively occupied with the fight against nature. They began to look for freedom not only for the slave as against his master, but also for themselves against the tyranny of the crowd. The masses of the people demanded that no man should aim above their own standards : the result was a mingling of licence with absolutism.[2] Such were the animadversions of the young Bonaparte on America, and they might with equal justice have been made of most English colonies. When he spoke of Republicanism, evidently he did not want anything

[1] Claudin : *Mémoires*, p. 330.
[2] Jerrold : ii, 8-10.

so conventional as the societies of the new world, or one in which the masses could dominate men of ideas. He wanted, as we shall see, a great freedom of development, and therefore a world endowed with the variety of a social hierarchy. What he missed in New York was the independence of the governing class in which in Europe he had always moved.

The Prince did not stay long in New York. A few days after his arrival there, his Mother had written him that she was expecting an operation. " In case it should not succeed," she wrote, " I send you my blessing. We shall meet again, surely, in a better world where you will come to join me, but not before you must. And you will remember that, in leaving this world, I regret only you ; only your gentle affection that has given some charm to my life. It will be a consolation to you, my dear child, to know that it was your care for her which made your mother as happy as it was possible for her to be. You will think of all my love for you, and take courage. Believe that our eyes remain fixed on all we loved here on earth in a gaze as clear as it is full of regard for their happiness. Have faith in this sweet thought : it is too needful not to be true. I press you to my heart, my dear one. I am quite calm and resigned and hope we may meet again in this world. Let the will of God be done."

But they did not operate on Hortense. They could not : they saw that her illness had already gone too far, and Conneau, her doctor, wrote to her son to hasten home. He arrived at Arenenberg in July to fix his eyes upon a dying woman. She was sleeping when he arrived : so they waited till she had awoken and then simulated the bustle of his arrival as seven years before she had simulated at Ancona the bustle of his departure. For weeks her son devoted himself to her while her fading glances watched his every movement. But with the warmth of the summer sun, her last powers of resistance left her. On 5th October she died in his arms. He himself closed her eyes and then fell weeping upon her bed : and there he long stayed kneeling, his head buried in his hands. " *Je crois bien qu'il pleurait*," said an old servant. " *Il y avait de quoi—comme elle l'aimait.*" [1]

Her body was taken to Rueil, and there, on either side of the High Altar, her body and her mother's hide their frailty beneath statues of white marble. Fifteen years later, her son made a song she had written in honour of her lover, into the National Anthem of France.

5

Louis Napoleon spent the winter at Arenenberg, setting in order the affairs of Hortense ; she was hardly in her grave before the Royal Government of France made representations to Berne that he should not be allowed to remain in Switzerland where he had already hatched one conspiracy. It is true that the Canton of Thurgau refused to give him up : but he settled the diplomatic difficulties by deciding that he would find a better centre in London.

Hortense had left him a considerable fortune, and he was able to take the place of an imperial prince in the central society of London. He had thought out his position, and carefully planned a course of action which would invite attention towards it. He took first Lord Cardigan's house in Carlton Terrace, and then Lord Ripon's in Carlton Gardens. He gave excellent dinners ; he rode a thoroughbred in the

---

[1] Jerrold : ii, 35, 36.

park; when he went to the opera, his A.D.C.s stood at his side as he entered his box; when he drove in the street, it was remarked that the Imperial Eagle was painted on the panel of his carriage door. He sent notices of his movements to the papers, and day after day *The Times* mentioned him in leading articles.[1] He made friends with the political novelists, Disraeli and Lytton, and he impressed them. " The Prince," in Disraeli's words, " encouraged conversation though he himself inclined to taciturnity. When he did speak, his terse remarks and condensed views were striking, and were remembered." [2] He was everywhere accepted as a royal personage. When he saw one of the sights of London, he was received with state formalities. When he went through the Bank of England, the directors gave him a breakfast. And as he watched the Lord Mayor's show from a window, the Lord Mayor himself gave him the greeting proper to a Prince of the Blood. The Duke of Wellington paid him particular attention. The Duke and Duchess of Somerset gave a dinner at Wimbledon to meet " Their Royal Highnesses the Prince of Capua and Prince Napoleon " [3]: for the Neapolitan Prince, though a nephew of Queen Marie Amélie, did not disdain to meet him as a friend, if not an equal.

English society was still dominated by the spirit of the eighteenth century, as the young queen was dominated by Melbourne. Although Lady Holland, Lady Blessington and the Duchess of St. Albans were not regarded as being within the true enclosure, young noblemen, as a whole, went where they felt

[1] F. A. Simpson : *Rise of Louis Napoleon*, p. 161.
[2] Disraeli : *Endymion*. There is a notable example of his conversation in *Endymion*, ch. xli.
[3] Jerrold : ii, 84, 85.

inclined for their relaxations. And among these the son of Hortense was not thought the worse for doing as he had always done. "He was no saint," says his official biographer, " he had his full share of some of the fashionable vices : he kept a mistress," but, in doing these things, he did them as they were done. If he was dissipated, it was noted, he was dissipated among gentlemen.[1] He had an eye for good horses on the Turf : he managed his thoroughbreds with a success that used to be noted in Rotten Row. He hunted : " I myself," wrote Lord William Lennox, " saw Prince Louis Napoleon sit a large field with the Quorn twice in one day." [2] He was a good though not a keen shot : he was an expert both with lance and sword : he prepared to fight a duel on Wimbledon Common with an illegitimate cousin, Count Léon. And he was present as an actor in that costly pageant, Lord Eglinton's tournament ; he wore a steel cuirass over a leather jerkin trimmed with crimson satin, a vizored helmet with a high plume of white feathers, and white satin hose. In the evening he appeared in a cassock of green velvet with shirt and sleeves of crimson satin, and a cap of crimson velvet with a yellow feather fastened by a jewelled aigrette, falling gracefully over the left side.[3]

" *J'ai besoin de mes petites distractions,*" [4] he used to say in after life ; and his alternations of elaborately organized sports, with occasional spells of dissipation, in a life of strenuous seriousness, present nothing surprising to a man or woman who knew the fashions

[1] Jerrold, op. cit.
[2] W. Lennox : *Recollections.*
[3] J. Bulkeley : *A Right Faithfulle Chronique of the Ladies and Knights who gained worship.*
[4] H. de Viel-Castel : *Mémoires.*

and tastes of those among whom he moved ; those among whom the sense of privilege and the taste for pleasure leaven the acceptance of responsibility. For to the rich and great, only those look able who are versatile ; their virility shows itself alternately in a magnetic bond with women, in sport, and in the management of men.

To the modern Napoleon, the management of men meant a thorough training in political economy. He toured industrial England, and looked closely at the factories and the shops. He once again thought out his position, and placed his views before the world in a new booklet : *Des Idées Napoléoniennes*. This is the most important of the many writings of Louis Napoleon. The central idea was that of the earlier pamphlet, the idea of the free instinct of the people accepting the guidance of authority : in other words, the dictatorship, founded on the plebiscite, and guided by ability, so as to make the masses of the people prosperous. He welcomed invention, he encouraged production, he urged commerce and intercourse among nations. His ideal, he pleaded, " gives work to all hands and capacities : it enters the cottage, not making empty declarations about the rights of men but providing means to quench the poor man's thirst, to quench his hunger and with a glorious story to awaken his patriotism." By its very nature it was for peace rather than for war. Its central principles were : justice, freedom, and authority. And it believed in religion, though it insisted that the clergy should play no political rôle. The spread of education, the extension of credits, the encouragement of industry, the fostering of agriculture pointed to an ideal for France and for Europe ; it was that of abler and more successful men leading people, through their own ability, to successful work, and so to well-being. Its dominant idea was that of a central authority : a monarchical authority such as France had recognized as her centre for fourteen hundred years. He aimed both at efficient direction from the centre, and the encouragement of local autonomies provided they remained in harmony with the central power. He would thus give all France the opportunity to make the most of her best brains and perfect the machinery by which as a whole she would enter into relation with other countries in Europe. For Louis Napoleon's idea was not merely French : he would make France a centre of harmony among nations ; hers was a sacred cause, and it was for her to spread through Europe those principles of justice, freedom, and authority of which she would be the example. She, in a word, through the person of her sovereign, was to be the arbiter of Europe.

Rhetorical, loose, but not impracticable, such was the broadly outlined philosophy which this remarkable young man had worked out and, which, as the years ripened, he determined to put into action. The book was published in 1839 ; and a copy of it was given to one of the ablest Englishmen of the time, the novelist, Bulwer Lytton.

" It is," wrote Lytton, " the book of a very able mind, with few ideas, but those ideas bold, large, and reducible to vigorous action.

" Very much depreciated at this day by the critics of a drawing-room, Prince Louis Napoleon has qualities that may render him a remarkable man if he ever return to France. Dogged, daring, yet somewhat reserved and close, he can conceive with secrecy and act with promptitude. His faults would comprise conceit and rashness ; but akin with those characteristics are will and enthusiasm.

He has these in a high degree. Above all, he has that intense faith in his own destiny with which men rarely fail of achieving something great, without which all talent lacks the *mens divinior*." [1]

6

In London, as earlier in New York, men were puzzled by the calm assurance with which the conspirator spoke of attaining the throne of France. He believed it with that faith which makes things hoped for into substance. Although the most attractive side of his elusive character was the boyish openness of his zest for enjoyment and for intimacy, one fixed purpose consumed the energy of his schemes.[2] He was dominated by the will to interpret in the practical speech of his own benevolence the ideals that he gathered from the career which had thrilled his memories and his hopes from early boyhood. In his long hours of study, in hardships and training, in the pursuit of women, whether he was loading the cannon, leading the insurgents, fleeing in disguise, or languishing in prison, one hope, one purpose, through good report and evil report, had hardened within him, as through its seed-time and its shooting the acorn hardens into a heart of oak. In the words of the poet Thompson, which the Prince used to quote, he strove—

"Still to employ
The mind's best ardour in heroic aims."

And these aims, feeding on the name he bore, were

[1] This is written in MS. by the 1st Lord Lytton in a copy of *Des Idées Napoléoniennes* preserved at Knebworth.
[2] Beyens : *Le Second Empire*, i, 418.

to renew in peace the story which was still spreading from the exploits of Napoleon ; so that his heir determined to make himself in turn the central man of Europe, and reign for the people's good.

His advocacy, his mission had been fitted to the hour. The name of Napoleon, an insistent music ever upon the lips of his surviving veterans, swelled up through France like trumpets pouring the summons to resurrection into the sepulchred ears of the dead. The dynasty of Bourbons, as though fearing dissolution into ashes, countered the menace by bringing from Longwood in 1840 all that remained there of Napoleon Bonaparte. But in the households of France, his figure was already present ; at every meal one met it, on plates, on knives, on forks ; it appeared again on pipes, on metal boxes and on bottles. Above the marriage bed, it smiled benign upon the lovers' joy. In innumerable statues of clay, of metal, and of wood, radiant in battle, or splendid in robes of state, the figure of Napoleon mingled with the daily life of France.[1] He already reigned from the column of the Place Vendôme : and now he was to rest in majesty beneath the crowning cupola of the chapel of his veterans.

Prince Louis, before such evidence of the claim which he believed to be personified in himself, could not be inactive. He knew that hundreds of thousands of Frenchmen had bought his little book. He had turned the figure of Napoleon from an heroic portent into a political programme, and he himself was prepared to make that programme into a new and immediate reality. His mind broke out into the fever of immediate conspiracy, and for the second time he determined to invade the realm of Louis Philippe.

[1] Lebey : *Les trois coups d'État*, p. 92.

7

On an August evening in 1840 the *Edinburgh Castle* sailed down the Thames. When the dawn came, the living eagle which had been tied by the leg to the mast looked on the choppy waves of the Channel. The little ship tacked many times ; the voyagers were seasick ; the eagle forlorn. Nor was there anything to encourage the conspirators when they landed next morning at Wimereux and marched on to Boulogne. An officer from St. Omer, Aladénize, had made the same preparations as Vaudrey had made at Strassbourg : but just as those preparations were nullified at Strassbourg by Taillandier, the hesitating troops were rallied to the King at Boulogne by a company commander, Col-Puygellier. In a short time the invaders were thrust out of the barracks. They then went on to the Column of the Grand Army—a column which commemorated another unsuccessful attempt at invasion ! From there they saw a large force of soldiers and police approaching ; Louis Napoleon said that he would remain at the foot of the Column : his companions dragged him away, and ran him to the shore. They rushed him into the sea, while their captain launched a boat. But the Captain of the port had boarded the *Edinburgh Castle*, and Louis Napoleon spent the night a prisoner in the Citadel of Boulogne.

On 28th September he was brought to trial in the Palais de Luxembourg by the peers of France. The peers saw before them a small and pale man of thirty-two, with a black moustache, a black beard, and a long hooked nose. He was dressed in black and wore on his breast the star of the Legion of Honour. What was his profession ? they asked. Slowly, impressively, he answered :

"A French Prince in exile."
Then he asked leave to address them. The leave was given. The Prince began by saying that at last he could speak in France to the French; and he had hoped to suggest to France that she had never taken away from the Bonapartes the imperial crown which she had given in 1804. He had felt it his duty to appeal to the people: to recall to a France which had lost its place in Europe, and was silent in the concourse of Kings, that Imperial France, so united within, so formidable abroad.

"One last word, gentlemen," he concluded. "I stand before you the representative of a principle, a cause, a defeat. The principle is the sovereignty of the people: the cause is the cause of the Empire; the defeat is Waterloo. That principle you have recognized; that cause you have served; that defeat you would avenge. There is no disagreement between you and me."

The peers listened: after a violent indictment of the Crown Prosecutor, the Prince's advocate finally addressed them in a speech which was rather an arraignment of the judges than a defence of the accused. It was all an impressive statement of the Bonaparte case. But none the less, the Prince was condemned to imprisonment for life; and on the day that the *Belle Poule* cast anchor at St. Helena to receive the body of the Emperor, Prince Louis Napoleon, his nephew, was conducted to Picardy to pass the rest of his life in imprisonment in the moated fortress of Ham.[1]

[1] This account follows that in Mr. Simpson's *Rise of Louis Napoleon*, ch. viii. Cf. also Lebey: *Strasbourg et Boulogne*.

IV

THE IMPRISONMENT AT HAM

> Return
> And make peace great, build the new France,
> Deepen her liberties, subtilize her laws
> And make her justice tender.
> TRENCH : *Napoleon.*

I

THE fortress of Ham had been built by the Comte de St. Pol in the middle of the fifteenth century as a place of defence against Louis XI.

St. Pol had engraved above the gateway the words : *Mon Mieux*, but his best was not good enough ; for Louis XI had invited him to Paris and then cut off his head.

The keep and walls have the massiveness and the proportion of the castles of the Middle Ages. They were thick and strong and handsome as they stood above the marshy plain around. For the country is flat and cheerless : not a single object attracts the eye to rest. For the greater part of the year the sky is cloudy, mists are common, and a menace seemed to the prisoner to hang in the heavy air which gradually blurred the monotony of the view. A stream flowed from the marsh to the very walls of the fortress, and gave a damp chill to the winter air. In the yard of the prison there is a small modern stone building, and there the Prince, with Conneau, his doctor, and Thélin, his valet, was confined in two white-washed rooms which an American visitor compared to a common kitchen.[1] They were furnished decently with the necessities, but so plainly that the Prince had to arrange planks to make his dressing-table. He also had shelves constructed in his sitting-room. He was allowed to pass from this on to a rampart some thirty yards long overlooking the moat; on the inner slope of the rampart, he made a little flower garden, and as time went on, he was allowed to ride in the yard. But he could not go out even so far without passing through two guard-rooms, and his prison was sentineled by a force of four hundred men. So the monotonous succession of the days and seasons for year after year from 1840 wore on him, as dripping water wears a hollow in a rock. The prisoner became rheumatic, and walked with a limp; he grew thin and looked sickly; and his emotional nature, which always swung between depression and self-confidence, became at first spiritless and dull. But before long there was a reaction.

For even here he found his opportunities; and in the very fact of being a prisoner he found a certain satisfaction. "I am in my right place," he wrote to Lady Blessington. "Bearing the name I do, mine must be either the gloom of the dungeon or the glare of power."[2] And if he was something of a martyr, so much the stronger was his appeal to the people's sympathy. The government recognized this: allowed him his horse if he cared to make a solemn perambulation in the prison yard; allowed his valet to go in

---

[1] Jerrold: ii, 199
[2] Ibid., p. 205.

and out of the fortress; and repaired the damp bricks on the floor, and told him that if he liked he could make further changes. But : " It is not my business," he replied, " to keep in repair the prisons of the State." [1]

At first the prisoner's nerves were restless, and his plans were desultory. But before many months had passed, he saw that the time of enforced quiet would mend the ravages of an unsettled life. He began to live less by his inclinations and more by the work of his mind. The habits which Le Bas had trained reasserted themselves; the Prince became a student. The books in the *Nationale* were placed at his disposal, and he began to arrange his theses, at first on subjects of history. He tried to controvert Guizot's thesis that Louis Philippe's accession was an analogy to that of William and Mary after the Bill of Rights. Louis Napoleon identified the Stuarts with the Bourbons, the Prince of Orange with himself. Yes, he was William : reserved, beset with difficulties, but reigning by and for the interest of the country, placing his claim to the throne on the national pride and in his claim for gratitude from posterity. The Stuarts, so wrote this new historian, could not gather the fruits of earth under a cloudless sky, but William of Orange could reap his harvest in a storm.

And from this story, the prisoner deduced three maxims :—

March in the van of the ideas of your time and these ideas will follow and support you.

March in the rear of them, and they will drag you after them.

March against them and they will destroy you.[2]

---

[1] See Jerrold : ii, 198.
[2] *Fragments historiques*, published in 1843.

THE IMPRISONMENT AT HAM

The Bonaparte Prince then turned his attention from the Orange revolution to beetroot. When France had been locked in by the British Navy, sugar could be obtained only from the beet-growers. It was an old problem of the Emperor's. Louis Napoleon saw in it issues in which he was particularly absorbed. For the modern Napoleon was more interested in the adjustment, than in the conquest of nations. How men were to work, how they were to be fed, those were the great questions. Great Britain, he pointed out, employed hundreds of thousands of workmen in her manufacturing towns : " but let any event shake public credit," he wrote, " close markets, or let over-production bring a glut, and in a moment the whole population, as we see to-day, is in the anguish of want, and presents all the horrors of hunger. The soil sinks under their feet, they have neither fire nor home nor bread."

So spoke Louis Napoleon in the hungry forties, thinking of England. He had noticed in Switzerland a happier system. Swiss industries were scattered over the country instead of being centred exclusively in cities. They are fixed wherever there is a watercourse, a highway, a lake, favouring their operations. The consequence of this system has been to accustom the agricultural classes to pass alternately from the labour of the fields to that of the factory . . . When a calamity strikes an industry, they suffer, no doubt, but they find in the fields a refuge and an occupation. The land must be the masses' buffer against the shocks of trade.

He returned to this idea three years later in his pamphlet on " The Extinction of Pauperism ". The chief idea was that of the people being fixed to the soil by possession and by training, but repairing to the towns for more profitable work when it was to be obtained. He showed once more his uncanny instinct of anticipation, and provided a remedy for the maladies inherent in the system of to-day. He foresaw that the factory system would always be subject to crises on account of the tendency to over-production, first, because when men are making money they always go too far with their schemes; secondly, because needs alter and methods improve. In fact, a world dependent on invention cannot but change with invention. So the crises recur. And they come—not only to the owner and the man of enterprise, but to the masses of his workmen. For these the remedy Louis Napoleon prescribed was neither insurance, nor—the dole. Anticipating the work of Miss Joan Fry to-day, he insisted that it was attachment to the land, and the possession of property. So alone could the masses always be assured of the means of sustenance. The worker must have fresh air, and direct dealings with nature.

"He has no capital except his arms: these, then, must be employed in a manner that will make them productive to the community. A place in society must be given him, and his interests must be rooted in the soil. He is without organization or social ties, without rights or a future. Rights must be given him, and his future must be assured. He must be raised in his own esteem by education, discipline, and association."

The ideas are vague, but the principle is fundamental. France, by keeping a sufficient number of small proprietors who work their own land, has given herself a stability which countries who have sacrificed agriculture to manufacture can never obtain. And yet the elaboration of a system by which agricultural enterprise can secure sustenance and wealth when manufacture has been overdone still needs to be completed and applied. The prisoner's instinct foresaw the needs of a century, but he had no opportunity of adapting his ideas to practical experiment : and, as we shall see, he lacked both the will and the definiteness which gave the first Emperor's successes a fatal immediacy. A peculiar sensibility would with surprising frequency fill his eyes with tears. If they shone at times like the great Napoleon's with the radiant power of empire, the glow even while it lasted was genial rather than resolute ; and then it faded into a languor which was habitual. His expression was not imperious but gentle : and he seemed a man made rather to charm than to command.

It was inevitable that the tendency to be " reserved and close ", which Bulwer Lytton had remarked, should grow upon a man who was always under surveillance. A prisoner with an active mind is not only a conspirator, he feels like the conspirator that he must never say a word that might betray his inward inclination against the power which restrains him. " I think I see him yet," wrote Louis Blanc in 1859, " walking with slow steps, his head bent ; I think I still hear his voice speaking low, lest the wind should carry his words to the gaoler." The conversation turned on the question whether Tacitus was or was not right in denouncing the Roman Emperors as tyrants. The argument of the Prince was that Tacitus was unjust. " I combated it," said Blanc, " and with a vivacity that led him to say ' Speak low ' ; and turning, he pointed out to me a man wrapped in a cloak who was following us at a short distance and never for an instant losing sight of us." [1]

[1] Louis Blanc : *Révélations historiques*, 1859, quoted in Simpson : *Rise of Louis Napoleon.*

"Still waters run deep." So Mlle Masuyer had written as she contrasted the quietness of his demeanour with the violent passions which moved so swiftly in the depths of his nature.[1] When the Royal Government had characterized him as a fool, they blinded themselves to his ability to "conceive with secrecy, and act with promptitude": for gradually men become the dupes of their own fabrications. With the conspirator's astuteness Louis Napoleon took advantage of every victory that had been scored against him. He was a prisoner, but he was now living in France; his misfortunes were a claim upon the sympathy of his countrymen; and with the doggedness which gives solidity to daring, he not only studied, but actually carried on his propaganda in a republican newspaper, the *Progrés du Pas-de-Calais*. He worked out his scheme for the Panama Canal—it is to be noted that in the interests of commerce he thought it ought to be cut through Nicaragua—; he made experiments in chemistry; he read widely and with care; but the importance of the imprisonment at Ham was that the prisoner used it to elaborate his campaign against the government which had imprisoned him.

He declared that there were more scholars in the Emperor's high schools and commercial colleges in 1812 than there were under Louis Philippe in 1840; that crime had increased under the monarchy; that the working classes were not so well off; and that the *prud'hommes*, or captains of working men, whom Napoleon had established had been ignored. And in relation to the poor man, he worked out his scheme for an established Church. For from this time on, we find no traces of Louis Napoleon being in

[1] *Revue des Deux Mondes*, 1915, iii, 867.

PRINCE LOUIS NAPOLEON
From a photograph in the Duke of Alba's collection.

" Still waters run deep. So Mlle Masuyer had written as she contrasted the quietness of his demeanour with his violent passions."

conflict with Catholicism : he had fallen under the influence of the prison chaplain and had found that, in a gaol, the chapel is a distraction ; doubtless, as his mind became more disciplined (and Madame Cornu noticed how much sharper and better it became at Ham), he realized the place of religion in the organism of society. " We have no right," the Emperor had said, " to deprive the poor man because he is poor of that which consoles his poverty." In other words, to withdraw State aid from the Church means that you make the clergy dependent on the rich. But on the other hand, Louis Napoleon did not want the clergy to be either supporters of the aristocracy, or to live as a caste independent of the lives of the people. For this reason the Emperor had discouraged monasticism. Louis Napoleon found his ideal in the clergy of Bavaria. " In their eyes," he wrote, " to be a priest is to teach morality and charity ; it is to make common cause with the oppressed ; it is to preach justice and toleration ; it is to predict the reign of equality ; it is to teach men that the political redemption should follow the religious redemption " : it was, in a word, to teach youth that " God had placed at the bottom of their hearts a faith to believe in good and a love to be extended to one another." [1]

And, indeed, as he looked over his life at Ham, he saw that his destiny was no plaything of a wandering star. His fate was one with his doggedness ; gradually he had been hewing his kingdom from the waste, and, inch by inch, had cleaned the acres for his sowing till now he was cutting a straight furrow to the end in view. A friend had advised him to be less active : less active ! Yes, he answered,

[1] Jerrold : ii, 266, 7.

that is what most people would say to a man on a desert island : " Wait till chance brings you a ship to carry you off ; don't try to build with the bark of trees a ship that will sink in rough weather."

" But that would not be my way," said Louis Napoleon. " I should say : ' Employ every effort to create for yourself instruments with which you will be able to build a ship. This occupation will be a moral support to you for you will always have an object before you : it will develop your faculties by giving you difficulties to conquer. It will prove to you, if you succeed, that you are above destiny. When your vessel is finished, throw yourself boldly into it ; if you manage to reach the continent you will owe your deliverance only to yourself.' "

And so he traced his life. " In 1832 I wrote a pamphlet on Switzerland in order to win the good opinion of those among whom I was compelled to live. Then I applied myself for three years to a work on artillery, which I felt to be beyond my strength, in order to win some hearts in the army, and to prove that, if I did not command, I had at any rate acquired the knowledge necessary to a commander. By these means, I reached Strasbourg. Afterwards I caused the Laity pamphlet to be published, not only to defend myself, but to afford the Government an excuse to demand my expulsion from Switzerland. This did not fail, and the hostility of the Government gave me back my moral independence, which I had in a manner lost by my forced liberation. In London I published, against the advice of everybody, the *Idées Napoléoniennes* to form the political ideas of the party and to prove that I was not merely an adventurous hussar. I tried, by means of the newspapers, to prepare men's minds for the Boulogne affair, but it did not suit the editors ; they wanted to live by polemics, and nothing more. I wished to profit by them. Here I failed at once ; but I could not help it. Boulogne was a horrible catastrophe to me ; but at last I am rising out of it, through the interest which people feel in misfortune, and through the inherent elasticity of all matured causes, which, although often compressed by events, regain with time their old position. What is left of all this chain of wants and cruel sufferings ? Something of immense value to me. In 1833 the Emperor and his son were dead ; there was no heir to the Imperial cause. France knew none. A few Bonapartes appeared, it is true, here and there in the background of the world, as bodies without souls—petrified mummies or aery phantoms. All the Bonapartes were dead. Well, I tied the threads together again. I raised myself from the dead by my own efforts alone and to-day, within sixty miles of Paris, I hang over the heads of its present governors a sword of Damocles.

"In short, I have really built my canoe with bark ; I have spun my sails ; I have taken my oars in my hands, and all I ask from the gods now is a wind to bear me forward." [1]

2

The wind to bear him forward came with the summer of 1846. The state of the prison buildings had become so bad that the Royal Government was forced to put them in better repair. Workmen had to come into the enclosure, had therefore to leave it, and the work went on for ten days. Louis Napoleon

[1] Jerrold : ii, 232.

talked to Conneau of assuming a workman's disguise; he watched the men, their clothes, above all how they came in and out of the fortress. It was noticed that they were passed in or out between two sentinels at the gates. It seemed hopeless. But as the Prince watched the men, he saw that occasionally during the hours of work a man would pass out carrying an old plank. He thought that he might try and do the same. He ordered his valet to go out and buy the clothes he wanted, a rough shirt, a blue blouse, blue trousers, and a workman's apron; and these were washed and ostentatiously soiled, made in fact dirtier than any decent French workman's clothes are on any Monday morning.

On 25th May (that day *was* Monday) he rose at daybreak; with Conneau and Thélin he peered down into the courtyard; soon afterwards they heard the chains of the drawbridge rattle, and just after five the workmen entered as usual between two files of soldiers. But the Prince and his two friends noticed also that the man on guard was the particular soldier who always scrutinized each workman as he passed. With him any attempt at escape would be hopeless. The chaplain had been coming to say Mass but he had been put off. At eight the Governor would take charge. At six o'clock, however, the perilous sentinel went off duty. The Prince changed into the workman's dirty blue clothes; he rouged his cheeks; a wig fell over his ears; he wore a peasant's hat, and thick clogs made him look an inch or so taller; and finally he shaved off his beard and moustache. In his pocket were letters of the Emperor and of Hortense: in his blouse a dagger.

Thélin lured the workmen away to have a drink, and then engaged the sentinel's attention at the door. The disguised workman, a clay pipe in his mouth, stepped out into the yard, holding a plank between his face and the guardian at the door. As he passed the first sentinel in the yard, the pipe fell and smashed, but the fugitive had the presence of mind to pick it up. At the gateway, where several men seemed to think his figure odd, Thélin distracted the sentinels' attention with the dog performing, while the Prince, holding a plank between his face and the sentry, went through the gate. Even on the drawbridge he met an official, on the other side he had still to pass another sentry.[1] When he was finally out, his life was in yet fuller danger because he had escaped : recapture this time would be death. He had hardly left the prison gates when he saw workmen approaching, but he kept his plank between his face and them, and they passed him with the words " *C'est Berthaud* ".[2] He plodded on in the clogs, carrying his plank : at last clear of the town, he left his plank in the field and knelt down before a cross in a graveyard to thank God for his deliverance. " There are instincts," he said, " stronger than all philosophies." A few minutes later Thélin had met him with a fly and a change of clothes, and they drove gently down the road to Amiens. He did not know whether his departure had been noticed at the prison. Conneau had said that he was ill, had taken medicine and must not be disturbed. To keep up appearances, Conneau (for it was before the days of water-closets) took a dose of castor oil himself. When this heroic measure failed to produce results in time, he made an unsavoury mess with chemicals. And thus he acted his part so that the Governor knew nothing till the evening. Then, entering the Prince's bedroom,

[1] F. Giraudeau : *Napoléon III intime*, pp. 113, 114.
[2] Loc. cit.

he saw that the form beneath the blankets was a bolster. "Then he has gone," said the Governor. "*Mais oui*," said Conneau. By that time the game at Ham was up.

The Prince, however, was well on his way. At St. Quentin, while he walked through the town, Thélin took a post-chaise, and found his master on the road to Valenciennes. Arriving there at two o'clock, they had to wait two hours at the station, and Thélin was recognized by a policeman who had known him at Ham, and who insisted on hearing all about the unseen Prince. A passport was demanded, but as in Italy, the Prince had obtained an English passport. With this he crossed the frontier, and hurried to Ostend. Next day he was in England, and welcomed, after his sporting adventure, with admiration for a sportsman.[1]

His father died in July, and, after a decent spell of mourning, the Prince renewed his friendship with Count d'Orsay and Lady Blessington, dallied with ladies who were respectable, and maintained an establishment for the faithful mistress, Miss Howard, whom seven years before he had won from Kinglake. But for the time he seemed to have no taste for adventure. Those long years had taken the edge from his activity: he had become both a thinker, and a dreamer: great ideas had absorbed him, he had worked hard at theories, he had developed his inventiveness. But the object of this was not so much to see his schemes carried out as to make propaganda; and from that time forward that habit never left him. Before he had been a man of action. For even a writer is a man of action; he assumes a power over both

---

[1] The full story of the escape is told with brilliant vividness of detail in Mr. Simpson's *Rise of Louis Napoleon*, ch. x.

men and things, and to writing Louis Napoleon had turned, as his uncle had turned to concise and pungent phrases to assume and express his mastery of a situation. But now Louis Napoleon found himself apt to consider without deciding, without coming to conclusions which demanded an immediate expression. Yet even so, as we have seen, his mind was clearer, his thought trained, and he had assumed a habit of listening and then expressing a decision. And yet it was not his habit to think the matter over and weigh the opposing means. He would light his cigar and dream. And as the ideas took form in his mind he would wait till one pleased his imagination. Then he seized it, and, moved with powerful excitement, would speak as one inspired.[1]

3

For the moment no conspiracy was as interesting as Lady Blessington's house in Kensington. Although her circle was made up of people like herself, at whom the inner great might look askance, they shared her charm. And as for Lady Blessington herself, though she was neither witty nor wise, she had a humour that enabled her to say almost everything without offending taste. It was said of her that " she never wrote a line that might not be placed on the bookshelves of an English lady ",[2] and those who saw most of her refused to believe the stories against her. She was at once so simple and so graceful, and her arch remarks, made in an Irish accent, were finished with a soft sweet laugh which those who heard it found impossible to resist.

[1] N. W. Senior : *Conversations*, ii, 116.
[2] R. C. Madden : *Life of Lady Blessington*, p. 81.

There was no one who was seen with her more often than Count d'Orsay. And no man in London had a personality of more distinction. His manners, like his dress, were perfect. He was singularly handsome; he had about him a sort of elevation, and when he spoke, he was a joy to hear. Belonging to an old family, he had been brought up as an Imperialist, and he gave a peculiar deference to Louis Napoleon, whose figure in 1839 he had sketched with that clearness and distinction with which he outlined everything on which he touched.

As for Miss Howard, whom Count d'Orsay presented, she captivated the prince and held him in thrall longer than any other woman. As for the real name and origin of this extraordinary person, she was the daughter of a Sussex brewer named Heriott. When Napoleon met her, she was living with a Major Mountjoy Martin, of the 2nd Life Guards. She had also been the mistress of Kinglake, who never forgave the Prince for winning her over. But in spite of her origin and her doubtful position, she entertained distinguished Englishmen—Lord Malmesbury, Lord Chesterfield, the Duke of Beaufort. She dressed superbly, rode well, and had accumulated a considerable fortune which she placed at the Prince's disposal on more occasions than one.[1]

When later she followed him to France, she modelled herself on La Pompadour, and it was thought that she entertained great ambitions. The Prince constantly visited her in the Rue du Cirque, and she did not scruple to appear in his company either in Paris or when he toured the provinces. This occasioned remonstrance which he answered boldly.

[1] Le Petit Homme Rouge (i.e. E. A. Vizetelly) : *Court of the Tuileries*, pp. 184, 5.

But, in the course of time, this relationship came to its inevitable end. She made demands for money, and they were honoured to the extent of five million francs. She died at a comparatively early age at her domain of Beauregard, near the outskirts of the Forest of Fontainebleau, and her son was ennobled with the title of Count de Béchavet.[1] And if afterwards she received vast sums of money, it must be remembered that at the beginning she gave it. In those years from 1846 to 1848 the Prince was very poor indeed. He did not even pay for his own lodgings : but was thankful to accept a bedroom in 29 Berkeley Square, after Lord Wenlock had shut it up and left it in the care of Mary Button, an aged and rather unprepossessing housemaid.

Miss Howard was not the only object of Louis Napoleon's attention : he also proposed to a demure and sober maiden, Miss Minnie Dawson-Damer. People who knew this lady in later years as Lady Fortescue, mistress of solid but not fascinating qualities in her square old-fashioned home in Devon, were intrigued to think of what might have happened if she had taken her chances with the heir of the Bonapartes.[2]

[1] H. Fleischmann : *Napoléon III et les Femmes* Révérend. *Titres du Second Empire*.
[2] Private information.

II

POWER

V

THE PRESIDENCY

> Be penitent, and for thy fault contrite;
> But act not in thine own affliction, son.
> Repent the sin; but, if the punishment
> Thou canst avoid, self-preservation bids;
> Or the execution leave to high disposal,
> And let another hand, not thine, exact
> Thy penal forfeit from thyself. Perhaps
> God will relent, and quit thee all thy debt.
> *Samson Agonistes*, 502–8.

I

THE chance for which Louis Napoleon had been so carefully preparing himself, for close on twenty years, came with the convulsion of 1848. There was disorder in Prussia, Vienna, London, the Papal States, and France. The Pope fled to the Pontine Marshes, Metternich, and Louis Philippe sought refuge in England: even before the dethroned King had landed, Louis Napoleon had already set foot in France.

The Republic was too weak, and too unpopular, however, to risk the presence of the heir of Bonaparte. Once again he was declared an exile. " I thought, gentlemen," he wrote in answer, " that after thirty-three years of exile and persecution, I had at length the right to find a home in my native land. You think that my presence in Paris at this time would be an embarrassment : I therefore retire for the moment. You will see in this sacrifice the purity of my intentions and of my patriotism." [1]

The request to leave turned out more helpful than permission to remain. It drew fresh attention to him ; it also left him clear of the intrigues and disorders of a disastrous year. He returned to London ; and with an instinct for order, he offered himself during the Chartist riots, and was actually enrolled as a special constable. " *Et que diable fait Monsieur Napoléon dans cette galère?* " asked an American friend who recognized him.

" Sir," answered the Prince, " the peace of London *must* be preserved." [2]

What was hardly less important, the people of France were enabled to see that a man who was taking his part in maintaining order in London would be a much more useful person in Paris than the agitators of the mob. On 4th June he was in four separate departments elected deputy. And from that time on, his name rose in France like the summer sun. His portrait was to be seen everywhere, and beneath it the single word : *Lui.* Before a fortnight had passed there were six Bonapartist newspapers. The Prince was still declared an exile, but, at the instance of Jules Favre, the Chamber decided it would be safer to withdraw the proscription. Men began to feel about it that, in the words of the British Ambassador, " it was unjust even if it was expedient, and most inexpedient even if it had been just." For " I desire

---

[1] Jerrold : ii, 393, 4.
[2] F. A. Simpson, *Rise of Louis Napoleon*, 278.

order," wrote the Prince to the President, " and the maintenance of a great, wise, and intelligent republic." [1]

So he was permitted to claim his seat. But he decided to submit his case to a supplementary election which took place on 17th September. Thirteen seats were vacant : for no less than five of them Louis Napoleon was elected. A week later he came back to Paris. His carriage rumbled over the cobble-stones of dark, deserted, ill-kept streets to a hotel in the Place Vendôme, that Place Vendôme where sixteen years before the first Emperor's statue had been set up on the central column. At last his career in France had begun : and not even in the case of the first Emperor had doggedness and daring given a Frenchman a more curious preparation for the exercise of power : for here was no successful general or administrator. Here was a wayward and artistic woman's son brought up in Germany and Switzerland : here was a man who had been an insurgent and for six years a prisoner. Here was a voluptuary and a pamphleteer. A third of his life he had spent in France, and of that third, half as a child in the Court, half as a man in prison. For the other two-thirds of his life he had been an exile. And now at last, recognized as having the power to lead and govern, he was for over twenty years to rule supreme—a reign as pregnant as any in French history.

2

It was eight years since Louis Napoleon, then at his trial, had been seen at any sort of assemblage in

[1] F. A. Simpson : *Rise of Louis Napoleon*, p. 288.

Paris. In the last few years his features had become almost unrecognizable. His foster-sister, Madame Cornu, hardly knew him. " What is the matter with your eyes ? " she asked. " Nothing," he answered. But when she went back next day, she looked at them more closely. She saw that the lids had fallen over them more heavily than ever, and that beneath they were empty and dead. And yet, if she had looked longer, she would have seen how on occasion their vacancy was exchanged for the most genial animation.[1] Years of study, of suffering, and of licence, however, had made Louis Napoleon at forty a middle-aged man.

As he mounted the tribune to make his maiden speech as a deputy, his enemies, whether Royalists or Republicans, saw that he was not a man whom henceforth they would be able to deride. His figure was small and slight, but it had a martial grace ; his bearing, as he walked through the Chamber, was quiet and easy ; and though his voice was firm and his attitude uncompromising, he had hardly begun to speak when those around him felt his peculiar power of winning the hearts of men. " For a long time, gentlemen," he said, " I have been able to give my country only the meditations of exile and captivity. To-day, the career which you pursue is open to me also. Receive me into your ranks, dear colleagues, with that affectionate sympathy I myself feel. You should not doubt that my conduct will always be inspired by a respectful devotion to the Law ; it will prove to all who have endeavoured to blacken me, that no person is more devoted than I am to the defence of order and the consolidation of the Republic." [2]

[1] H. W. Senior : *Conversations*.
[2] Jerrold : iii, 16, 17.

And yet there was something rotten in this talk of " Republic ". Louis Napoleon did not want it : he knew that the claim he made on the people was that they did not want it either : he knew that the actual President, Cavaignac, was fighting for the sake of principle and not for a majority behind it ; he knew that principle to be specially odious to Thiers, and the followers of Louis Philippe. One of them, Bugeaud, had actually compared the President to a cow in the skin of a hyena.[1] All of them were prepared to support Prince Louis against him in the Presidential election of December. And meanwhile the Prince, who by sympathy and cogitation, had become the modern man, who already fifteen years before had been speaking words which fall so apposite a hundred years later, laid down his general principles: order re-established, authority strengthened, liberty intact, religion, the family and property protected, the press preserved from both tyranny and licence.

"As regards practicable reforms," he said, " here are those which appear to me to be most urgent : To admit every saving that, without disorganizing the public service, will allow the reduction of the taxes which press the hardest on the people ; to encourage undertakings, which, by developing agriculture, say in France and Algeria, give work to those who want it ; to provide for the old age of working-men by establishing benefit societies ; to introduce into our legislation modifications tending, not to ruin the rich for the benefit of the poor, but to base the prosperity of each in that of all.

" To restrain within proper limits the employment which depends on the State, and which often makes

---

[1] Earl of Kerry (now Marquis of Lansdowne) : *Secret of the Coup d'État*, p. 58.

a free people a nation of beggars. To avoid that shameful tendency which leads the State to undertake works which private enterprise can do as well—or even better. *The centralization of interests is the essence of despotism.*" [1]

The manifesto was addressed to the men who then made, and have ever since continued to make the strength of France, the small proprietors, the men who had never had very much but had found their satisfaction in increasing by their own work and enterprise their store from year to year. Such is the solid body of conservative but not reactionary tradition which makes France, taking it as a whole, socially the most secure of nations, and which leaves it strong when both invasion and political dishonesty have done their worst: it gave the Citizen Napoleon Bonaparte of 1848 a vote of 5,434,226 votes out of a total of 7,327,345; his runner-up, Cavaignac, having 1,448,107. And French opinion remained equally solid behind Louis Napoleon for over twenty years. It would be difficult to find a man who retained so much of the public confidence for so long either in France or in any other country.

3

But his exercise of power did not begin easily. It was still but a year since Karl Marx had first issued his manifesto. The Socialists were carrying on a strong propaganda, which succeeded in winning an election in Paris on 10th March, 1850. And three weeks later the President, as he passed through the Faubourg St. Antoine, was greeted with an ugly

[1] Jerrold: iii, 37, 38.

demonstration, shouting " Down with the Tyrant ! " It was an anxious moment. " Paris," wrote Hübner, " bears on her darkened forehead, and on her tightened though still smiling lips, the marks of the situation. People dance, they play their music in their drawing-rooms, but at the same time they lay in stores of gold and take their passports." [1]

Whether or not Louis Napoleon was capable of affronting such a situation was considered doubtful. He had in the previous autumn, on the 31st October, strengthened his hand, and assumed the full responsibility for the situation, with all its risks. But then he had relaxed into his recurring torpor. " A marked distaste for business," wrote the Austrian envoy, " has overcome this Prince, who is temperamentally weary, indolent, and fatalistic." [2] But that mood had passed, and the very success of the Socialists in Paris came to him as a reinforcement when he asserted the power of order. He made adroit use of it in a speech at Lyons on 8th August, 1850. " Before a general danger," he said, " all personal ambition should disappear. At such a time, patriotism can be assessed in the same way as, in a famous case, the judge determined which of a child's two claimants was the mother. By what sign was the real mother recognized ? By her renouncement of the rights which would have endangered the child she loved. Let the parties who love France never forget this magnificent lesson." [3]

That argument was addressed not merely to the Socialists, but to the leading Parliamentarians of the Monarchy. From the beginning (and it was to be so to the end) Louis Napoleon found his most

---

[1] Vienna National Archives (referred to hereafter as V.N.A.), Baron Hübner to Prince Schwarzenberg, 3rd April, 1850.
[2] V.N.A., Hübner to Schwarzenberg, 15th December, 1849.
[3] *Moniteur*, 19th August, 1850.

formidable adversary in Adolphe Thiers. Thiers was then the greatest orator of France. He was born into a class so low, that even when he had risen to supreme power, a subscription was raised to save his relations from famine and prostitution. But he was a great historian, an able politician, and he had secured the idolatry of a wealthy wife. This lady looked after him with the constancy of a baby's nurse, and the regularity of a chronometer. His coffee, his soup, the wine with which he moistened his lips in the pauses of his ringing speeches, the springs of his carriage, the cut of his clothes, the temperature of his rooms, were all carefully arranged and tirelessly supervised. Everything was devised to prevent an accident.[1]

And yet there was an accident. For from the beginning Thiers was hostile to the President. He had, as we have seen, objected to Miss Howard being entertained where Louis Philippe's blameless queen had once been châtelaine. "*Il me déplait, ce petit Louis,*" said Thiers to Hübner, "*je n'ai pour lui, ni goût, ni estime, ni espoir.*" He looked upon him as a blockhead dead to the force of logic, and in the beginning of 1851, believing that France was then safe from anarchy, he set to work to undermine the President's position : it was a work carefully planned and never to be relaxed : and it was then concentrated on the vote for the President's civil list. " I am not his cook," said Thiers. " Those details are scarcely my business. He can arrange them himself with his cook, his butcher's and baker's bills. But the Chamber would be inexorable if he dared to submit his proposals. They would never grant him his millions." [1]

[1] Villemessant : *Mémoires*, iv, 369, 370.
[2] V.N.A., Hübner to Schwarzenberg, 22nd January, 1851.

But there Thiers was wrong. The President demanded a great income, and he got it. His capacities, negative as they often were, had been displayed with the skill of a master. Calm, reserved, confident, in his star, he had listened, careful but unperturbed, to the speeches sometimes sarcastic, sometimes furious, but always venomous, which were made against him in the Chamber. The Army had been hesitating, not knowing which was master, the President or the Assembly: but already in the autumn of 1850, on the plains of Satory, Louis Napoleon had heard the cry of *Vive l'Empereur*! And everyone knew that the speeches in the Chamber made no impression in the country as a whole, where there had been an enormous increase of prosperity. " I am much deceived," wrote Hübner, " if the real prestige of the name of Louis Bonaparte comes less from the grandeur of his uncle than from the hope that he will free the country from government by talk." [1] What fascinated France was the tone of authority. The Emperor's predilection was turning back to the Constitution of the year VIII and that was particularly congenial to the army. " I would not say to you : ' March and I follow you,' " declared the President finally. " What I would say is : ' I march : follow me.' " [2]

The adjutant this commander needed had come forward with his accession to power.

4

A few months after his election, the Prince President received at the Elysée the son of Queen Hortense and of the Comte de Flahault. Flahault had married

[1] V.N.A., Hübner to Schwarzenberg, 3rd November, 1851.
[2] V.N.A., ibid., 8th November, 1851.

a Scottish baroness and lived in London : but his mother, Madame de Souza, had brought up the child to whom Hortense had given birth. Auguste Demorny had become at will the Count de Morny, and he had more than the usual share of talent, energy, charm, and unscrupulousness. Early in life he had become a cavalryman, and served in Algeria. He had distinguished himself at the siege of Constantine and been given the Legion of Honour for saving the life of his general. He returned invalided to France, and saw that business offered bigger prizes than the army. In a very short time he showed himself to have the shrewdest head for business : in fact, at the age of thirty, he was the head of the sugar industry of France, that industry which his half-brother, while still in prison at Ham, had so energetically vindicated. He then entered the Chamber as deputy, and distinguished himself by his talent for finance. His connections had always been with power : he was now rich, and he combined his financial foresight with a brilliance of manner and wit which made him irresistible. For he inherited both the distinction of Flahault, the amorous attraction of Hortense, and the cunning of Talleyrand. His grand manner made him at home in the world of fashion ; his wit cut through his difficulties, and his opponents, it was said, wilted in the sparkle of his smile. Even when he was twelve years old, Talleyrand had foreseen that he had a political future. But his greatest gift was insight. " When you talk to a man," he said, " listen to what he thinks, not to what he says." And he never saw too much to disturb a rapid and ruthless decision. Yet, though he had the prudence which safeguards success, his greater gift was the cavalryman's instinctive power in the face of danger. " Where is there not danger ? " he used to say, and he loved it, because he could seize its opportunities. Yet he would watch events, and listen to advice. "In spite of his indifference," wrote Ollivier, "he was capable of friendship. Like all men who have had many love affairs, he had no gentleness of affection; in its stead, he had grace, an easy wit, tact, cordiality, a seductive charm.[1] There was no pose in his manners, no surliness, but a captivating spontaneity. He was always gracious and, although very busy, never appeared in a hurry. It was impossible to approach him without feeling at once attracted, and there were few who did not find him finally congenial. Amiability in a word varnished the hard grain of his unscrupulousness, as experience had sharpened to the finest edge the polished steel of his heredity. He had been a guest at shooting parties in Scotland, he had talked politics with the King of the French, he had found favour in a circle of *grandes dames*, and he had been commended for his talents by the chaste Guizot. He was a wit and a man of action, a courtier, and a financier, a man of fashion and a politician. In all this, however, he was "*brillant plus par son esprit que par la chaleur de ses convictions.*"[2] As Lord Cowley said of him, at his death, "he had it in him if he had been honest to have become a very great man."[3]

This was the man who, when he felt assured that the Prince President was secure at the Elysée, decided that he himself might found a claim on his relationship to Hortense. Louis Napoleon was much moved.

[1] Emile Ollivier: *Le 19 Janvier*.
[2] V.N.A., Hübner to Schwarzenberg, 15th December, 1849.
[3] F. Wellesley: *The Paris Embassy*, p. 281. The authoritative biography of Morny is one which M. Quatrelles L'Epine was preparing at his death at the end of 1932. That of M. Boulenger is also reliable.

Here then, at last, was a brother : here was one who could fill the void which insurrection and measles had made at Forli so many years ago : and here was one who shared his own feelings for reform, not merely on beet sugar. " Moderate concessions," so Morny himself had written, " intelligent reforms, conscientious study of financial and social questions, a pious zeal in the rich in favour of the poor classes, and at the same time a courageous opposition to the factions which prevent the evils which menace us. Let the sufferings of the working classes be studied with fervour : let savings banks, crêches, day schools, tontines, general workshops, councils of *prud'hommes* be created—here is the solution of the problem." [1]

But when the brothers met, they did not speak of these things ; they did not mention her who gave them the secret of brotherhood. It was bond enough that their hands clasped. Louis Napoleon saw in Auguste de Morny the qualities which are priceless in the ally of a conspirator : shrewdness, hardihood, and initiative. Here was the man who was to raise him to the throne of France. Here was one who, having in his possession papers that proved him the son of Hortense, while she was still the wife of Louis, saw that it would be wiser not to claim the style or title of imperial brother.

The Prince President was still a conspirator at heart. " Cavaignac had scruples," says La Gorce, " and prided himself on inspiring with them the men around him. Bonaparte, if he appeared to have them himself, was marvellously clever in preventing his friends from being embarrassed by them." [2] He saw

[1] Véron : *Mémoires d'un Bourgeois de Paris*, v.
[2] La Gorce : *Deuxième République*, bk. x, ch. iii.

that against him he had not only the Royalists but many of the Republicans. The Assembly had in fact become his enemy, and were seeking to get him out. The Orleans Princes (for Louis Philippe died in 1850) were beginning to feel that their time was ripe. Thiers had narrowed the suffrage, and the men who were left were politicians who represented their own ambitions rather than the instinct of the people. Thiers had made an entente with the Duchess of Orleans. Royalists had once more joined Republicans, and this time against the Prince President.[1] For his power in France was getting too strong for them. As for him, he had been convinced of his hold over the country when he toured it in 1850. Although he had long called himself a Republican, he meant by that merely that he would not force the Empire on people before they knew that they were ready for it. In his heart, as he feared and detested the Bourbons, so he feared and detested universal suffrage; but he knew that, without it, the pinnacle of power would be beyond attainment. He could not decide what to do. "What," he asked the Austrian Ambassador, "do you think of my last idea—to give the vote to every married man?"[2]

But in his heart of hearts, he knew that he could employ a stronger power than any suffrage; beside the general instinct of the people, and their enthusiasm for his name, he had, for the most part, the loyalty of the army. Beyond that again, he had another power, which from the time of the First Empire up to now is the real power in France, the administration of the police.[3] While his adversaries in the Assembly were deriding his incompetence, while his

[1] V.N.A., Hübner to Schwarzenberg, 8th November, 1851.
[2] Hübner: *Neuf Ans*, p. 35.
[3] Hübner: *Neuf Ans*, i, 15.

speech in November of 1851 had been judged
" insipid, not to say stupid ", while the deputies
discussed his inability to manage them, and his
ineptitude in all the arts of parliamentary government,
they lost sight of the very secret of his power, that he
did not really believe at all in the phantom cavalcade
which was called democracy, and behind which the
politicians of France and England had, in their own
interests, driven for thirty years the sovereign people.[1]
Louis Napoleon was astute enough to look facts in
the face. He knew that the people knew that he
wanted them to be well off : he knew that the real
power was the combination of the artillery with the
police : in place of the arts of a Parliamentary leader,
he had the skill of a conspirator : he could " conceive
with secrecy and act with promptitude ".

4

Once again, in the autumn of 1851, he found
himself faced with the contrasting alternatives of
imprisonment and empire. On the one side he had
his parliament against him : and on the other he
knew from Morny, and Morny's father, Flahault,
had given warning, that the Bourbons were acting
with the Chambers.[2] The Prince met his peril with
the sudden violence which laborious stratagem
prepares, like gunpowder, to explode into action
from the underground procedures of the conspirators'
brain. Reckless of his oath as President, he planned
to arrest his enemies, and make a direct appeal to

[1] Hübner : op. cit., i, 51.
[2] Kerry : *Secret of the Coup d'État*, pp. 176, 199.

the people in the twin names of suffrage and of order.

Few were his confidants. Morny was the first, and perhaps in Morny's brain the plot was conceived: for Flahault, won over from the Bourbons by a shrewd estimate of the claims he might make on the newly discovered capacities of the son of Queen Hortense, was also told the secret. To Morny the Prince President added Mocquard, his private secretary, and two others who were also friends of Morny. These were General de St. Arnaud, lately returned from Africa (he it was whose life Morny had saved), and M. de Maupas whom Morny had brought up from the provinces to be made the prefect of police. No others were informed, except Persigny, whom the President, for auld lang syne, refused to leave out.

The first of December was the anniversary of Austerlitz; in the evening the Prince President gave a great reception at the Élysée : but as he moved among the guests, no word, no look, no gesture gave the slightest hint that he was within a few hours to set at work the machinery of a great issue.[1]

Only Maxime du Camp noticed that, as he passed among the guests, he drew aside one officer to exchange words with him in a low tone. The words which no one heard were an order that the réveillé should not sound in the morning for the guard who, in fact, when they did wake, were to find their drums pierced and their powder wet. Nor did Maxime du Camp know that in the few minutes in which the President withdrew from the assembly that it was to mark certain papers with the word *Rubicon*.

At eleven, the guests departed : only Maupas, Mocquard, and St. Arnaud remained. Later they

[1] Hübner: *Neuf Ans*, i, 35.

were joined by Morny who came on from the Opéra Comique, where he had been seen in the box of one of his lady friends.

"They were just saying to me, my dear Count," she said, "that the Prince was going to sweep out the Chambers. What will your part be?"

"Madame," answered Morny, "if the broom is to be put at work, I shall try and stick with the handle." [1]

5

Next morning, early, he was installed as Minister of the Interior: in other words he was in charge of the administration of France—and under a government that had been made absolute.

For before they left the Elysée, the conspirators had made their compact final. The papers marked *Rubicon* had been handed by the President to his confederates, the *coup d'état* was made. Barricades were erected in the streets, and the army, under the command of St. Arnaud, had power over all Paris. The feeling of the men in power is summed up in a terse message from Maupas to St. Arnaud: *Du canon, du canon et du courage.*[2] Every parliamentary leader, or military officer—there were eighty of them—who could head a faction, had been arrested and taken to prison. The workmen when they woke in the morning saw not only the barricades, but proclamations telling them that their vote and their liberty had been restored. And recalcitrants to the

---

[1] Véron : *Mémoires d'un Bourgeois.*
[2] Archives du Quai d'Orsay. *Papiers de Cerçay.*

number of something like fifteen had been killed or wounded.[1]

The President had been called in the morning at five, and wrote with his own hand an invitation to join him on horseback at eight o'clock. At the head of a cavalcade of his supporters, he rode amidst a scene of wild enthusiasm from the Elysée to the Palais Bourbon. The cry of *Vive l'Empereur*! was already heard on every side, and when at times, workmen countered it with *Vive la République*! the troops were ordered to shout louder still *Vive la République*!

At lunch time the President was expected at a luncheon at the Ministère des Affaires Étrangères. For an hour the host and guests waited, and then sat down in desperation. The Prince had retired so exhausted that he had forgotten to excuse himself to his hostess.[2] He must have learnt in the meantime of those casualties not only among the soldiers, but the innocent citizens of Paris who, like the baby victims of Herod, had been sacrificed to make him safe. Always shocked, and exhausted, at the thought of bloodshed, he was to hear two days later of a much higher list of casualties.[3] Louis Napoleon was nearly always impassive ; he was never ruthless ; and though the tears came less easily now than when he was a young man, his temperament was still extremely emotional. Morny, on the other hand, had the calmness of his phenomenal efficiency, and struck his father as heroic.[4]

---

[1] The number, which has been the subject of much controversy, is apparently settled by Maupas' confidential report to Flahault. Kerry : *The Secret of the Coup d'État*, 21, 22, 155–7.
[2] Hübner : *Neuf Ans*, i, 34.
[3] Paléologue : *Entretiens*, 31.
[4] Kerry : *Secret*, 120.

Paris, and in fact all France, seemed to accept the change with calm, and in some cases with enthusiasm; and for the most part, the distinguished foreigners in Paris were pleased. Hübner was gay, and the minister of King Bomba, like the Princess de Lieven, was in ecstasies of joy.[1] But the plenipotentiaries both of England and Belgium looked very far from pleased.

The most important of the men arrested was not Cavaignac, but Thiers. Thiers, though he must have eight hours of sleep in the twenty-four, took one after each meal, and so could rise at five in the morning and was always at work by six. Although he rose so early, the birds of the *coup d'État* were earlier still, and caught their worm. Though disturbed in bed, he at once reminded his captors that as a deputy he was immune from arrest but, seeing that they paid no attention, he realized at once that parliamentary government had been suspended, and began to dress.

"I should very much like to shoot you," he said to the police sergeant.

"I doubt if you could," was the answer, "and in any case I shouldn't allow it." So Thiers went off to Mazas quietly, contenting himself with asking for café au lait on his arrival. But he never forgave the man who had dared to ignore him. To have had to flee to London like a mere Pole—that consummated his antipathy and rankled through the busy years while he wrote his history and waited for revenge.[2]

But the arrest of Thiers and the deputies was not the gravest detail of the *coup d'État*. The Tuesday

---

[1] Hübner: *Neuf Ans*, i, 35. Kerry: op. cit., 122.
[2] Villemessant: *Mémoires*, iv, 369, 379.

passed off quietly: it was not until the noon of Thursday, 4th December, that Maupas became nervous as to what was happening in the workmen's quarters of Paris. " The news," he wrote to St. Arnaud at 1.15, " becomes very grave: the insurgents are occupying the houses; shopkeepers are handing over weapons to them. The *mairie* of the 5th *arrondissement* is in the hands of the insurgents; and there they are making fortifications. To allow them to increase now would be an act of gross carelessness. Here is the moment to strike a decisive blow. One must have the boom of cannon and its effect. Above all cannon and AT ONCE." Half an hour later he sent a still more urgent message. " We are surrounded by revolutionaries. They are shooting at my door. The *mairie* of the 6th *arrondissement* is captured. There is not an instant to lose. In the name of the country, which you *will give up to ruin* if you wait one minute, send troops. Send to my headquarters a regiment and cannon." [2]

So it was that to put an end to all resistance the troops came out once more into the streets, and fired.[2] On that terrible afternoon the casualties rose from about fifteen to more like six hundred.[3] That figure brought resistance to an end, but the number of the casualties was never forgotten either by France or Louis Napoleon.[4] The country, it is true, endorsed his action: and since she endorsed it, his responsibility for breaking his oath is no longer personal. He did break his oath certainly, but that is not the question. There are circumstances which are stronger than any pledges, and the people of France tacitly released

[1] Archives du Quai d'Orsay. *Papiers de Cerçay.*
[2] Simpson: *Louis Napoleon and the Recovery of France,* 152, 3.
[3] Kerry: *Secret of the Coup d'État.*
[4] Paléologue: *Entretiens,* 31.

him from his oath. But Thiers did not. As for Count d'Orsay, he described the coup d'État as the greatest political swindle ever practised in the world.[1] "*Les choses qui se passent en France*," wrote the Duchess of Kent to Lady Douglas, "*sont horribles.*"[2] We are not told what Miss Howard thought.

Miss Howard had been brought over to Paris and given an apartment not far from the Tuileries: and such were the standards of the time that Napoleon felt he need not make a secret of it. " The Prince has brought over from England," it was said, " the most beautiful horse, and the most beautiful woman in Paris." But she did not absorb the attention of her lover. He renewed his suit to Princess Mathilde, the cousin who had once so thoughtlessly rejected him. Princess Mathilde, however, had been married to a rich Russian, and, though he had long left her to herself, she could produce no grounds for dissolving the marriage. So the Prince must look elsewhere for a wife, as he looked elsewhere for a mistress. As early as 1849, there had been a brilliant young Spanish lady, who he had met with Princess Mathilde, Doña Eugenia de Guzman, the daughter of one of the great ladies of the Court of Queen Isabel, whom the Prince had invited to dinner in the forests near St. Cloud one summer evening, and not for the *bon motif*. But this young lady had settled the affair by leaving her admirer with her mother on his arm— so tactfully did she insist on the precedence of courts —and then she travelled off to Germany.[3] Miss Howard's position, therefore, was undisturbed. And

[1] R. R. Madden : *Lady Blessington*, i, 359.
[2] V.N.A., Hübner to Schwarzenberg, 18th December, 1851.
[3] Filon : *Souvenirs sur l'Imperatrice Eugénie.*

the Prince President seemed absorbed in the triumph of his position. He was in every sense of the word the master of France.[1] " France has enough vitality to recover her energy," it was neatly said, " but is ill enough to need being taken in hand." [2]

It was not until the next autumn that he realized how the descending mantle of his uncle's glory had enveloped him with magic. But then he made a great tour in the centre and in the south of France. What better cry to greet him than the old cry *Vive Napoléon* ? And when one put three exclamation marks after it, the printed notice read already *Vive Napoléon* ! ! ! . From that it was natural to cry *Vive l'Empereur*. The people who had greeted him had found that their business during the three years of his power had become solid ; to them he personified both the comfort of the good old times, and the hopes of a radiant future. From the East of the Cevennes to the West of the Pyrenees, village vied with village, and valley with valley, in their enthusiastic welcomes. Old soldiers who had known the Emperor came with their descendants, often more than a hundred miles, to scan the features of the nephew for that something which they had worshipped in the uncle. At Nîmes, they slept on the tiers of the amphitheatre by thousands. At Toulouse the grave mountaineers of Andorra mingled with the men who had grown up by the thousand streams that flowed into the Garonne.[3] There was one man who sent the Prince a pair of high boots which he had worked garishly with pictures of the Emperor, of his generals, of his battles. The Prince received it with a roar of laughter, and then he realized that behind this crude offering

---

[1] V.N.A., Hübner to Schwarzenberg, 14th May, 1852.
[2] La Gorce : *Deuxième République*, vol. ii, preface.
[3] La Gorce : *Deuxième République*.

was the heart of one filled with a sacred devotion as of the nun who embroiders a frontal for the altar, or a vestment for the Madonna.¹ That great mystic tribute which the hearts of men were wont to give to consecrated authority, this, in the autumn of 1852, with the magic syllables " *Vive Napoléon* ! " came flooding up through France like the lapping waves of the deluge to the quiet little man who bowed silently as he passed through the crowd, and who answered it by repeating a succession of phrases : " commercial progress," " railway enterprise," " improvement of agriculture," " provision for the poor," and " peace." ² At times he struck a deeper note. " I have henceforward but one end," he said at Lyons, " it is to build up once more in this great country—which has been convulsed with such countless commotions, and such countless Utopias—a peace founded on conciliation between men on undeviating principles of authority, of moral duty, of love for the men who toil and endure, and on the dignity of the nation as a whole."

At last, on 12th October, at Bordeaux, he gave his final acceptance to the long ovation : there was no more need for his followers to cry *Vive la République* ! After the enthusiasm of such a Lupercalia, Persigny could well press him to take the eagle crown. And, now in the tone of the Emperor, he could speak of the people of France pressing forward as his soldiers. But these soldiers were not to march abroad to kill and conquer : they were to be the soldiers of prosperity in the Empire of peace. They were to bring back " to religion, to morality, and to opulence that still numerous proportion of the people which

---

[1] Paul de Cassagnac : *Souvenirs*.
[2] *Morning Post*, 21st July, 1852.

in a country possessing a faith has no knowledge of the precepts of the Saviour, which in the bosom of the most fertile territory on earth scarcely obtains the common necessities of life." " Peace," he said, " was the desire of France ; peace, active, fruitful ; and making glorious conquests but only in the arts and sciences where every victory was a benefit for all men,[1] which would allow the country to cultivate her waste lands, to open new routes, to render her rivers navigable, to finish her canals, to complete the network of railways, to assimilate to herself the vast kingdoms which she possesses in Africa, to bring her western ports nearer to America by that rapidity of communication yet lacking, to restore ruins, to overthrow false gods, to make truth triumphant."

Such was the speech of 12th October at Bordeaux. The apostle of modern France had voiced for her the course of her civilization as we see it to-day. His words rang through France, the trumpet of a prophecy, And the orator returned to Paris to accept the crown on the anniversary of the day which made him absolute, the day of Austerlitz, the imperial date on which both Alexander and Franz Josef had ascended their thrones. On 2th December, 1852, he was proclaimed Emperor. And it all happened so easily that it was regarded as inevitable. The Empire seemed to have come with the unquestionableness with which the summer sun ripens the wheat to harvest.

But in reality, this was no natural process. It was a human triumph, the triumph of a man who so far had shown himself resourceful to the most remarkable degree, and who through such strange

---

[1] See the *Moniteur*, 27th November, 1852, for an admirable paraphrase of the Bordeaux speech.

adventures had pursued what he felt to be his destiny. Reserved and close as he was, he had doggedly pressed his aim through rare vicissitudes. As a child he had been banished from his country : as a youth, he had fought as an insurgent against the soldiers of the Church and escaped as a footman through the Austrian lines ; as a young man, he had appeared as a rebel in France, been arrested and deported to America. Four years later, he had made the same attempt, again fled before French bullets, been again captured, tried for his life, condemned to perpetual imprisonment, and finally, after six years, escaped, disguised as a mason. And after all this, his faith and enthusiasm still undaunted, he had returned yet once more to France, at forty years of age, and in a few weeks had been chosen by the people as their head. As President, he rapidly overwhelmed all adversaries. Three years later he had made himself absolute. Then, in a year, he had convinced France that there was only one thing to do : to crown him with the glory of Empire, and leave him free as sovereign to do as he thought best, for were not his counsels those of the *mens divinior* ? And yet the *mens divinior* was not his strongest asset : already the words Socialism, Communism, were in the air, and even those who had little love for him preferred him to such an alternative. " To vote for him," said Montalembert, " is not to approve all that he has done ; it is to choose between him and the total ruin of France."

And though the *coup d'État* seemed ruthless, seemed unscrupulous, if we wish to understand why it was endorsed, we must never forget the tact, the solicitude, or the sympathy of the man who was responsible for it.

If we wish for an example of his tact, let us listen to him speaking as he revisits Ham. " When one has seen," he said, "how many troubles the justest revolutions bring with them, one hardly understands one's audacity in having attempted to assume personally the terrible responsibility of a change. So I do not complain that here, in six years' imprisonment, I expiated my temerity against the laws of the country, and I am happy that in these very places where I suffered I can propose a toast in honour of the men who, in spite of their convictions, are determined to respect the institutions of their country." [1]

This sensitiveness to the claims of an authority against which he had rebelled was equalled by that of his solicitude for the poor and mean and lowly. Of that we have evidence enough in Morny's circular to the prefects after the *coup d'État*. "One must show the greatest warmth and kindness," he wrote, " to the humblest and the weakest : lower officials often think they can increase their importance by creating difficulties and embarrassments. They do not know how many curses, how much unpopularity they bring upon the Government." [2]

And finally let us observe a typical gesture of the Prince President on the eve of the *coup d'État*. In distributing five Crosses of the Legion of Honour to those who had been given awards in the Crystal Palace, the Prince said : " Allow me to encourage you to make great efforts. Undertake them fearlessly, they will prevent unemployment this winter. The Government behind you is solid. It has the rights with which the people have invested it, and the strength which comes from God."

The next day M. Charrière, a manufacturer of

---

[1] Véron : *Mémoires*, p. 55.
[2] V.N.A., Hübner to Schwarzenberg, 20th January, 1852.

surgical instruments, was invited to dine at the Elysée. Before he started his employees had presented him with his Cross of the Legion of Honour, which he showed to the Vice-President, M. Boulay de la Meurthe. Boulay in turn showed it to the Prince. Without a word, Louis Napoleon took it from its box and placed it on his breast, putting in its place the cross of diamonds which he had inherited from the First Emperor. Next day, the Vice-President himself went to the workshop of M. Charrière, and explained how the Prince had been delighted to give this unique decoration to encourage a good employer, and to show his sympathy with artisans.[1]

And even when it was suggested to give the name of Hortense to the new boulevard which had taken the place of the Canal St. Martin, he insisted that it should be called after Richard Lenoir, who had risen from a simple labourer to be a great and beneficent manufacturer.[2]

[1] *Moniteur*, 26th November, 1851.
[2] Quai d'Orsay. *Papiers de Cerçay*.

VI

INAUGURATION OF THE EMPIRE

Nach diesen trüben Tagen
Wie ist so hell das Feld
Zerriss'ne Wolken tragen
Die Trauer aus der Welt.

Und Keim und Knospe mühet
Sich an das Licht hervor,
Und manche Blume blühet
Zum Himmel still empor.

Ja, auch sogar die Eichen
Und Reben werden grün.
O Herz! dass sei dein Zeichen
Werde froh und kühn.

Hoffman von Fallersleben.

I

"*La grande question est décidée,*" said Fould, the Jewish Minister. "*Nous nous appellerons Napoléon III.*"[1] The ascent of a new Bonaparte to the throne of France startled and dismayed the ancient monarchies of Europe, as the advent of the first motor-cars on the roads afterwards shook the nerves of horses. No one felt more disquiet than the Czar, and he even addressed a personal letter to the President to warn him against assuming the title of Napoleon and above all the numeral III.[2] Lord Cowley, the new

---

[1] *Cowley Papers*: Cowley to Malmesbury, 4th November, 1852.
[2] Simpson: *Louis Napoleon and the Recovery of France*, p. 198.

British Ambassador, asked for an audience to argue that that number suggested that the Bonapartes could claim the throne by hereditary right. The Emperor was not unequal to the situation. If that were so, he answered, he would be Napoleon V.[1] He was not trying to count either his father or King Joseph, but he could not ignore the fact that the King of Rome had been proclaimed Emperor as Napoleon II. But anxious as the royal families were not to admit the Bonapartes as a dynasty, the Northern Courts—the Courts of Russia, Prussia, and Austria—liked almost less the alternative contention that Divine right was claimed through the will of the people, and that a rebel against the Bourbons must be again accepted by their Majesties as a brother. The word " brother ", which etiquette henceforth required, stuck in the throat of the Emperor Nicholas. But Napoleon III was secure. He had his people with him, and it rested with France to keep the equilibrium of the Continent. " When France catches cold," said Prince Schwarzenberg at Vienna, " Europe sneezes." " When France is satisfied," Louis Napoleon had said at Bordeaux, " the world has rest." [2]

Of this few felt more assured than the English. *The Times*, it is true, had been very rude ; and some of the British Ministers had sympathized, but none could approve. Lord Granville decided to write to the editor : he compared the Emperor to a naughty boy, *The Times* to a sort of butler. " A strong, energetic schoolboy, vain, irritable, without principle, and latterly much spoilt, walks

[1] *Cowley Papers* : Cowley to Malmesbury, 11th November, 1852.
[2] Simpson : *Louis Napoleon and the Recovery of France*, p. 194.

about the Square with a lighted candle. A fellow-servant of mine, very influential with my master, in mild and dignified language, complains every morning to the schoolboy that he is an unmitigated little scamp, who deserves to be well whipped."[1] So Lord Granville tried to mollify the editor, who, perhaps, himself realized that he had been not unlike the bumptious little boy himself. For, as a matter of fact, *The Times* was neither mild nor dignified. The *Morning Post* in fact compared it to a barking cur.[2] But the *Morning Post* had become—who knows by what influence?—the voice of the French Ambassador, and to it whatever the Emperor did, had done, and was henceforth to do, was right. The immense majority of Frenchmen felt likewise. "What I feel magnificent," said Napoleon III, "what satisfies my *amour propre* is that actually to-day—just think what that means—the people of France, really 'the people' themselves, of their own free will bury the Republic." As the new Emperor spoke these words, he seemed like one inspired, like one who had received a power from on high.[3] He had received his title and prerogatives from the men of France by a majority of more than thirty to one. It was prodigious.

2

The adversaries, of course, suggested that the figures had been faked. But it was no longer easy to play with the figures. The counting was done in public by the Mayor and councillors, who had themselves

[1] Lord E. Fitzmaurice : *Life of Lord Granville*, i, 68.
[2] *Morning Post*, 14th October, 1852.
[3] V.N.A., Hübner to Schwarzenberg, 21st November, 1852.

been in turn elected. They could hardly falsify the returns before the people who knew them best. And as a matter of fact, young men and old in place after place had gone to the Hotel de Ville, and to the cry of *Vive Napoléon*! had voted in delirious enthusiasm for the man who had freed them from the tyranny of the deputies, from the threat of the Bourbons returning, and above all from the disorder of the anarchists. With him, they felt that business, the family, the Church, would all be safe, and as in the days of the great victories, France could rejoice in glory. Her people did not want another Terror, such as Maret Dufraisse seemed to threaten when he vaunted the execution of Louis XVI; they felt that a speech of M. Thiers against the President, running into three columns of eloquence in the newspaper, was simply an interruption of business.[1] They had their eye on other things, and so had their Emperor.

He established his workmen's leaders to adjust relations between employers and employed. The army was reduced. Parliament met and reduced the budget by 5,000,000 francs. The Ministry of Police was exchanged into the Sureté Générale, which concentrated on the suppression of that special indulgence of revolution, pornography. In the time of scarcity, a price of 4*d.* was fixed for the 2 lb. loaf. The corn duties were reduced, and so were those on the importation of cattle. New railways were hurried forward, and in return the tariff was reduced on iron and coal.[2] France rushed forward to take her place as an industrial nation, and the people, not less thrifty and hardly less industrious than before,

[1] *Morning Post*, 21st July, 1852.
[2] Jerrold: *Napoleon III*, ch. ix.

found that by a sudden turn the ill-fortune of the forties had changed and that they had swung back from poverty to riches. Capital had reason confidently to engage in new enterprises, manufactures throve and were distributed by the new methods of transport, taxes were low, and the new Emperor showed that he understood those principles of *The Wealth of Nations* which he had read at Ham. France became once more the centre of Europe, and Paris the capital of civilization. And the Emperor chose Paris as the one creative expression of his ideals. He summoned from Bordeaux its prefect Haussmann, and gave him charge of Paris to make it what it is. " If Europe leaves me in peace," he had written to Haeckerer in Vienna in 1852, " I shall make of Paris the finest city in the world." [1] We shall see how.

When he accepted the Presidency in 1848 he had made with the ablest survivor of the reign of Louis Philippe, Drouyn de Lhuys, an agreement to maintain the international treaties ; to respect the Church ; and not to try and destroy the old parties.

Now on assuming the crown, he could go further. He could begin to dream, however vaguely, of remoulding Europe. He meant religion to be a force working for the well-being of the poor ; he meant the workers to live in comfort, and as for the parties, let the best men all join in one national *fascio*.[2]

He did not mean to eliminate poverty : his hope was to alleviate it. " Each man for whom I win comfort," he used to say, " is a recruit from the ranks of Socialism." And how was he to guarantee comfort ? To drain marshes, to build up farms, to cultivate the dunes, to plough great stretches of land, to

[1] Granier de Cassagnac : *Souvenirs*, ii, 213.
[2] Paul de Cassagnac already used the word of Mussolini to describe the Emperor's idea.

distribute implements, to give a subvention to the Trappist cultivators ; to construct in the great cities workmen's houses ; to make food cheaper, to found co-operative societies and workmen's banks ; these were among the means he encouraged and inaugurated. He inspired About to write *Les Echasses de Maître Pierre*. But he had seen now that material provisions could not guarantee society against unrest unless men had work, unless there were family life, and unless ambitions were controlled and elevated by religion.[1] Such was the scheme of the Modern Emperor.

As for his methods, there was first the search for men. In this the time did not help him. There was hardly one outstanding figure in any department of life in the Second Empire, except Victor Hugo, and not only did he refuse to co-operate with the régime, but his misrepresentations of it were fantastic. The Emperor had first to surround himself with his own family. Old Jérome, who had spent nearly thirty years as the Prince de Montfort, became again " King " Jérome, and was appointed the Governor of the Invalides. His handsome daughter, Mathilde, even though held by the Church beyond the reach of suitors, was still the elder daughter of the Court ; his son Jérome, who was always known as Prince Napoleon, was heir to the throne and a centre of discontent. His father was managed by him, said the Emperor, as a weathercock by the wind.[2] He had always been a spoilt child. " *Son petit caractère entier, despote et colère,*" wrote Mademoiselle Masuyer when he was twelve years old, " *n'est pas compensé par un cœur très sensible. Bien loin de là.*" [3]

[1] Granier de Cassagnac : *Souvenirs*, ii, 210, 211.
[2] V.N.A., Hübner to Schwarzenberg, 4th April, 1849.
[3] *Revue des Deux Mondes*, June, 1915.

He was now a stout young man of thirty-two, with raven black hair, and regular Italian features, extraordinarily like those of the great man. "To his mental gifts, which are incontestable," wrote Hübner, " he adds a will of iron, and the appearance of a Roman Emperor of the Decadence."[1] Lord Cowley, taking a directer tone, called him a " brute ".[2] He was a professional gambler, plunged in debaucheries and connected with the dregs of the immigration into France of the revolutionaries of every part of Europe.[3] He was able enough and ambitious enough to want the first place. Yet he owed all his honours to the abilities of one whom he was inclined to suspect was not a Bonaparte at all. He was in a recurring sulk, which caused him always to appear at the most gorgeous ceremonies of the Court in black. Yet he could easily assume the position of a Prince, and at will moved from his habitual disdain to a brilliant charm. His powers of mind expanded in the presence of his friends : but when his tastes, his theories, or his position were questioned, he would burst out into a violent temper, his eyes shot lightning, and his words were storm. There was no one in the entourage of the Emperor more difficult than Prince Napoleon.[4]

Floating in on the turn of the tide came he who was known to be the son of the First Emperor by the Countess Walewski. Although he never admitted his real paternity and had become a diplomat under Louis Philippe, he had early made friends with Palmerston, his claim on Louis Napoleon had been too strong to ignore, and he had been in 1848

[1] V.N.A., Hübner to Buol, 16th July, 1853.
[2] *The Paris Embassy*, by F. H. Wellesley.
[3] V.N.A., Hübner to Schwarzenberg, 22nd January, 1850.
[4] Maupas : *Mémoires*, ii, 120.

appointed French Ambassador in London. Although bullied by Lord Clarendon, and sometimes thought a fool,[1] he had proved himself not unequal to the task of representing France, and in time to come was to make an entente with England. His round face lacked the fierceness of Prince Napoleon's: but the resemblance to the First Emperor was as undeniable as that of Morny to Napoleon III.

Close, too, at hand was Persigny, the man whom everyone felt to be honest, the man who believed in the Bonapartes at least more ardently than any of the family itself. Devoted to the Emperor with a knightly ardour, he was now in the triumph of his joy. And behind came the crowd of old friends, for not one was forgotten who had rendered a service, or shown a kindness. The prison chaplain, Tirmache, was made a Bishop; the valet, Thélin, Keeper of the Privy Purse.[2] And behind the personal friends came the old Bonapartists, the Duc de Bassano, the Marquis de Cambacérès, the Princesse d'Essling, the Murats. The quiet, unprepossessing, awkward little man, whose manners were so modest and easy, became the centre of a Court the ceremonies of which were as impressive as the people's feeling for him was enthusiastic.

3

No hero could look less romantic. The short legs, the heavy head leaning towards one side, the coarse shaven pallid cheeks, the imperial (for so the sudden sprout of beard on the chin was henceforward to

---

[1] Maxwell: *Lord Clarendon.*
[2] Jerrold: *Napoleon III*, iii, 408.

be known), the thick lips, the spreading waxed moustache, the heavy hook of the nose, the weighted eyelids over the pale weary eyes, the greasy hairy hands, the suggestion of something unkempt, almost unclean in the whole loose dissipated figure, with all this he could easily be caricatured into a horned satyr. The marvel was that, in spite of all this, his glance irradiated charm and his bearing dignity. No one could explain how, yet no one could deny that the whole of this odd figure was instinct with a curious mixture of unusual power and unusual kindness. He liked to laugh, and he laughed loudly.[1] But amongst a people who are expert talkers, he was habitually silent : unlike them, he loved to listen ; they arrive at once at decisions they can pointedly express ; he pondered long. They were excitable ; he phlegmatic and mild. They were definite, he was vague.[2] Yet when he did speak, his manners were so affable, and at the same time so distinguished, that he won deference rather than commanded it. His voice was sweet, clear, and vibrant like his mother's[3] ; and his illustrations were at once so familiar, so playful, and so much to the point that it was not easy to resist them. Discussing the freedom of the Press for example, he said he would leave the journalists free to run about, but with a string to their paws, that would pull them down if they ran too far.[4] So without discussion he would settle hard questions by a playful metaphor, for though he reflected slowly, his wit was quick.

And this was the man whose doggedness and daring

---

[1] Cassagnac : *Souvenirs*, i, 52.
[2] Ibid., p. 96.
[3] Tascher de la Pagerie : *Mon Séjour aux Tuileries*, ii, 179.
[4] Granier de Cassagnac : *Souvenirs*, ii, 85.

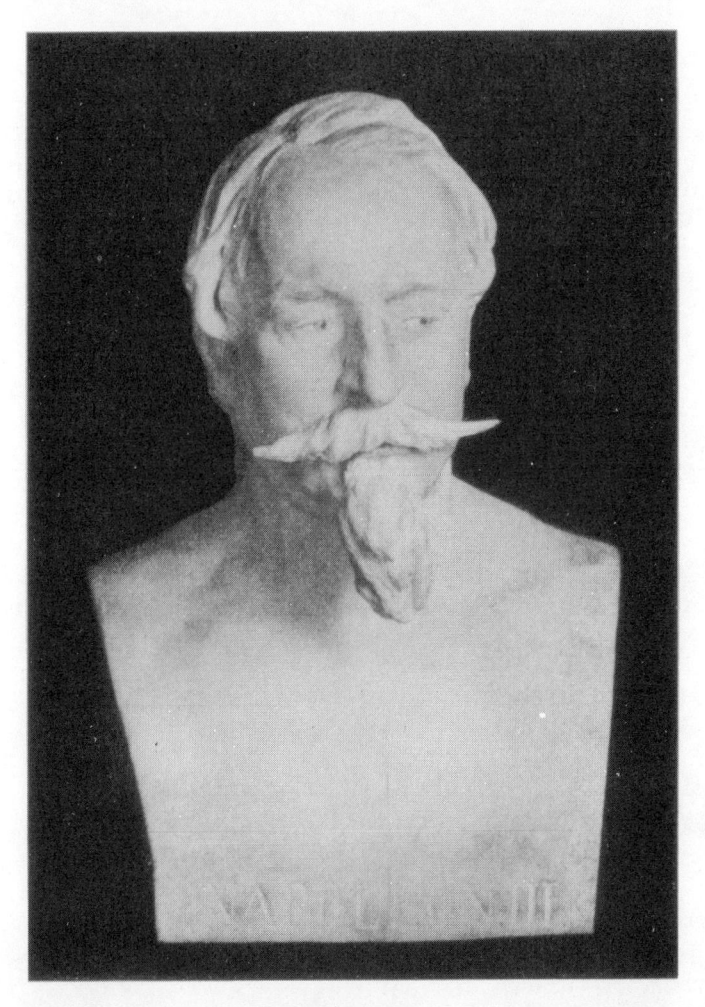

Napoleon III
From the bust by Carpeaux at Malmaison.

"This was the man whose doggedness and daring had won the throne."

had won the throne. But as a curtain seemed to veil his eye, so he seemed to have cultivated that counterpoise to each of his stronger qualities which would disguise it in the central position which would henceforth, wherever he moved, centre hundreds, and even thousands, of eyes upon his person. The face in repose had the sleep and much of the coldness of marble.[1] His temperament was violently emotional. His temper could be violent : the first sign was the swelling of his nostrils, like those of an excited horse. Then his eyes burned, and his lips quivered.[2] But his habitual glance was dead, and his pleasant voice, even on great occasions, never really thrilled with eloquence. Nothing in his manner or appearance showed either the will, the enthusiasm, or the courage which, at the end of his ordeals, gave him a warrior's crown. The processes of his psychology were all hidden : he seldom conferred, he seldom appeared to reason, he listened in silence, and then in his quiet voice he gave his decision, brief and clear, as a general in a hot engagement.[3] The secret of all this can be given in a phrase : that he was not a creative thinker, that he lacked initiative, and that his resolute will was a power of resistance to his inertia.[4] The mountains of Empire did not rise to a peak but to a mist driving over blunted ground. " When the Emperor gets an idea into his head," wrote Cowley, " he broods upon it until all difficulties disappear in his imagination."[5] As General du Barail said : " If his brain was large and deep, it was rather lacking in that definiteness of which his

[1] Viel Castel : *Mémoires*.
[2] N. W. Senior : *Conversations*, ii, 117.
[3] Granier de Cassagnac : *Mémoires*, ii, 95.
[4] Madden : *Lady Blessington*, quoting *La Gueronnière*, i, 474.
[5] *Cowley Papers* : Cowley to Clarendon, 24th October, 1855.

uncle had too much.[1] " He was as it were the figure of a thought," wrote Madame Tascher de la Pagerie ; " he never stops dreaming." [2] And as a dreamer, he has been stigmatized by almost every Frenchman. The truth is that he was less a dreamer than a schemer. Unable to create his opportunities, he was always waiting to take advantage of those left to him by others. And in after years, he even boasted that he did not drive Louis Philippe from the throne, but, when it was abandoned, so acted as to be asked to take it.

The great writer, who was the noisiest of his enemies, described him as vulgar, commonplace, puerile, theatrical, and vain, " a man captivated by the noise, the glitter, and the glamour of power," one whose taste was " for spangles, feathers, and embroidery ".[3] Such words are a monument to blindness. And Lamennais was as grossly deceived as Victor Hugo. " This man," he said, " has no feeling of good or evil : his only feeling is for himself." No, his great ambition was to be the protector of the poor. It was not until the reign was far advanced that a critic pierced to his real weakness. Ste. Beuve, in the *Nouveaux Lundis*, was writing of the Emperor's *Life of Cæsar*. For the writer, Ste. Beuve wrote, was, indeed, another Cæsar, but not one of those who, in their range and variety, in their lofty valiancy, as in their vices, in their precision and their surprise, prove that their gifts are an overflow of Heaven's profusion. The other order of Cæsars are, on the contrary, more like manufactured images of genius ; such he suggested was the new Napoleon's : he had

---

[1] Du Barail : *Mémoires*, ii, 291.
[2] *Mon Séjour aux Tuileries*, i, 179.
[3] Victor Hugo : *Napoléon le Petit*.

tried to become the god-like man, and by long effort succeeded. He had repeated his part until he knew it. Born in the purple, or beside it, he had been inspired with a child's trustfulness in the glory that hung around his cradle, and never for a moment had he doubted that he, too, was of the blood of the gods. Even when captured and banished, he was undismayed. The ambition he had set before him and never let go, his self-education, however incomplete, yet tending always to a single end, had raised his mind and thoughts till he was able to assume the place of Cæsar. Faith had given so much to one of even the manufactured great. " Do not ask them, therefore," said Ste. Beuve, " to have no superstition. Their power in politics is inseparable from a faith in destiny. It is so that they have an instinct for grandeur, a mastering confidence, a coolness, a presence of mind, a sense of being superior to all that passes around them." But can one of these coolly direct the hazards of war? Was not Louis Napoleon even hesitant and impractical in the problems of civil government? He had really only one will : to be the Emperor.

That he was. Its mark was on his forehead. He had the august presence, the leisured step, the impressive silence, the rare phrase. But he had aspirations rather than a plan, and the means of his success betrayed the limits of his power.

Long before, another observer watching him at a review on the Place de la Concorde had made a similar observation.

"I watched his pale corpse-like imperturbable features not many months since, for a period of three hours," said this witness.[1] " I saw 80,000 men in arms

[1] Madden : *Lady Blessington.*

pass before him, and I never observed a change in his countenance, or an expression in his look which would enable the bystander to say whether he was pleased or otherwise at the stirring scene that was passing before him, on the very spot where Louis XVI was put to death. He did not speak to those around him except at very long intervals and then with an air of nonchalance, of ennui, and eternal preoccupation with self : he rarely spoke a syllable to his uncle, Jérome Bonaparte, who was on horseback somewhat behind him. It was the same with his brilliant staff. All orders came from him, all command seemed centred in him. He gave me the idea of a man who had a perfect reliance on himself and a feeling of complete control over those around him. But there was a weary look about him, an aspect of excessive watchfulness, an appearance of want of sleep, of over-work, of over-indulgence, too, that gives an air of exhaustion to face and form, and leaves an impression on the mind of a close observer that the machine of the body will break down soon, and suddenly—or that the mind will give way—under the pressure of pent-up thoughts and energies eternally in action, and never suffered to be observed or noticed by friends or followers."

The truth was that the man's will was not as strong as his emotional nature. He could, and did, at times work prodigiously—the vital energy was there. But it was dissipated. It was followed by long spells of languor or by the hot pursuit of pleasure. The conflict between ruthlessness and kindness, between will and emotion, between religion and selfishness, between the Bonaparte and the grandchild of Josephine, had been born with him. His parents had both been over-emotional. Each had suffered from a disease which seldom fails to affect the temperaments of their children. There was, therefore, an inheritance of nervous abnormality which showed itself in waves of exaltation and depression. After the spell of torpor and relaxation, when he again assumed the rôle of Cæsar, he would believe himself the chosen of providence. It was this alternation, this conflict between the different elements of his nature which he had been forced to veil—in a veil so thick " that the breath of his body was stifled within it ".

At the moment he assumed the throne, his constitutional disequilibrium was about to be accentuated. At the age of forty-five, a normal man, even if he has been licentious, expects to be less amorous. But Louis Napoleon, who had in his youth been a rebel to the Church, had never attained to a true faith in it. He approved it as a social institution, he did not go to it for inward peace. It was not peace but satisfaction that he craved, and satisfaction he found in intimacy with women. Wherever he had been he had demanded sexual adventures, and so morbid had seemed the alternative that they had been allowed to him even in prison. Even as a child he felt that the influence of women in his life would be overwhelming.[1] From the age of sixteen, when he was a schoolboy at Augsburg,[2] for now nearly thirty years, he had surrendered heedlessly to the wanton play of his inclinations. " Every day shows more and more," wrote Lord Cowley at his engagement, " how little his passions are under control." [3]

---

[1] V. Masuyer : *Revue des Deux Mondes.* 1st August, 1914.
[2] Hübner : *Neuf Ans,* i, 441.
[3] *Cowley Papers* : Cowley to Lord John Russell, 9th January, 1853.

Such a life not only deadens the spirit; it drugs the vital energies, it weakens the will, it dulls the nerves: for it makes the nerves, and therefore the mind, vibrant to fingers clumsier than those of reason, and on strings thus jarred, reason disdains to try her masterpieces. To natures sexually indulged the caprices of selfishness begin to shout their orders. The sense of social adjustment is forfeited. The extremes of emotional alternative become more violent; impulses are more capricious. Dissolute men, when placed in power, do not create the destinies of nations. They wait and see.

So was it with the new Emperor. And he was just beginning to feel the effects of the dread disease which twenty years later was to kill him. His brain was to be clouded over by uric poison; his nervous energy exhausted by the tortures of the stone. But this was not yet. At present, the man who was so magnetic, was specially subject to the claims of beauty. The month after his enthronement, the British Ambassador wrote to London that " The great adventurer of all has been caught by an adventuress ".[1]

4

It was typical of the Emperor that at the moment when he had been proposing marriage to a Swedish Princess, and that his Ambassador at London was pressing his suit with a niece of Queen Victoria, he himself should be running hot foot after the brilliant young Spaniard whom he had invited three years before to sup in the forest at Villeneuve L'Etang.

[1] Wellesley: *The Paris Embassy.*

That young lady's mother was the greatest matchmaker of her age : her elder daughter reigned already in Madrid as Duchess of Alba in a position hardly less than royal : and at the advent of the Emperor, she had returned with the younger to Paris and resumed the brilliant social amenities to which her rank not less than her abilities entitled her. This lady was the daughter of a wine-merchant, who was himself a younger son in a family of Scottish gentry, but she had married into one of the greatest families of Spain. She was mistress of a splendid fortune : she had a remarkable power of interesting the ablest men, and she had been for a time in the supreme official position among the ladies of the Spanish Court.[1]

But she had not had an easy time with her younger daughter who had fallen in love with a dissolute young nobleman who used her as a means to press his presence on the young Duchess of Alba. The daughter was highly strung, and her nerves after this adventure were badly shaken. The mother insisted on taking her daughter away from Madrid, and so worked that Eugenia never heard the name of the man she had loved. In the year 1852, one of the greatest nobles of France, the Duc de Doudeauville, had proposed to her and been refused.[2] This was the lady whom in 1849 the Prince President had tried to compromise in the Forest, and who, at the critical moment, had slipped aside and left him with her mother on his arm.

When the Prince met her again three years later in those days when his hard-won crown was glittering with its fairest novelty, his old ardour became a

[1] Llanos y Torriglia : *La Condesa de Montijo, passim*, R. Sencourt : *The Empress Eugénie, passim*.
[2] Private information.

devouring flame. He had invited her to his hunting party at Fontainebleau in the middle of November, and paid her such attention that Drouyn de Lhuys already spoke of a possible marriage. A few weeks later she was at Compiègne. There, the Emperor presented her with jewels, with a horse,[1] he crowned her at dinner with a wreath of violets, he left the fireside at midnight to find her a flower in the freezing dark. He rode home from the hunt with her at his side at the head of the cavalcade.[2] It is said that opening a secret door he even appeared at night in her bedroom, only to be reminded that she did not doubt he was a gentleman.[3] It is true that one evening as he sat at dinner at Compiègne she refused to appear, and his conversation with his neighbours languished. He scribbled notes and handed them to an A.D.C. : and at last she appeared in a black robe sewn all over with fresh rose petals, and she lovelier than her flowers.[4] Those present whispered at table, or wrote to their friends, to anticipate the moment, as Hübner wrote, " *quand la brèche serait ouverte et quand se rendrait la forteresse.*" [5] But the Emperor assaulted in vain. He was always expecting, was always being disappointed, and the lady, who was invited to Compiègne for a few days, was pressed again and again to prolong her stay. So also were Lord and Lady Cowley, who, although recommending a marriage connection with England, were compelled to watch from day to day the manœuvres and intrigues which were supposed to lead to the fall of

---

[1] Filon : *Souvenirs*.
[2] Jerrold : *Napoleon III*, iii, 425.
[3] Private information.
[4] Ibid.
[5] V.N.A., Hübner to Buol, 26th January, 1853 (Secret).

INAUGURATION OF THE EMPIRE 137

the young Spaniard, but which ended by raising her to the throne.[1]

For when, as one afternoon in the gathering dusk, the new Emperor had pressed his audacious proposals on his huntress, she had whispered " *Oui, quand je serai impératrice.*" And as they rode on alone in the forest, both their watches had stopped at the same hour. To natures like theirs in whom the sense of destiny was strong, such happenings were not taken as coincidences.[2]

The two were stricken with a sort of awe which was one with the romance which tingled through them in that exhilarating winter air when fate was dazzling them both with his new splendour and new success. The opposition to Doña Eugenia was most violent. Her game needed all her skill. With the Emperor, the vivacious freedom of her manners would suddenly freeze into propriety and she became the picture of virginal reserve. Her critics were astonished. Was there, they asked, more art, or cynicism, in a game played for such stakes before so many witnesses?[3]

The situation was the more exciting because here were two natures which possessed in the highest degree the qualities of magnetism. He was the man of the hour, the conqueror, the chosen of France, and—not least—absorbed in her with all the generosity of love. This was the woman whose every movement enhanced her distinction, whose wit, whose courage, whose coquetry were at the service of a character as chaste as it was tense. She had entirely mastered him, and if at such a time Count Walewski had succeeded in persuading Queen

[1] Ibid.
[2] Llanos y Torriglia : *La Condesa de Montijo*, p. 137.
[3] V.N.A., Hübner to Buol, 16th January, 1853 (Secret).

Victoria to give her niece, he would have found himself in a very embarrassing position.[1]

But on the other hand, the conflicts were strong. His family and the Ministers saw how things were going, and they were furious. Miss Howard was still in evidence, and did not make his position easier. But at last, on 14th January, at a reception at the Tuileries, a certain Madame Fortoul pushed past the Spanish Countess with insulting words about the prominence given to a questionable foreigner. The Emperor saw that his love was furious. " To-morrow," he said, " no one shall dare to insult you." After all he had placed her in a vulnerable position : only in one way could he repair the harm he had done to the woman he had come to worship. Next morning the Countess of Montijo had in her hands a written proposal of marriage. And so passionate was the Emperor's suit that in a fortnight from that date, Doña Eugenia de Guzman had been married to him in Notre-Dame, and reigned in France as sovereign.[2] A figure more different from that of Minnie, Lady Fortescue at Castlehill could hardly be imagined.

5

Fate was singularly indulgent to his passion when she placed in his way so superb a creature as the Empress Eugénie. Born of a family so noble as to be the kinsmen of kings, thrice a *grande d'Espagne* of the first class, Doña Eugenia enjoyed in her own right as a younger daughter the titles of Countess de Teba and Marchioness de Moya. But her education had been peculiarly modern. Brought up in loyalty to the Bonapartes, she had been from childhood

[1] Greville : *Mémoires*, vii, 38–41.
[2] R. Sencourt : *The Empress Eugénie*, 67, 68.

THE EMPRESS EUGÉNIE
By De la Fosse, in the possession of Mr. Julian Sampson.

"Fate was singularly indulgent to his passion, when she placed in his way so superb a creature."

a believer in social reform, even to an extreme degree. She had been taken as a child to Paris, and received her education in one of the smartest of Paris convents, while her private tutors, Merimée and Stendhal, had been two of the greatest masters of French who ever wrote romances. She spoke and wrote French, if not faultlessly, very finely, with a striking power of charming and picturesque imagery. She had been at school in England, and she had grown up intimate with an ancient court, and cognizant even at an early age of the political intrigues of which it was the centre. She had been presented at Buckingham Palace. She was a gymnast, with a supple body trained to endurance. And she had all the social arts of a woman of the world.

Her mother, though hardly less remarkable in her way than Queen Hortense, owed her success to vivacity, not to languor ; not to her artistic gifts but to her wit. She was a moral woman, yet like Hortense she knew how to play upon the hearts of men.

And it was not alone the incomparable slope of the daughter's shoulders, or the ripening of her breast, which won the Emperor. Beneath the red gold of her hair (and the rose she often placed in her curls made them look particularly coquettish), the dress of Doña Eugenia was faultless in its taste, and her features showed the fineness of her race.

> Her eyes, and oh her eyes !
> In all her beauty, and sunlight to it
>   is a pit, den, darkness.
> Foam falling is not fresh to it, rainbow
>   by it is not beaming.
> In all her body, I say, no place was
>   like her eyes.

Those deep blue eyes sparkled, as she spoke, like the Mediterranean in a breeze, but in spite of her radiant health and of the gracious curves of her figure, their expression was often sad. What her heart had craved, it craved still, and the devotion of the man who at last so passionately loved her brought to her nature a promise of joy which that very nature could not of itself ever fulfil. These two were phenomenally magnetic, but they could not live intimately without discovering that what he craved and offered, especially in intercourse with women, was too much of the trombone to make one carol with her shrill flutings. He could not, as a husband, satisfy a wife who had won the crown by her resistance to his attempts to ruin her. Her passion was too high, too tense to hold such a husband for long, and its rarity was enhanced not by gross physical responsiveness but by a rich vein of sorrow, sorrow which is to the soul what sun is to the plant, needful for the germination of the seed, the opening of the flower, the ripening of the fruit.

If God had given her everything she most desired, she was to say in years to come, it was to take back from her, one by one, each joy that He had given. From the beginning she felt this would be so : and, fascinated by the thought of Marie Antoinette, she was often possessed by a premonition that she, too, would die the ghastly death of the guillotine.

Hers was to be a longer martyrdom, a martyrdom so long, so virile, that in the end she was to taste its final triumph. Her nature from the beginning had too much of the heroic in it for her to be a normal woman ; and she could never build in the heart of the people, or even of those closest to her, the solid place won for more normal women by their warmth of heart. For that she was too high-tempered, too vibrant, too lofty. " Endowed with all the qualities of the soul," her bridegroom said, " she will be the ornament of the throne, and as in the day of danger, she will be its unflinching defender. Catholic and devout, she will raise to heaven the same prayers as I for the felicity of France."

Yet, firm as her religion was, she was neither a mystic, a devotee, nor a theologian. Her faith was that of an intellectual. She had been educated not only by free-thinkers in France : even in Spain, her family traditions had been those of the most liberal Catholics in the country. Her feeling for her Church and for its head was a reasoned allegiance ; loyalty, with honour, was the root of all her chivalrous virtues. But on the things of faith and morals she knew no compromise : and this made her most irritating to the revolutionaries who hated the social and spiritual traditions of the Church as wholly as those of ancient privilege. These never tired of pretending that this most rational of Catholics was a bigot.

Her Catholicism taught her charity : and her heart was full of sympathy for those in need. But she preferred the traditions, and therefore the power, of Catholic countries to the dominance of Protestant or material civilization ; her sympathy was always with Catholic influences and consecrated monarchies. Loyalty to Spain, and keenness on reform found in her broad life ample room for each other. Through all, she loved sport and exercise and games and play. Hers in every fibre of mind and body was the spirit of adventure.[1]

And when she ascended the throne, her mind was far from being balanced. It was the lighter rather than the more serious side of her character which was most in evidence. Those who were best able to judge her summed her up as anxious to charm,

[1] See Sencourt : *Empress Eugénie, passim.*

and sure to charm all, but especially men ; full of coquetry and animation ; fonder of jokes than wit, and with more wit than prudence ; mad for whatever was new, astonishing, unforeseen ; fond of every sort of movement of mind or body ; and in political matters, among the most advanced parties in Spain, with a taste for liberalism, and recalcitrant to old ideas of authority ; capricious and eccentric, illogical in her ideas, but endowed with a force of will, and a physical courage rare amongst women of any nation. As for her manners, they went far beyond the general freedom, advanced as that was, of Spanish girls, and therefore often occasioned ill-natured gossip while in reality she was the most virtuous of women—*Sans faute véritable mais péchant par les apparences.* An ardent imagination, a passionate heart which had burnt already with romantic ardour, though never unchaste ; a woman who could not help attracting and fascinating such a man as her husband, whom she would strongly influence, for good or ill, according to the caprice of the moment ; a woman also who, if love should give way to disillusion, might revive in the Tuileries the tragedies of its past, or even, in a fierce gesture, tear away the very bonds which held her to the throne.[1]

So, at the moment of her marriage, was she described by one who had known her long and had every opportunity to hear the truth. She to whom, in England in her girlhood, a gipsy had said : " An eagle will carry you into the highest heaven and from there you will drop." [2]

At the time of the marriage and for long after, there were indeed few people who understood how

[1] V.N.A., Hübner to Buol, 26th January, 1853 (Secret).
[2] Private information (Major Oakley).

extraordinary were the qualities of the woman whom the new Emperor had raised to share his throne. There had been a splendid ceremony both at the Tuileries and at Notre-Dame : but the crowds in the streets, in spite of some bursts of enthusiasm, had left at least on the Ambassadors an impression that there was little real enthusiasm. " The Emperor's foolish marriage," wrote Lord Cowley, " has done him an infinity of harm in the country. It was, of course, ill-received at Paris, even by the Emperor's friends, and it has set all the women against him. Clergy and army disapprove. The people believe that he has married his mistress. In general everyone sees in it another proof of the headstrong will which sets everything at defiance." [1] The Emperor did not seem to care. Business itself was put in the background, while he gave all his dreams to his bride.[2] The passion for Empire had ceded to the Empire of passion. And when the Diplomatic Corps was received in the gallery of Diana on the eighth day after the wedding, the Emperor struck them as a man intoxicated with his joy. " I would never have thought it possible," wrote the Austrian Ambassador, " that at his age and with his experiences, he could be so single-heartedly and so manifestly in love." [3]

But in another ten days, they saw that he had a thought for other things : for gas, for sewers, for railways, for town-planning in Paris.[4] As for his foreign policy (and it was on that which all was to turn), no one could guess it. He was alone on an ocean of complications, and, if he had a compass,

[1] *Cowley Papers* : Cowley to Howden, 10th February, 1853.
[2] *Cowley Papers* : Cowley to Clarendon, 5th May, 1853.
[3] Hübner : *Neuf Ans de Souvenirs*, i, 109.
[4] *Cowley Papers* : Cowley to Clarendon, 5th May, 1853.

he kept it hidden. Lord Cowley seized the opportunity. That shrewd diplomatist had not been sent for nothing to replace Lord Normanby. In a few months he had won the Emperor over to compare England to Eugénie : a wife after his mistresses. The Emperor was furious that the Crown Prince of Belgium had married an Austrian Archduchess, and France, remembering the Spanish marriage, suspected another Coburg plot. But the British Ambassador reassured him. " I cannot say," said the Emperor to Cowley at St. Cloud on 6th June, " how glad I am to find myself acting cordially with England. I desire to do so on all questions, even if this crisis passes over. . . ."[1] The Modern Napoleon was already even anticipating the Entente Cordiale ! For perhaps the most special of his secrets was to avoid his uncle's mistake of ruining his victories by alienating England. If we track out the plans of Napoleon III, we shall see in general how his idea of copying the Conqueror was subsidiary to the intention of avoiding the mistakes which led to St. Helena.

At St. Helena itself, however, a new error was conceived and vaunted—the cause of nationalities. And this, which was for the uncle a pose became to the nephew a passion. It was that passion which above all both made the Europe of to-day and destroyed the man whose greatest claim on our attention is that famous procreative power. Whether the procreation may not be in the end as ruinous for us as for him is a question which makes his career all the more suggestive to the modern world.[2]

[1] *Cowley Papers* : Cowley to Clarendon, 6th June, 1853.
[2] F. A. Simpson, *The Times Napoleon Supplement*, 5th May, 1921.

VII

THE CRIMEAN WAR

> He's a fool
> That being a cold would thrust his hands i' th' fire
> To warm them.
> WEBSTER : *The Duchess of Malfi*, I, ii, 129.
>
> Wherever there is war there *must* be injustice on one side, on the other, or on both. There have been wars which were little more than trials of strength between friendly nations and in which the injustice was not to each other, but to the God who gave them life. But in a malignant war of the present ages there is injustice of ignoble kind, at once to God and man, which *must* be stemmed for both their sakes. It may indeed be so involved with natural prejudices and ignorances that neither of the contending nations can conceive it as attaching to their cause; nay, the constitution of their governments, and the clumsy crookedness of their political dealings with each other, may be such as to prevent either of them from knowing the actual cause for which they have gone to war.
> RUSKIN : *Modern Painters*, IV, xviii, 32.

I

ALTHOUGH it was now more than half-way through the Nineteenth Century, the absolute monarchies of the Northern Courts dominated the diplomacy of Europe. Austria, in league with the Rome of Pius IX, and swayed by the Archduchess Sophie, was reactionary. Prussia was a militant aristocracy, still cultivating the traditions of Frederick the Great. And beyond these loomed up through Europe, Asia, and America the dominions, vast as the very surface of the moon, and still extending, which touched Prussia, Turkey, Thibet, China, and British Columbia—the Russias of the Czar.

The Northern Courts were all united in antipathy to France, and Napoleon III regarded it as the great failure of Louis Philippe that he had done nothing against them.[1] It was not only the range, the expansion, and the military power of Russia which threatened Europe : Liberals were exasperated to think that in this country the majority of men were still serfs, and Protestants were outraged to admit that the religion of this vast tract, centred as it was in the person of the Emperor Nicholas, was hardly more reformed than Roman Catholicism, perhaps much less so. All this in itself was troublesome for those who wanted to keep the world's powers in equilibrium : and when Russia began to overbear the administration of the Sultan, it seemed intolerable to diplomatists as a whole and especially to an overrated survival of ambassadors acting on their own initiative : for Lord Stratford de Redcliffe had gone in the spring of 1853 to represent Her Britannic Majesty at the Sublime Porte.

The trouble began in a dispute at the Holy Sepulchre. The great Church where the body of the Crucified Redeemer had rested was in the hands of Latin monks ; unless they opened their door, no one could reach the chapel at its side which was in the possession of the Orthodox. And thus met the spear-points of ancient antagonism between Rome and Constantinople. Great national cultures were still involved. France and Austria were, in their different ways, protectors of the Papacy : the Czar claimed a sort of supremacy over all Eastern

---

[1] Hübner : *Neuf Ans*, vol. 1.

THE CRIMEAN WAR 147

Christians. Thus a national, a personal ambition was easily confused with a sacred duty. And the Czar had so long disposed of arbitrary power that he was no longer quite normal mentally. "There is something wild about him,"[1] wrote Queen Victoria. He had come to feel that to question his decisions or thwart his desires was a sort of blasphemy.

He found a suitable agent of his absolute will in Prince Mentschikoff who came to Constantinople with a great military train not merely to settle the dispute at Jerusalem, but to assert a sovereign power over all Turkish subjects who shared the religion of the Czar. Those subjects numbered not less than a dozen millions.[2] Outrageous as this claim was, it was made still worse by the arrogant tone in which it was delivered, and by the fact that this Ambassador Extraordinary did not even observe such a common courtesy as calling on the Minister for Foreign Affairs.[3] "All that savours of the Middle Ages, or at least of Peter the Great," said Lord Clarendon to Count Walewski, "but that quaint sort of show is not without its dangers."[4] It began to dawn on Europe that Mentschikoff had objects far more sweeping than to dictate the pieties of pilgrims, the custody of a key, or the restoration of a cupola. In fact, Turkey could not give in to the demands of Nicholas without abandoning her rights as a sovereign state.[5]

Now for Russia to extend her sway to the Dardanelles, and to have a free opening to the Mediterranean, was a thing that no power in Western

[1] T. Martin : *Life of the Prince Consort*, vol. iii, ch. li.
[2] Quai d'Orsay. Angleterre. Walewski. 21st May, 1853.
[3] La Gorce : *Second Empire*, i.
[4] Quai d'Orsay. Angleterre. Walewski. April, 1853.
[5] *Morning Post*, 19th May, 1853.

Europe wanted, least of all either France or England. Each Government, agitated by the same instinct, desired to draw nearer to the other, and the English sent to France the Will of the First Emperor. Napoleon III wrote to Lord Clarendon a letter with his own hand to thank him, and sent a *tabatière* stamped with the Imperial Arms to Dr. Dyke, of Doctors' Commons [1] : he did not stop at little courtesies. By 31st May he had given orders to his fleet to sail for the Dardanelles, " not to take the initiative in aggression, not to excite Turkey to refuse any sort of terms, but to provide a guarantee against immediate danger, and to reserve to diplomacy as she needed them the resources which would be too late if the struggle was against facts already accomplished." [2]

The Czar indeed seemed to be threatening Turkey with an ultimatum. " But if he does," said Lord Clarendon to Walewski, " one need only publish the documents you have shown me to show how monstrously unjust his claims are. And besides, after such precise assurances given by the Cabinet at St. Petersburg to Paris and London, how could he dare to go back on his word so obviously and so blatantly ? " [3]

The Czar did not mean to go back on his word. The summer wore on, the autumn came. The Turks stated their terms, the Czar accepted them ; but then, lured on by the unscrupulous Stratford, who had an old grudge against the Czar,[4] the Turks

[1] Quai d'Orsay. Angleterre. Walewski to Turgot. 23rd February, 1853.
[2] Quai d'Orsay. Drouyn de Lhuys to Walewski.
[3] Quai d'Orsay. Angleterre. Walewski to Drouyn de Lhuys. 21st May, 1853.
[4] Thouvenel : *Nicholas Ier et Napoléon III*, p. 121.

THE CRIMEAN WAR

pushed forward still more demands, and on 10th October Russia and Turkey were technically at war, though hostilities had not actually commenced. The Emperor had been working hard for peace. "The time for conquests is over,"[1] he insisted. Even Prince Albert could not withhold a tribute to his statesmanship.[2] "He is so anxious to preserve peace," wrote Lord Cowley, "that he would not look closely into any arrangement (that is, whether it would be acceptable to Turkey or not) provided he could induce the Four Powers to say to the Porte, 'You shall accept it.' Indeed, the only anxiety I feel in regard to our own alliance with him is that the desire to see the question terminated may overrule all other considerations."[3] He did not, of course, mean Russia to extend her territories, but he steadfastly hoped that the Czar would be generous and prudent enough to be satisfied with humbling the Turks; for the Turkish Army, he knew, was a very bad one and would probably be beaten.[4] From the commencement of the trouble he had made up his own mind not to send a soldier to the East.[5]

But circumstances were gradually becoming too strong for him. He could never forget the need of his diplomacy to weaken the alliance of the Northern Courts against France: he knew it in the meanwhile to be imperative to act as fully as possible in understanding with England. The Allied Navies, therefore, were induced to enter the Black Sea together; and the Turks, after having provoked the Russians in several small naval engagements, had suffered signal

---

[1] *Moniteur*, 2 Mars, 1854.
[2] Martin: *Prince Consort*, vol. iii, ch. li
[3] *Cowley Papers*: Cowley to Clarendon, 11th November, 1853.
[4] *Cowley Papers*: Cowley to Clarendon, 21st November, 1853.
[5] *Cowley Papers*: Cowley to Clarendon, 13th January, 1854.

punishment. In their own harbour at Sinope, their fleet had been smashed to pieces. When this news reached Constantinople, Lord Stratford was happy. " That means *war*," he said. " The Emperor of Russia chose to make a personal quarrel with me, and now I am avenged." [1] He knew that with Lord Palmerston, the Liberal papers and the people of England all anxious to fight for democracy, he could snap his fingers at the peaceful Courts of St. James or the Tuileries. The feeling was so strong against Prince Albert that it was even proposed he should be shot at dawn in the Tower; there was a rumour that even Queen Victoria had been arrested, and it was sober fact that the crowd in London had transferred its homage from her to the man who appeared at her court as the representative of Turkey.[2]

As for the Emperor of the French, he had forgotten the key and the cupola at Jerusalem: he had been involved in the diplomatic struggle which the prestige of England, with that of France, was waging against the might of the Czar. The Russian troops still occupied Bessarabia. But the Emperor still insisted that war could not be justified till every offer of peace had been rejected. He took his Empress into his counsels. " I could see from her manner," wrote Lord Cowley, " how alarmed the Emperor is, and how desirous he is to preserve peace." [3]

There is one word which is fatal to the welfare of a great nation. Lord Cowley breathed it: *Honour*.[4] Although there was still some denominational friction,

[1] F. A. Simpson : *Louis Napoleon and the Recovery of France*, p. 239
[2] Greville, i, 1st February, 1854.
[3] *Cowley Papers* : To Clarendon, 24th January, 1854.
[4] Quai d'Orsay : Drouyn to Baragney d'Hilliers, 18th January, 1854.

the Emperor was thinking most of that now, the honour of France. But he tried one more expedient. On 29th January, 1854, he wrote a personal letter to the Czar. Firm but conciliatory, he indicated the alternatives : a thorough understanding, or a violent rupture. Let the Russian troops return from Bessarabia, the Allied Fleets from the Black Sea and Russia treat direct with Turkey.[1] But the Czar refused to treat. He answered haughtily that the Russia of 1854 would be found the same as that of 1812.[2]

So Napoleon's diplomacy had failed : " I will take care of the Turks—England will act as I wish," he had boasted, but now he only wished that the Czar should be duly punished for his outrageous conduct.[3] He planned an attack on Sebastopol by land and sea at once : and plunged into plans for a siege, with estimates of the shipping at Sebastopol, of the expenses of the campaign, with inquiries about the attitude of Berlin and Vienna, and the question of a Turkish loan : and he suggested that the Polish recruits should be encouraged to desert.

He had sent out St. Arnaud, and St. Arnaud was not equal to the command of such an arduous campaign. In the first place, he was not trusted by the Army, and he had failed wholly to realize that an army marches on its stomach.[4] He knew himself that even the bravest and strongest of his men cared no longer for renown ; they were restless and were out of spirits. Afraid that cholera or fever might attack them at any moment, they had lost interest in any other enemy.[5] Besides that, the French

[1] La Gorce : *Second Empire*, I, 211.
[2] *Cowley Papers* : Cowley to Clarendon, 15th February, 1854.
[3] *Cowley Papers* : 1st February, 1854.
[4] *Cowley Papers* : Cowley to Raglan, 9th August, 1854.
[5] *Cowley Papers* : Cowley to Clarendon, 30th August, 1854.

and English Embassies were quarrelling in Constantinople.[1]

In September, Prince Albert came over and met the Emperor at Boulogne. Albert had no predilection for Napoleon; he shivered at the idea that this dissolute parvenu should have that prize of distinguished innocence, the Garter.[2] But there was a war to win, and it was not for the Queen's husband to fail in courtesy to her ally. Which was to take take precedence? Albert's position always made difficulties, he was the Queen's husband, but he was not a sovereign; in fact, in Germany, his position was that of the younger son of a Duke, and his title not Royal Highhess but "Durchlaucht". The Prince demurred at the moment when it came to enter the Emperor's carriage, but to the Emperor's insistence that the Prince should receive the politeness due only to a monarch, Albert graciously deferred and finally took the seat on the right side.[3] The days passed by according to plan; though the fields were too full of corn for Napoleon to attempt manœuvres on the grand scale. The Emperor pressed the Prince hard for information as to how England was governed, and received the most courteous answers. "It is trying to make acquaintance as it were in public," said the Emperor to Lord Cowley, "but the Prince has made it easy. I am more pleased than I can say with all that I have heard from him."[4] And then there had been a most gracious letter, written in perfect French, from Victoria herself.

[1] *Cowley Papers*: Cowley to Clarendon, 31st July, 1854; to Stratford, 4th August, 1854. Cf. L. Thouvenel: *Nicholas Ier et Napoléon III*, ch. iv.
[2] *Cowley Papers*: Cowley to Clarendon, 8th September, 1854.
[3] *The Times*, 7th September, 1854.
[4] *Cowley Papers*: Cowley to Clarendon, 6th September, 1854.

THE CRIMEAN WAR

Albert, too, had been forced to reconsider his prejudices. He found Napoleon quiet, indolent, phlegmatic, and extraordinarily ignorant on certain subjects, but thoughtfulness and shrewdness made some compensation for the lack of knowledge.[1] And the Prince could not help liking the gay, humorous talker who spoke with such ease and openness, an openness which astonished Greville [2] and always made an impression on Lord Cowley. Here in this astonishing conspirator was a sincerity almost impossible to resist. Before the Prince left on the night tide for Osborne, on 8th September, he had said that the Queen hoped to receive the Emperor and Empress in England. Napoleon was too overjoyed to accept this coveted invitation in becoming terms, but answered awkwardly that he hoped to see the Queen in Paris. Much as he wanted, much as he needed the endorsement of Windsor, he knew that the time for the visit was not yet come.[3]

The winter that followed in the Crimea was to freeze the strongest hearts. France had 90,000 men between Constantinople and the Crimea : ill, chilled, and almost starving. Prince Napoleon came back, and with him the Duke of Cambridge, each under suspicion. The man who looked so much like the great conqueror had found his nickname of Plon-Plon had been changed to Craint-plomb. He was thoroughly disgruntled, and he argued in Paris that Sebastopol was impregnable and that the war ought to stop. The Alma, Balaklava, Inkerman, these had meant a thrill, but from all the army had endured of disease and hardships, of wounds and death,

[1] *Cowley Papers* : id., 7th September. H. Bolitho : *Albert the Good*, p. 221.
[2] Greville : *Queen Victoria*, vii, 170.
[3] *Cowley Papers* : To Clarendon, 2nd February, 1855.

what had been gained ? Nevertheless, the Emperor refused to give up all for nothing. He had begun to work out sweeping plans to establish Austria in Bessarabia, to make Poland into an independent kingdom. That he dimly felt was his destiny, to reorganize the map of Europe. But for that he must have victory.

Even a year before, the dramatic notion had entered his mind that he must take command in the Crimea himself. In the spring of 1855, that notion began to lodge within his thought as master. The position in the Crimea struck him as serious. " There is no plan of action there, no decision," he said to the British Ambassador, " not even a plan for future operations. I do not pretend to be a military genius, but if I go I shall at least relieve the Generals from the responsibility which is weighing them down, and of which I am not afraid. If something is not done we shall go from bad to worse. Army after army will rot before Sebastopol." [1]

It was supposed that the paladin spirit of the Empress had conceived this idea. This was not so. Was it likely, she asked, that in lightness of mind she would advise that which placed the Emperor in danger ? No, the fact was that he had a mental conviction, which she could not counteract, that he alone could retrieve the deadlock in the Crimea. She had not been satisfied till she consulted General Vaillant, and Vaillant was convinced that the Emperor was right.

But suppose the Emperor failed !

" Oh, if Providence is against us," cried Eugénie, " nothing can be done ! " [2]

Both of the Sovereigns trusted that the stars in

[1] *Cowley Papers* : Cowley to Clarendon, 28th February, 1855.
[2] *Cowley Papers* : Cowley to Clarendon, 8th March, 1855.

their courses were fighting against the Czar. And yet it was not less necessary to adopt the most energetic plans ; if Sebastopol was impregnable, then another plan of campaign must be adopted. If 60,000 men were left before Sebastopol, and he could move about another army of Turks, English, French, and Sardinians, he might obtain in that way the great success without which the war could hardly be ended. Everyone around the Emperor was pressing him hard for peace : and he wanted to show that something had been gained. The Holy Places had faded from his mind. He kept thinking of the independence of Poland, or, if not independence, at least the rights which had been guaranteed to Warsaw in the Treaty of Vienna ; and he had even proposed that England should have Sinope, or some other port on the shore of the Black Sea. " You might convert it into another Gibraltar," he said to the British Ambassador, " Asia concerns you more intimately than it does us." [1]

3

Prince Albert's decision at Boulogne came to flower next spring. It was on 17th April that the Emperor, driving through London at a walking pace, showed the Empress the lodging in King Street where he had lived after his escape from Ham.

Evening was falling when they drove up to Windsor, and Queen Victoria, filled with " indescribable emotion ", was waiting to greet them as they alighted from their carriage. The Queen at once fell under the fascination of her guests. They were shy, but that gave them a deferential grace most flattering to their hostess. It was not merely that the Emperor was civil and well-bred ; his low soft voice, his

[1] *Cowley Papers* : Cowley to Clarendon, 14th March, 1855.

quiet frank manner, his tactful talk, and that magnetic mystery which few normal women could resist (the Queen was a quite normal woman) at once worked their spell.[1] He danced, she noticed, at the Ball that evening, with great dignity and spirit. And next afternoon, after a council of war in the morning, she admitted her ally to the most signal mark of her approval. With Prince Albert on one side, and the Duke of Cambridge on the left, she " buckled the Garter on the left leg of His Imperial Majesty, the Chancellor pronouncing the admonition ". And then she rose, and completed the ceremonial by receiving him in her arms.[2]

Next day the French Sovereign drove to lunch at the Guildhall. Gay with floating banners, and swaying with crowds, the streets of London rang with acclamations from tens of thousands who had come out to do him honour. The reception of the public, wrote the Queen on the first day of his arrival, was *immensely* enthusiastic. What was she to say of it now? Her heart was full. And what were his feelings as at last he rose among England's great to tell them how the affection for England, which he had felt as an exile, guided him to alliance now that he was on the throne of France? " If I have acted in accordance with my convictions, it is that the interests of the nation which has chosen us, no less than that of universal civilization, has made it a duty. Indeed, England and France are naturally united on all the great questions of Politics and of human progress that agitate the world." [3]

This great pronouncement of the Modern Emperor having been made in the heart of London to England's

[1] Martin : *Prince Consort*, iii, 241, 2.
[2] *London Gazette Supplement*, 20th April, 1855.
[3] *The Times*, 19th April, 1855.

leaders, he drove back with his consort amid shouts louder than before. " Since the time of my Coronation, with the exception of the great Exhibition," wrote the Queen, " I don't remember anything like it. To-night we go in State to the Opera."

Next day, the Queen drove him to the Crystal Palace, and as it was his birthday, she gave him a pencil-case.[1] She had each day been more impressed: his manners were so perfect, and majesty came as natural to him, she said, " as though he had been born a king's son and brought up for the place." [2] She seemed to have forgotten for the moment that he had been born a King's son. Yet even his royal bearing was subordinated by a power peculiarly personal. For when she wrote that she felt " safe with him ", what did she mean but that she found him deliciously dangerous? " That he *is* a very *extraordinary* man with great qualities there can be *no* doubt— " she wrote in her journal on the day of his departure, " I might almost say a mysterious man. He is evidently possessed of *indomitable courage, unflinching firmness of purpose, self-reliance, perseverance and great secrecy* ; to this should be added a great reliance in what he calls his STAR and a belief in omens and incidents as connected with his future destiny which is almost romantic, and at the same time he is endowed with a wonderful *self-control*, great *calmness*, even *gentleness*, and with a *power of fascination* the effect of which upon those who become more intimately acquainted with him is most sensibly felt." [3]

Queen Victoria's portrait of Napoleon was neither more nor less than an unconscious paraphrase of what Lytton had observed sixteen years before.

[1] Martin : *Prince Consort*, iii, 249
[2] Ibid., iii, 252.
[3] *Queen Victoria's Letters*, i, bk. iii, 132.

"Your Majesty," the Queen wrote to his Empress, "has a way of winning every heart." [1] And of both the Queen said to Monckton Milnes: "They are the pleasantest people I have ever met." [2]

After returning, Napoleon wrote a charming letter to Victoria: "Although it is three days since our return to Paris, I am still in thought present with Your Majesty, and my first need is to repeat how deep is the impression left by the gracious and affectionate kindness of your welcome. It was political interests which drew us together," he continued, "but now when it has been vouchsafed to me to know Your Majesty personally, the real link between us henceforth is a feeling of warm and respectful devotion: and, indeed, it is impossible to live together intimately for a few days without falling under the charm of the picture of a household so august and so happily united. Your Majesty has also deeply touched me by Your gracious thought for the Empress; for nothing gives one greater pleasure than to see her whom one loves the object of such flattering attentions." [3]

The Emperor added to these polite phrases a promise hardly less welcome, not to go to the Crimea. Though he had politely deferred at Windsor to military suggestions which the Prince Consort pressed on the part of Lord Raglan, but which he thought strategically weak, he had returned to Paris with the feeling that his presence alone could set things right in the Crimea. But now it appeared that the dangers of the war were less serious than the dangers of Paris. His cousin, even his Ministers, might play him any trick. What government could be formed if he went abroad? What set of men could he, could

---

[1] R. Sencourt: *Empress Eugénie*, 122.
[2] Merimée: *Unpublished letter.*
[3] *Queen Victoria's Letters*, 1st series, iii, 118.

anyone trust ? " You did well on the 2nd December to risk a little in order to gain much," had been the advice of Persigny. " Do not risk all now to gain a little."[1]

The Emperor had hardly finished his letter to the Queen when an assassin gave him a sharp reminder of the precariousness of his position. He was riding in the Champs-Elysées, when an Italian, a certain Pianori, came down a side street towards him, and fired twice from a pistol at close range. Neither ball touched the Emperor. He continued to ride at precisely the same pace as before to the Bois de Boulogne : and it was only by the strongest representations that he allowed the law to take its course upon the criminal.

4

To maintain the English alliance was not easy. The country wanted peace. " His position is too hard," wrote Lord Cowley on 21st May, " surrounded by men who do nothing but *din* the word peace into his ears."[2] And he was well aware that no one in the Crimea was able to work out a plan of campaign, and contradictory orders were being sent out from Paris and London. Lord Raglan still kept pressing the idea which Prince Albert had commended, the idea of making a base of Eupatoria. On 23rd May there had been a great reverse ; as the Emperor looked at the figures of the casualties, he saw that they were greater than those of Austerlitz : and all for an indecisive result ! He was almost in despair. He maintained that it would be madness to storm

[1] V.N.A., Hübner to Buol, 27th February, 1855.
[2] *Cowley Papers* : To Clarendon.

Sebastopol before it was invested.[1] Pelissier had taken over the command, but the only result had been more losses and no further advance; and the Emperor felt much inclined to recall Pelissier. Vaillant, at the Ministry of War, however, persuaded him otherwise.[1] On 5th July he was still dreadfully out of spirits but he must make preparations for the return visit of the Queen which was now arranged for August. She was to arrive on the 19th accompanied not only by the Prince Consort, but by the Prince of Wales and the Princess Royal. If the little Princess did not come, Napoleon said, it would break his heart.[1]

He carefully thought out the questions of precedence, especially in relation to those nice points which kept pricking up out of the equivocal status of the Prince Consort. The Queen above all must be gratified. "*En même temps que la reine*," he said, anticipating the delicacies of Disraeli, "*il faut voir la femme.*"[2] He himself took the greatest trouble in preparing her rooms at St. Cloud, and she said that it was all so much as she wished that if only her little dog was with her she would feel perfectly at home. The Emperor said nothing but, three days later when she came in, she found the dog greeting her with a bark. A special messenger had been dispatched at once.[3]

The host knew that his guest felt a melancholy sympathy with Louis Philippe, whose daughter had married her uncle. So he suggested himself that they should drive out to Neuilly and see the old King's château. At the Grand Trianon they saw where his Queen had been married; at the Tuileries, the room where the King had signed his abdication. And

[1] *Cowley Papers.*
[2] *Papiers Secrets des Tuileries*, iii, 397.
[3] Emily Crawford : *Victoria, Queen and Ruler*, pp. 311, 312.

everywhere the Queen noticed with what delicacy of feeling the new Sovereign had left the memorials of his predecessor untouched. " Nothing," she wrote, " could exceed his tact or kindness." And nothing evidently could express her own enthusiasm. " We have been to the Exposition," she said in a letter to King Leopold, " to Versailles, which is most splendid and magnificent—to the Grand Opera, where the reception and the way in which ' God Save the Queen ' was sung was *most magnificent*. Yesterday we went to the Tuileries ; in the evening *Theatre ici* : to-night an immense ball at the Hôtel de Ville. They have asked to call a new street which has been opened after me." And there it remains to this day—the Avenue Victoria.

The ball at the Hôtel de Ville was brilliant. The Queen gave herself to her partner's dancing with even more enthusiasm for his mingling of dignity with spirit than she had done at Windsor. And yet, wherever the little lady moved, the air of majesty enveloped her with uniqueness, and kept even the closest at a distance.

But there was a moment when her remoteness was violated in a most surprising manner. In an interval of the dance, the Emperor presented some Arab chiefs who approached each in his great burnous, as though a human balloon. As the tallest of the chiefs came forward to do homage, a man of great height with all the menace of the wilds in his expression, and knelt down before the Queen, he seized her by the calf. *Honni soit qui mal y pense.* Was the Arab to renew the institution of the Garter ? The Queen neither swooned nor uttered cry : if she was nonplussed, it was by the effort to keep herself from laughing. For this intimate approach was designed to do her a Biblical reverence according

L

to the words : Lay hold upon my thigh—only that in the passage of ages the sign of obeisance had dropped below the knee.[1]

This charming adventure (not reported in gazette or newspaper) was no doubt but one of the experiences which made the Queen feel that her sojourn in Paris was " fairylike ", was " overpowering ". " I am *delighted, enchanted, amused,* and *interested,*" she wrote, " and I think I never saw anything more *beautiful* and gay than Paris—or more splendid than all the palaces. The reception is most gratifying—for it is enthusiastic and really kind in the highest degree ; and Maréchal Magnan says that such a reception as I have received *every day here* is much greater and more enthusiastic than ever Napoleon on his return from his victories had received ! " [2]

There was an impressive calm one evening in the roar of homage, which day after day thrilled the heart of the Queen. Late one evening the Royalties arrived at the Hôtel des Invalides, so late that it was felt they had abandoned their visit. Veterans were given torches which shook in their trembling hands. As she came before the high altar of the chapel, Victoria read the words : " I desire that my ashes should rest on the banks of the Seine." She descended to the vault. The great sarcophagus of porphyry was not yet ready, and the body of the First Emperor rested in a chapel hung with velvet, beneath a velvet pall embroidered with golden bees. A golden eagle stretched his sheltering wings above. The star, the order of the Legion of Honour, the hat worn at Eylau, the sword of Austerlitz, rested beside the tomb.

It had been the hottest day of a stifling week.

[1] Merimée : *Unpublished Letter.*
[2] *Queen Victoria's Letters,* i, bk. iii, 136.

The air was overcharged. Thunder clouds had darkened the sky, and now from their congregated might, black rain and lightning burst after a roar as from a hundred cannon. " Kneel," said Victoria to her son, " before the tomb of the great Napoleon." And while the future King of England knelt among the shooting shadows before the tomb of England's sternest foe, the lightning flashed down more eerily on to the vault, the thunder pealed its salvoes. And then the organ raised its measured boom to greet the Queen of England in slow notes which filled all hearts.

> God save our gracious Queen,
> Long live our noble Queen ! [1]
> God save the Queen !

At last the visit was over, the pleasantest, and most interesting and most triumphant ten days, wrote Queen Victoria, that she had ever passed. Her heart was full as she said good-bye : her sorrow heavy when at last she lay down in her yacht to sail away from France. " Now those long days are passed," she wrote, " they seem like a vision or a dream, so lovely that we can scarcely believe it." [2] " As for the Emperor and Empress," she wrote again, " we all simply love them dearly." Even Prince Albert admitted that it was extraordinary how very much attached one became to the Emperor. And of him the children had grown excessively fond. " You know," said the Prince of Wales, as the Emperor drove him through Paris, " you have a fine country here. I wish I were your son." [3] " In short," the

---

[1] Sonolet et Fleury : *Souvenirs du Second Empire*.
[2] *Unpublished Letters to Lady Cowley*.
[3] Merimée : *Unpublished Letter*. T. Martin : *Prince Consort*, iii, 351.

Queen wrote of her host, " without *attempting* to do anything particular to make one like him, or *any* personal attraction in outward appearance, he *has* the power of *attaching* those to him who come near him and know him, which is quite incredible." [1]

5

On 8th September, Sebastopol fell, and there was a period of what Victoria called ecstasy [2]—both in France and England. At the *Te Deum* in Notre-Dame on the 13th, the Emperor, whose features lit up so rarely, seemed like one inspired [3] : but soon, in France at least, there was a strong reaction ; and before the month was over, the Emperor felt very differently from the English as to the point of pressing on the war. Money was running short, and he did not want to ask for another loan. He still hoped to occupy the whole Crimea, and to blockade Russia until she came to terms, but whether he could carry his people with him to an end attainable only by sacrifice, became more questionable with every autumn day. Apart from the question of the loan, he was solicitous for the troops who had already endured the rigours of one winter.[4] And in any case, how was he to make the war more popular unless he could interest the people of France in some immense scheme, like the liberation of Poland, and with it a change in the whole map of Europe ? The wildest ideas flitted through his mind : but it was questionable if even the most grandiose schemes would make the

[1] *Queen Victoria's Letters*, i, bk. iii, 139, 140.
[2] Strachey : *Queen Victoria*.
[3] Hübner : *Neuf Ans*, i, 340.
[4] *Cowley Papers* : Cowley to Clarendon, 22nd September, 1855.

French enthusiastic. Success did not rouse the nation, and Bourqueney, the Minister at Vienna, on returning to Paris found to his horror that the old military spirit of France had been exchanged for a love of the things that belong to peace.[1] Lord Cowley had become so insistent with regard to the war that the Emperor began to evade him.

Napoleon had his firm plan for peace : Poland was left out, Wallachia and Moldavia were to be united under a foreign Prince, the Danube was to be entirely freed from Russian jurisdiction, the Black Sea neutralized ; and the religious question settled as the Western Powers thought best. On 10th November his patience with England had given out. He had closed the exhibition with a speech in which the desire for peace was very openly expressed. In the evening he saw the Duke of Cambridge, and told him that as the English Government proposed nothing, the generals nothing, and yet none accepted his own proposals, there was little sense in going on with the war. The next day, Prince Napoleon made a speech on the Crimea without the slightest reference to the British Navy having been there at all.[2]

6

It was not only the English and the French who were involved in the Crimean question. Austria was watching it very closely, and negotiating with the allies as to whether she also should declare war against Russia. In October, 1855, Vienna had broken off diplomatic relations with St. Petersburg. And that was much. It would mean an additional weight

[1] *Cowley Papers* : To Clarendon, 13th October.
[2] *Cowley Papers* : Cowley to Clarendon, 11th November, 1855.

against Russia in settling the terms of peace, and had not Prince Albert said that the war was as much an intellectual campaign as a matter of the musket and the cannon?[1] But apart from Austria, there were two rising nationalities in Europe, each with a rising patriot. Queen Victoria had met at Versailles the diplomat, Bismarck. And the Sardinian Cavour had actually sent troops to fight on the French side.

His sovereign, Victor Emmanuel, therefore made visits as ally to Paris and to London. Neither his manners nor his appearance served as an advertisement for his country: and he brought back from London to Paris a very mischievous piece of gossip. " There has been the devil to pay at Compiègne," wrote Lord Cowley to Lord Clarendon on 10th December, 1855, " in consequence of the King of Sardinia's indiscreet *Cancans*. He has brought over stories of Palmerston's language respecting the Emperor which have raised not without reason the imperial ire—but the word is that he has also reported a conversation with the Prince [2] which the Emperor has taken much to heart.

The King's story about Palmerston is—that the latter said " that His Imperial Majesty was in the hands of a parcel of adventurers, that he could not stand up against them, and that yielding to their exigencies, he was ready to conclude an ignominious peace—that England did not care a fig for the French—that the Emperor might withdraw his army from the Crimea if he liked ; but that if the Sardinians would remain firm, they and the British troops were strong enough to carry on the war alone, and bring it to an honourable conclusion ".

[1] Quai d'Orsay : Walewski to Drouyn de Lhuys, 5th June, 1855.
[2] i.e. Albert.

The language reported of the Prince was that it behoved England to be very watchful of an alliance between France and Austria, for that they might then turn round upon England and dictate to her hereafter.

"The Emperor," concluded the Ambassador, "came open-mouthed to me as soon as this was told him, and I never saw him more hurt or annoyed. He said that he had done nothing to merit these reproaches—that he was as determined as we were to obtain honourable conditions of peace and to prosecute the war until they were obtained. It was a mere question of strategy whether the war should be prosecuted in the Crimea or elsewhere, a point which could only be determined by the Council of War." [1]

A month later he was able to give a convincing proof of his sincerity. He showed Lord Cowley a letter from Drouyn de Lhuys in which the Minister advised using England as long as it was worth while, and then abandoning her for her more useful allies. To this the Emperor had answered that if others could be drawn to his side he would be very glad, but that alliance with England was the keystone of his policy.

On the anniversary of the sovereigns' wedding-day there was a great ball at the Tuileries. The Empress was talking to Lord Cowley and asked him if he was satisfied with everything he had been hearing from the Emperor. The Ambassador answered that he was always satisfied with everything he heard from His Majesty who was to him the soul of honour and loyalty : but that it was a different matter with the Ministers. The Empress did not disagree. She knew how great a difficulty the Sovereign had in finding

[1] *Cowley Papers.*

honest men to serve him. Over and over again, he had said that there was not a statesman in France. "And there at all events," concluded the cynical British diplomat, "he speaks the truth." [1]

7

By the 17th January, 1856, the Russians, now ruled by Alexander, the new Czar, had so far agreed to the allies' demands as to make an armistice possible, and, early in the spring, the Congress of Paris met to arrange the Treaty of Peace, and to take some steps towards readjusting in favour of France the articles of the Congress of Vienna. The English were particularly glad to have the Congress held in the one place where the one Frenchman on whom they could depend was present, and was supreme. And the Emperor did not disappoint the Foreign Secretary. " I like him better and better, the more I know him," said Lord Clarendon. And so on the 30th March, a treaty was signed, which was marvellously courteous to Russia, and settled nothing. Lord Stratford's ghastly war, which had originated out of trifles,[2] had been all in vain. The capture of Sebastopol had not been worth while," wrote the old Metternich of the Congress of Vienna who still lived on : " There is peace, but not the peace of order." [3] " I have a presentiment," said the Emperor himself, " that the present peace will not last long." [4]

[1] *Cowley Papers* : To Clarendon, 31st January, and 3rd February, 1856.
[2] Napoleon III to Hübner, 15th May, 1858 : " *Quelle était l'origine de la dernière guerre ? C'était la sotte affaire des vieux saints et les bêtises de M. de la Valette.*"
[3] Metternich : *Mémoires*, viii, 395.
[4] Paléologue : *Cavour*, 77.

The man to whom those words were spoken was the envoy from Sardinia : and before long more Italian assassins were to reinforce the pleadings of Cavour with Pianori's argument—gunpowder. For the Second Empire, alas, did *not* mean peace. " I fear that the current will drag me in," said the Emperor to the Austrian Ambassador, a month after the peace. " I am horribly afraid of it." " To side with England and Piedmont," answered the Ambassador, " would be to surrender to revolution. You would be terrible : you would do Europe as much harm as you have done her good," he continued, " but you would hurt no one as much as yourself."

" That is true," agreed the Emperor, " and that is why I am anxious." [1]

But the tendencies of which he was the agent were ruthless : and before long old James de Rothschild, chuckling in his German accent " *bas de baix, bas d'Empire* ",[2] was pointing his finger towards the fatal policy, so pregnant in history, which alienated the Emperor's sympathies from Austria, and gave them to such sinister foster-children as Piedmont and Prussia. Then might Napoleon have remembered how sharper than a serpent's tooth is ingratitude from those who owe one their life, their growth, their rise to strength ; and a jester might have recalled the words of Lear's fool :—

> The hedge sparrow fed the cuckoo so long,
> That it had it head bit off by it young.

But those times were not yet : for all men spoke of was still peace : peace founded on victory. And if Poland was not yet liberated, nor Rumania yet created, the Congress of Paris had established laws

[1] Hübner : *Neuf Ans*, i, 429.
[2] Ibid., ii, 273.

for the freedom of the seas. Piracy was to be abandoned, the merchandise of the enemy to be sacrosanct, under either neutral flags or its own. War was still regarded as a matter for armed forces only : it was not meant to involve civil populations, and, even during the War, Russia had been invited to send her contribution to the Paris Exhibition. And at the end of the Congress, Walewski, its president, had invited the plenipotentiaries to speak on other subjects than those in hand. So did the Modern Emperor inaugurate the contemporary systems of international conferences, and sow the seed of the League of Nations.[1]

[1] René Arnaud : *Deuxième République et Second Empire*, 99.

VIII

THE APPARENT TRIUMPH

> Thou rainbow on the tearful lash of doomsday's
>   morning star,
> Rise quick, and let me gaze into that planet
>   deep and far,
> As into a loved eye ;
> Or I must, like the fiery child of the Vesuvian
>   womb,
> Burst with my flickering ghost abroad, before the
>   sun of doom
> Rolls up the spectre sky.
>
> BEDDOES : *Doomsday.*

I

" THEY are doing all they can to concoct a child." So in a letter of 4th August, 1855,[1] did Lord Cowley refer to the most immediate result of the visit to London when Eugénie was given counsel both by Sir Charles Locock and the Queen. Long since it had been felt that only British physicians could settle this question of an heir. And Victoria at St. Cloud had been delighted to discover that her advice was being followed meticulously, with hopes of good success. Congratulations in the provincial papers greeted the expectant mother in words of intimate enthusiasm.[2] But many critical months were to pass before those moments arrived which proved the most critical of all. The Congress was just drawing to an end when on 15th March, 1856, its deliberations were interrupted by an announcement that a very interesting thing was about to happen. But as the

[1] *Cowley Papers* : Cowley to Clarendon.
[2] Archives Nationales : F 10, I 135, BB 18, 1657, d 2, 7498.

day wore on, it did not happen. Mother and child were in such danger that the Emperor was consulted as to which should be sacrificed : and his decision was that they should spare the mother. But at last nature and physician resolved the hours of torture. The Emperor wept to find himself the father of a son, born at the very moment when most he needed a pledge of keeping the future secure. His heart was so melted with joy and gratitude that as he passed out through the Tuileries he embraced everyone he met.[1] There was not a statesmen in Europe but shared the relief of Napoleon. " *C'est un évènement international*," said Lord Palmerston.[2] Théophile Gautier went much further :—

> *C'est un Jésus, à tête blonde,*
> *Qui porte en sa petite main,*
> *Pour globe bleu, la paix du monde*
> *Et le bonheur du genre humain.*

A wave of satisfaction poured over France : and one commune after another sent its felicitations in a tone which was at once respectful and affectionate. The societies of authors, of composers, of painters, and of actors were to have a donation, and so were the poor in each of the towns ; all the children born on the same day as the new Son of France could claim the Emperor and Empress as their godparents. Finally, a general political amnesty was declared.[3] " I am happy," said the Emperor, in closing the Congress of Paris, " that Providence has granted me a son at a moment when general reconciliation is dawning upon Europe. I will bring him up imbued

---

[1] Persigny to Walewski, 17th March.
[2] Archives du Quai d'Orsay : Persigny to Walewski, 17th March, 1856.
[3] *The Court of the Tuileries*, par Le Petit Homme Rouge.

with the idea that nations must not be egotistical, and that the peace of Europe depends upon the prosperity of every nation."

"A dynasty," he had said a few days earlier, " can only hope for stability by remaining faithful to its origin and by devoting itself to the popular interests for whose service it was created."

2

It was the inevitable consequence of the *coup d'État*, and indeed of the whole principle by which the Napoleons governed, that they had to work to a large extent alone.[1] In allowing no place for politicians, they seemed to have left none to statesmen. Victor Hugo and his friends refused to return. Thiers, hard at work on his history, remained irreconcilable, and it was hardly wise to offer power to avowed Republicans. The Emperor therefore kept almost all the power in his own hands. He dispensed most of it through Morny whom he had made President of the *Corps Legislatif*, and who supplied him with two men of ability, Rouher and Magne. And though there were among the unsympathetic deputies powerful speakers, such as Montalembert, Morny managed them well. His superb manners set a standard that made a rough demeanour or even a serious tone seem rather ridiculous : and it was by a suggestion of ridicule that his mocking smile and quick wit, which always kept the members both amused and docile, robbed critics of courage to attack the government.[2]

He felt that there were other things more important than to talk in Parliament. When Louis Napoleon

[1] Simpson : *Louis Napoleon and the Recovery of France*, 373.
[2] La Gorce : *Second Empire*, ii, 29, 30.

was made President, the railway lines amounted to no more than 3,600 kilometres against 10,000 in England which is hardly more than half the size of France. These 3,600 kilometres were divided amongst more than twenty companies which each had its own fares.

It was not a week after the *coup d'État* before Morny and the President had made a belt line to join the principal stations on the right bank of the Seine. In 1853 the Midi Company was founded, in 1854 l'Est, in 1855 l'Ouest. On the 12th September the Emperor showed his personal interest by writing to Rouher, his Minister of Public Works, to ask which were the best means of joining by rail Bordeaux and Mulhausen, Bordeaux and Lyons, Lyons and Calais, Nantes and Marseilles.[1] In 1858 the lines from Marseilles to Paris and from Paris to Cologne were opened. At the end of the following year, there were more than 16,000 kilometres running; in 1869 there were 23,000, while lines to Boulogne, to Basle, to Havre, and to Bordeaux, opened up fresh intercourse both to Europe and to the sea. In 1857 a subvention was given to three Transatlantic steamship lines: from Havre to New York; from St. Nazaire to Mexico and the West Indies, and from Bordeaux to Brazil and Buenos Ayres. The telegraph had been opened to private communications in 1850, and when in 1855 the wires reached Mende there was no prefecture which was not in immediate touch with Paris.[2]

During the Empire more than 25,000 kilometres of roads were built. New ease of communication and transport provided an enormous stimulus to

[1] Quai d'Orsay: *Papiers de Cerçay*.
[2] La Gorce: *Second Empire*, ii, 10, 11, 12,

industry, and factories sprang up to pour wealth into the pockets of capital. It was a time of boom, and, thanks to Morny, all that it produced was encouraged by the government while, at the same time, nothing interfered with the freedom of private enterprise. In all this the Emperor took a personal interest, writing letter after letter by his own hand to Rouher, whom he invited to come and stay with him at Biarritz. With this great work in hand, the Emperor was too occupied to apply very carefully the schemes he had worked out at Ham. But the masses of the people were not forgotten, and, stimulated by his sojourns at Biarritz, he pressed forward with his schemes for the cultivation of the forests and swamps in Les Landes.[1] On the 10th June, 1854, he introduced a law to facilitate the drainage of marshes.

"Walewski," said the Emperor, one day in January, 1858, "I am going to make you a present."

"Your Majesty is very kind."

"I am going to give you a marsh."

"What—a marsh?"

"Yes, a marsh. I have just bought one in Les Landes. I shall have it drained, and the men who run the business assure me that in three years it will bring in an income of £4,000 a year: and in three years I shall give it to you." [2]

A credit of 100,000,000 francs had been opened to assist farmers to drain their own marshes.[3]

The figures for exports and imports increased from 1,645,000,000 millions in 1848 to 4,593,000,000 in 1857; in 1869 it amounted to 6,228,000,000. In 1850 the wealth per head was counted at 500 francs

[1] Quai d'Orsay: *Papiers de Cerçay*.
[2] *Cowley Papers*: Cowley to Clarendon, 30th January, 1858.
[3] Evans: *Mémoires*, i, 186.

and in 1870, in spite of the great increase of population, the wealth per head was almost double.[1]

The Modern Emperor introduced into France from England the Building Society System in the Société de Credits Fonciérs. In 1859 he personally contributed 100,000 francs to improve the houses of workmen in Lille. In 1864 he spent 15,000,000 francs in building workmen's homes, and in 1867-8 he built 42 houses for workmen at Vincennes.[2]

He seldom visited a town without making inquiries as to overcrowding, drainage, and water-supply. And in 1852 his Government voted 10,000,000 francs for improving conditions in manufacturing towns. In 1856, just after the Prince's birth, he toured flooded districts, and took steps to safeguard the future against deluges to come. A debate in Parliament, a " unanimous report ", this was easy to obtain ; but what he insisted was that the building of dykes should begin at once. " I hold it a point of honour," he said, " that during my reign rivers as well as revolutions should keep to their beds and have no chance to break out." [3]

While these works were pressed forward, under the personal supervision of the Sovereign, while his consort busied herself with the sick, the poor, and the expectant mothers, the Court itself was organized with a brilliance of ceremonial, and a frequency of entertainment, which not only made Paris the centre of the world, but kept the money in it in frequent movement. The Empire was inaugurated with great balls. To dance : this was no simple physical pleasure, no mere gallant diversion : it took a central place in one's duty towards the people.

[1] Evans : i, ch. v, *passim*.
[2] Evans, id.
[3] La Gorce : *Second Empire*, ii, 41.

It was *une œuvre sociale*, in this reign of muslin and taffetas.[1] And after dancing, then listening to the concert, after attending the opera, to sit in quiet rooms in the dark around a table till the table talked was another function, half scientific, half preternatural, a substitute both for the perfumes of incense and the ranker odours of the laboratory. At the court of the Tuileries, all was to be modern : and meanwhile the great expression of the Emperor's mind, his ideals for society, his sense of progressive order were to find their principal expression in the planning and organization of his capital.

3

"The Emperor has done wonders for Paris," wrote Queen Victoria to King Leopold on 23rd August, 1855.[2] The complex and rather disordered result of centuries of conflict, Paris was an epitome of France. It is through Paris, Paris as it had grown, Paris as he found it, Paris as it is now, that we shall go furthest towards appreciating the modern Emperor. For the capital, in inviting him to express his ideals for France, formed them in telling him what France had been.

Paris, of course, is not merely the capital of France. The exacter truth is that France is the country which has grouped itself round the nucleus of Paris which is central not only in France but in Western civilization. Hugh Capet had first given it importance by making it his capital in 987. Then, indeed, it was born to life and movement as the winged insect bursts from the chrysalis : it took the very form of a butterfly with La Cité as its body and the Ville and

[1] Beyens : *Le Second Empire*, i, 416.
[2] *Queen Victoria's Letters*, i, bk. iii.

l'Université as its wings. Philippe Auguste, reigning from 1180 to 1223, first gave it a conscious plan, framing the streets and encircling them with a towered wall. Charles V of Valois finished the feudal Louvre and threw back the walls, or *bohlwerke*, to the present lines of the boulevards.

But it was with the Sixteenth Century that Paris began to take the form of a modern city. Before that, its Gothic gables and stone were those of a medieval city like Nuremberg or Hildesheim. Within its formidable walls, its spires were spears, Its temper was one of fear, and, therefore, of fanaticism. Women eating meat on Fridays were liable to be burnt alive, cruelty was no small ingredient in the hearts of those whose worship was lit by the fiery glass of the Sainte Chapelle, or by the tapers which shone like stars upon its central altar of Notre-Dame de Paris, and sparkled in the gloom of its long aisles. Paris was still to see the Massacre of St. Bartholomew, and the Journée des Barricades. It was still to endure the four years siege of Henry of Navarre.

It was after him that Paris, like Rome itself, became a Renaissance city. The dear disorder of its gables began to give way to buildings spacious, regular, and elegant. Energy attained refinement, glory found its complement in culture. In a North no longer barbarous, taste, honouring the Latin virtues, conquered not with a man's will but with a feminine attraction. Passion found a new function, as we see, in the household where reason was master, and if the Church of the Counter-Reformation showed in the new architecture how secure was its dominion, no doubt one reason for its victory was its guarantee to maintain a woman secure at the apex of creation.

Under Anne of Austria, convents arose regal ; and then the capital fell under the spell of Mansart.

He led the movement which transformed Paris from a city of timbered walls and gables like Brunswick into what we see ; then arose the Savonnerie, the Gobelins, the Invalides, the Place Vendôme. Elegance grew out of wantonness and held savagery in check at the same time as mysticism undermined formality.

Such was the temper of the modern City when the Reign of Terror reminded the world that the ferocity of the Gothic spirit was still a strong ingredient of the Parisian genius. And on this mingling of dark, narrow streets, of medieval windows and spires, of picturesque survivals with the superb grace of Mansart's buildings, the first Napoleon stamped his sense of universal Empire. He extended the Quais and ensured for his city that ample beauty of a wide free river, flowing between trees and palaces. He bridged it with the Pont de Jéna. He built the Bourse so that commerce on the grand scale might have a Roman theatre. He raised the Vendôme column to bear his statue. Copying the arch of Septimus Severus, he raised the Arc du Carrousel between the Tuileries and the Louvre, and on this arch he placed the bronze horses of San Marco which Theodosius had first taken to Constantinople from the Temple of the Sun. He transformed the Madeleine into a *temple de gloire* in honour of his armies. Finally he extended the Champs Elysées to the Etoile and built the Arc de Triomphe. But the Great Napoleon, having stamped his organizing genius upon a few central spaces, did not stay to transform the streets and lanes of the city. When his nephew re-established the Empire, the central inspiration was there, above all in the sense of space and fitness inherent in every view of the Place de la Concorde. That sense which, taking a lesson from the Piazza del Popolo, set up in the centre the obelisk of Luxor, which had completed the Champs Elysées with the Arc de Triomphe and placed at the entrance of the avenue the Chevaux de Marly, which had arranged on one side the garden and the façade of the Tuileries, and on another the Dome des Invalides and the columns and pediment of the Palais Bourbon, and on the fourth the buildings of the Ministere de la Marine with others used for private purposes, so that these should open, on the Colonnades of the Madeleine—displaying on its imperial pediment a relief in which the Lord of earth and heaven arrests the ministers of judgment to speak in mercy to a woman taken in adultery ; that sense might subjugate the Second Emperor even while it whispered to him how great a part women of doubtful virtue had played in the Courts which preceded his : it insinuated the names of Gabrielle d'Estrées, Madame de Maintenon, Madame de Pompadour. And was there not in the chapel at Vincennes a window where Diane de Poitiers stood naked in the midst of Saints ? [1]

4

So, and so always under the influence of woman, did Napoleon III dream of dominating Europe from Paris. He was profoundly conscious of the universal influence of French civilization : and of this he meant to make an epitome of Paris as a whole.[2] For this, therefore, he summoned Haussman to Paris, and set him to work with Belgrave and Alphand. He built not only the Place de l'Etoile and its twelve great Avenues for the enriched Bourgeoisie who arose in his reign, and attended his Court. A great boulevard swept from the Gare de l'Est to the Ile

[1] See Hoffbauer : *Paris à travers les âges.*
[2] R. Escholier : *Paris.* M. Poëte : *Une vie de cité.*

de la Cité, and then on to the Porte d'Italie. Another connected the Place de la Republique with the North. The Rive Gauche was crossed with others, and over their wide spaces grew the shade and freshness of countless acacias, elders, planes, and poplars. Everywhere trees added their charm to the achievements of architecture and freshened the city air. Balzac had complained that one of the most unsightly and unsavorous slums touched the Louvre itself. The Emperor changed it into a garden. Yet another group of hideous and infected houses were destroyed to give place to that sumptuous playground, the Parc Monceau. Yet another garden made at this time was the Parc Montsouris. And at either end of Paris spacious woods were reserved, and laid out with lakes so that the people of the City might have for ever at their gates the freshness not only of unspoiled country, not of a mere park, but actually of the lake and forest ; and every device of art was exerted in them to retain the tang and freedom of the wild.

Appropriate spaces were given to every façade, not only to those of the new Hotel de Ville, the Opéra, and the Grand Palais, but both to railway stations and to Churches. St. Augustin, La Trinité, St. Francois Xavier, were built ; the spires of St. Clotilde arose to give a new nuance to the Place de la Concorde, and on Notre-Dame itself became more significant by the addition of its flèche. The two banks of the Seine were joined by the new bridges of the Invalides, St. Michel, Solférino, and l'Alma.

So came the modern city. When Napoleon III began his reign gutters still ran through the middle of the streets, every corner was a rubbish heap, the lighting was wretched. Then, too, all over Paris one private garden joined another, and white chestnuts or lilacs flowered quietly in what are now the roaring thoroughfares of the Rive Gauche. Children played blindman's buff or shuttle cock in the busiest street. Match-sellers and fried potato men, shoe-blacks, cat-doctors, and shearers of dogs plied their trade on the Pont Neuf facing those delightful houses which still survive from the sixteenth century over against the statue of Henry of Navarre. A deep ditch ran round the Place de la Concorde. Paris ended at what is now the Rond Point Clémenceau. Beyond it there was only a sort of Faubourg with here and there a mansion, a coach-builder's factory, or a warehouse. High walls closed in the paved roads that led away from the Arc du Triomphe.

So the old was reorganized to harmonize with the order of the new. Many beautiful details were sacrificed, but Paris became a whole, dedicated to decency, cleanliness, traffic, air, and play. Macadamized roads not only made the drive comfortable, they took away the paving stones which used to be built into barricades, and Paris ceased, a little too soon, to be afraid of her own citizens. For once again the city was to be ravaged by the mob, as a healthy body may be laid low by a fever in its entrails.

But Napoleon III did not stop at a prophylactic for political distempers. He gave Paris fresh water and drainage. It is to him she owes it that her sewers are the most impressive in the world, and that her water supply vies with that of ancient Rome, as it is to him likewise she owes it that her children play in fresh air.[1] And it must not be forgotten that social life was comparatively quiet, and its moral

[1] The best account of the work of the Emperor in Paris is in Sylvain Blot: *Napoléon III*.

PRINCESS RICHARD METTERNICH
From a portrait in the possession of Her Serene Highness Princess Oettingen.

" Tous les étrangers ravis s'élancent vers toi, Paris."

convention rigid, while Paris was prepared to witness processions of kings and queens.[1] They passed through it in uniforms and crinolines. They found it the centre of Western civilization. It was not merely the place where fortunes had been made : it was above all the place where they were spent, spent on superb dressmakers, on wine and cooking, and what was called joy :

> On accourt, on s'empresse
> Pour connaître, ô Paris,
> Pour connaître l'ivresse
> De tes jours, de tes nuits.
> Tous les étrangers ravis
> S'élancent vers toi, Paris.

In the centre of this glittering, and now illumined, capital stood the Tuileries, lit night after night, for the sumptuous entertainments of the Court. There were to be seen from year to year not merely sovereigns with their trains, not merely the members of old families, but men of eminence from every walk of life and every part of Europe. There Americans were especially welcome. There, not less welcome, were often to be seen Princess Colonna, Prince Poniatowski, Princess and Prince Richard Metternich, the Duke of Alba and the great of Spain, the Duke of Hamilton, Lord Clarendon, Lord Palmerston, Lord Lansdowne, Lady Ely ; but there also were Merimée, Sandeau, Octave Feuillet, Ferdinand de Lesseps, Meyerbeer, and Offenbach. It is true that the finest talent was not always recognized : as inevitably a Winterhalter rather than a Millet will become the Court painter. The authors of *Madame Bovary* and *Les Fleurs du Mal* were prosecuted for indecency in the Imperial Courts. The Empress,

[1] Beyens : Le Sécond Empire, i, 413, 414.

though the pupil of Stendhal and Merimée, was no protector of Flaubert. The one protégé of the Court was Wagner, whose *Tannhaüser* was greeted in the Opera with hisses. But though the Emperor appeared to belong in his artistic tastes rather to that epoch than to this, it must not be forgotten that it was at his personal suggestion that an exhibition for rejected painters was opened, and that there appeared the work of Corot and Daumier.[1]

The Modern Emperor is not perhaps less modern because he accepted the tastes of his own period. For his age, like our own, alternated between severe constructive effort, and a frenzy for diversion. Of that alternation the Emperor's own character was itself typical. It was a mistake of the time, a mistake that has often been made since, to think of the Sovereigns of the Second Empire as a pair of harlequins. They were not such. Because they threw themselves with all their hearts into a hunt, a picnic, a charade, or a masked ball, it was forgotten that after their bouts of frivolousness, they worked long and regularly. They both had unusual funds of energy, shining social gifts, wide sympathies. They were both, behind the changing functions of their Court, simple and busy people. They rose early and worked hard. And Modern Paris gives the key to her Modern Emperor's secret.

Occasionally its monotonies are a little jejune, and there is much that is pompous and extravagant in its detail. Nowhere is that clearer than looking up the Avenue de l'Opéra. The suggestion of grandiosity is as distinct as that of hollowness. But the staircase and the foyer of the Opéra are a noble frame to the pageant of imperial society. That

[1] A. Bellesort : *Société du Sécond Empire.*

THE EMPEROR IN HIS BEDROOM AT THE TUILERIES
From a painting in the Duke of Alba's collection.

"He rose early and worked hard."

ordering, that cleansing, that constructive spirit which mark the work of Napoleon III in Paris show the profoundest instinct of his mind. It is the incoherence and the excess of detail which show the elements of weakness in his nature. The churches built in his reign have impressive façades, but they are vapid within. So was it with Napoleon III. He might be described in the phrase of Keats as " mad with glimpses of futurity " : or, if not mad, too dazed to be observant. His instincts were prophetic, his intentions generous, his work was wide. But other men moved him towards their ends because he never could resist " the love of love and her soft hours ".

His ends were so disguised with conflicting motives, that he was always projecting alliances with his enemies, and war against his allies. The conqueror is made of harder stuff. There is in the work which is efficient on the grand scale a clearness of decision, an energy and continuity of purpose, and a grasp over both the men and the events which are immediate, which show that behind the generous impulse the giant will is set sure upon its end. The will to have his uncle's crown, to restore France to a place of power in Europe, and then to change the map : with so much was this mysterious man endowed, and so he is the agent of more momentous changes in history than his uncle. But he did not accomplish this change by his efficiency ; it came in ways he had not calculated, as the result of his intrigues.

IX

PLOTTING ON THE GRAND SCALE

> *Quanto sia laudabile in un principe mantenere la fede e vivere con integrità, e non con astuzia, ciascuno lo intende. Nondimanco si vede per esperienza ne nostri tempi quelli principi aver fatto gran cosa che della fede hanno tanto poco conto, e che hanno saputo con l'astuzia aggirare i cervelli degli uomini, ed alla fine hanno superato quelli che si sono fondati in su la lealtà.*
> MACHIAVELLI : *Il Principe*, xviii.

> The expense of spirit is a waste of shame
> Is lust in action ; and till action, lust
> Is perjured, murderous, bloody, full of blame,
> Savage, extreme, rude, cruel, not to trust ;
> Enjoy'd no sooner, but despised straight ;
> Past reason hunted ; and no sooner had,
> Past reason hated, as a swallow'd bait,
> On purpose laid to make the taker mad ;
> Mad in pursuit, and in possession so ;
> Had, having ; and in quest to have, extreme ;
> A bliss in proof ; and, proved, a very woe ;
> Before, a joy proposed ; behind, a dream :
> All this the world well knows ; yet none knows well
> To shun the heaven that leads men to this hell.
> SHAKESPEARE : *Sonnet CXXIX.*

I

THE most redoubtable opponent of the Crimean war had been the Duc de Morny. His objective mind had been left cynical—and perhaps his jealousy had been aroused—by his experience of his father's connections with England. He had never fallen under the spell of Lord Palmerston, even when

Lord Palmerston's head was handed over by Lord John Russell as the price of approval of the *coup d'État*. On the other hand, he was devoted to the Princess Lieven, that brilliant lady who, born as Dorothea Benckendorff, acted as the spy for Russia in the very heart of the French capital. Her salon said that Thiers was the " observatory of Europe ". She had been presented in St. Petersburg at the court of Paul I in 1799 and had been busy with high politics ever since. There was not one great personage of all those fifty years whom she did not know. She had become an institution, a woman not so much of wit as of the world ; and behind her grand manner, she had an unparalleled experience of diplomatic intrigue. " To pick up information," said Hübner, " to divine the secrets of those with whom she talks, and then to give those secrets away as she feels inclined with an indiscretion so charming that one can hardly grudge it her, and still to keep on finding trustful people who confide to her what they would have done better to keep to themselves is the object of her life, her incessant craving, and now at the end of her long life the only passion which moves her cold and worldly heart." [1]

But Morny did not need Princess Lieven to teach him indifference to the quarrels in the Holy Places, or distrust of the outraged pride of Lord Stratford de Redcliffe. From the beginning Morny had been against the Crimean War : all through it, to Lord Cowley's fury, he had worked in almost undisguised intimacy with Princess Lieven to bring it to an end,[2] and now after the Congress of Paris, he was fitly chosen as Ambassador to the Court of the Czar to cement the peace. He did that, as we shall see,

[1] Hübner : *Neuf Ans*, i, 216.
[2] *Cowley Papers* : *passim*.

with a thoroughness that might almost be called excessive.

"*Je vois en Russie*," he began by writing, "*une mine à exploiter par la France.*"[1] And from that moment, his enthusiasm was a flood overflowing the banks of exactness. He was soon reporting that Russia was consumed with not merely respect but admiration for her enemy of a year before. The Russians had an absolute faith in Napoleon's word and Prince Gortschakoff proclaimed to Morny that now he could obtain what really had been the object of his policy from thirty years back. France and Russia in his view were natural allies, as long as France was kept in order by an unyielding authority. And in Napoleon she had that authority. Napoleon could speak in a tone as absolute as the Czar. Under him, said Gortschakoff, she was no mere flying comet impelled through space by revolution. She was a fixed planet moving in an ordered circle by the guidance of a firm and able hand.[2]

The Emperor, however gratified by these flatteries, was too shrewd to accept his Ambassador's dispatches as wholly reliable. Reports came to Paris that gave him flatly the lie. And after all, between the absolute monarchy of Russia and the government founded by a plebiscite, there were some differences of principle, not least in regard to the governments to be encouraged in other states. "The Emperor is very touched by the forethought and the kindly actions of the Emperor Alexander," wrote Walewski (now Foreign Minister) to Morny on 12th September, 1856, "but friendly relations can be established only by sharing interests and pursuing similar conduct with regard to questions under decision, and if, as in the past, we always find

[1] Quai d'Orsay : Morny to Walewski, 8th August, 1856.
[2] Quai d'Orsay : Morny to Walewski, 5th September, 1856.

Russia in the opposite camp, whether in Italy, or in Spain, or in Germany, or in Belgium, it would be difficult to maintain such friendly relations as we should wish." [1]

With regard to Spain, for instance, the Czar of Russia had never recognized the government of Queen Isabel, for he wanted something far more reactionary. With regard to Germany and Belgium, Russia wanted to be the predominating influence in the interests of reaction ; in Naples, she was unprepared for changes, though changes there soon must be. But Morny hoped to adjust those little points : he would have Count Benckendorff at once dispatched to Madrid to recognize Queen Isabel.[2] He could promise that what the Emperor desired would be approved. Napoleon, however, determined to be prudent. " I shall send you a letter for the Emperor Alexander," he said. " And you may trust that in the meantime I shall act ceaselessly in your interests : but stay in Russia till they are solved." [3]

Morny had another reason for remaining in Russia. After the Czar's coronation at Moscow, where the sumptuousness of his palaces and the warmth of his enthusiasm had overshadowed those of Lord Granville, he began his pursuit of a Russian Princess, who was a favourite at the Court and who was said—but incorrectly—to be a daughter of the late Czar : the truth was that Nicholas had learnt of a liaison between her parents, and insisted on their marrying before she was actually born.[4] Frail as a reed, with a face delicate as a rose-petal and hair yellow as ripe corn, Sophie Troubetskoi had brought her brilliance and passion

[1] Quai d'Orsay.
[2] Quai d'Orsay : Morny to Walewski, 14th September and 18th September, 1856.
[3] Quai d'Orsay : *Russie*, vol. 213, p. 217.
[4] M. Boulenger in his *Morny* is not quite accurate.

from the schoolroom into society when the bald Ambassador of France—at that time a little weary of his mistress—was persuaded to pay court to her. He yielded to the adroit proposals of his friends, and she to his, and, when he returned to Paris, he joined her influence with his in favour of Russian diplomacy. The effect on the modern Emperor was, as we shall see, more than any could have guessed.

For it chanced to coincide with, and to dovetail into, another engagement. That engagement led to what was in Napoleon's foreign policy at once his most radical mistake, and his most pregnant achievement. France remembers him to-day, and Thiers recognized him long since, as *l'accoucheur de l'enfant terrible* : that child is Italy.

2

After the visits of Victor Emmanuel to Paris and London, the Emperor had written to him : " Your Majesty can count on me as a true friend." That phrase meant much. It was the affairs of Italy which had been discussed, with many sharp criticisms and re-vindications from Lord Clarendon, in the talk at the end of the Congress of Paris, when Walewski declared that the Congress would be open for a general debate. When, after the birth of the Prince Imperial, the Archduke Ferdinand Max had arrived at the Tuileries on a visit from Vienna, it was about Italy that he required assurances—and Napoleon gave them.

But immediately afterwards Napoleon's policy took another turn. His doctor, Conneau, Count Arese, who had been his friend ever since the days of New York, and a certain Signor Bixio, had all fallen under the influence of Cavour. They approached the Emperor in turn and reawakened in him the Italian passions of his youth.[1] The Crimean War had left him with his craving to correct the map of Europe unappeased. Peace had been made, and nothing had been done to change the settlement which Metternich had guided at Vienna in 1815. Indeed, after the war was over, and especially in the spring of 1858, a feeling of discouragement and almost despair began to weigh upon the sovereign's heart.[2] The plain fact was that his disease was gaining upon him. Spasms of hideous pain would interrupt him even as he was speaking, and compel him to keep silence. He would sit down and find himself unable to rise. He struck the Duke of Saxe-Coburg as being in a state of the plainest physical decay.[3] And yet no one quite knew what was the matter. His doctors in the summer of 1856, however, advised him to go to the Vosges and take the waters at Plombières. There, with his disease undermining his energy and warping his judgment, he commenced an intrigue with a new mistress. That lady was, in the words of M. Paléologue, thrown into the Imperial bed by her cousin, who was using her to involve her lover in another intrigue, more fatal, more far-reaching. For the Countess Castiglione was the cousin of Cavour.

When the Emperor returned from Plombières to Paris on 9th August, he had regained his vitality. When it was found that the door of his carriage was jammed, he jumped out of the carriage window. "I am afraid," wrote Lord Cowley, " he has been what is called ' going it ' at Plombières." [4]

[1] M. Paléologue adds the name of Madame Cornu, but this is in conflict with her own statement. N. W. Senior : *Conversations*, ii, 117.
[2] *Cowley Papers* : Cowley to Clarendon, 22nd January, 1858.
[3] Duke of Saxe-Coburg : *Mémoires*, iii, 193. F. A. Simpson : *Louis Napoleon and the Recovery of France*, p. 374.
[4] *Cowley Papers* : To Clarendon, 10th August, 1856.

3

It was impossible to go further into the Italian question without involving friendship with Austria. Napoleon, however, had already begun to lose patience with Austria : he had not been able to win any real assistance from her either during the Crimean War or in the Peace Congress at Paris. Her ambassador, Hübner, had never won the Emperor's confidence. It was not only that Hübner had a way of lecturing Napoleon : but his origin was so obscure that his presence at the French Court seemed a reminder to the Sovereign that Franz Josef looked askance at him.[1] It was said that the Ambassador was the illegitimate son of Metternich : by others that his father was a tailor in Moravia. But the fact is that no one could guess who his father was, and few realized how he had risen into such a brilliant position in society.[2] England itself had not been quite so responsive as Napoleon had hoped, and *The Times* was inclined to resume its old truculent tone. Among the Emperor's Ministers there was not one who liked England. Most of them, disgusted with the way that Stratford had jockeyed them into war, and the British Government had allowed it to drag on rather in British interests than in those of France, felt for England a feeling not short of detestation.[3] On the other hand, while Morny was pressing for reconciliation with Russia, Cavour was winning Napoleon over to a new policy.[4] Instead of playing England's game, the Emperor began to scrutinize her.

[1] *Cowley Papers* : Cowley to Malmesbury, 26th December, 1858.
[2] Private information from Dr. Engels-Janosi, who is preparing a book on Hübner.
[3] E. Fitzmaurice : *Life of Lord Granville*, i, 208.
[4] Paléologue : *Cavour*, ch. ix.

"People who love another," he said in his playful way to the British Ambassador, "are apt to be jealous."[1] The point of this characteristic metaphor was that he could not conceal a certain anxiety on seeing how, since Buol had arrived at the Congress, the British Government, which had been as much annoyed as he with Vienna, had been drawing closer and closer to it. France, on the other hand, had finished under the influence of Morny as the friend of Russia. And then the whole of French policy had been changed by happenings as far away as the Danubian Principalities of Moldavia and Wallachia. For at this time Napoleon III began to develop yet another of the most modern of his schemes. He began to plan to create out of the old Latin colonies on the northern confines of the Turkish Empire the great modern kingdom which we know as Rumania. Madame Cornu came forward as the champion of nationality[2] : again emissaries from the East pressed into the Court of the Tuileries, and again the whole machinery of intrigue on the scale of high politics was set working.

As we have seen, it was on behalf of those Christians that the Czar had at first advanced his claims on Turkey : and in the reconciliation, guided by Morny, the Emperor of the French found himself slipping into the same moral responsibilities as the Czar. That in these wide and fertile districts, placed as they were near the mouth of the great waterway of the Danube, men of business, like Morny, should also have an interest, is not improbable ; and French influence both in them, and under the newly appointed Thouvenel at Constantinople, was made the subject

[1] *Cowley Papers.*
[2] Paul Henry : *l'Abdication de Prince Cuza*, p. 65, n.

of complaint.[1] It was not only Turkey which was interested in the question : Austria was hardly less so. For in Transylvania was a Rumanian population which might easily claim independence if their countrymen in the Danubian Principalities were already combined as an independent state. Austria therefore combated the French manœuvres, and for a time with great success. But Napoleon was irritated. " I have made war in the East," he said. " Austria has not. If she had fired a single shot, I should find it very natural that she should exercise in the East— which is close to her, and far from France—the dominant influence ; but as I have made more sacrifices than she, or any other power, I feel that I have the right to exert in Turkey a power in proportion to my sacrifices : well, that is what annoys Austria. She opposes me everywhere, in the great things and in the small : and that is what embitters our relations." [2]

The truth was that in the ironies of the situation, the Emperor who owed his throne to a plebiscite was drawn into unity with the Czar. Both wanted an independent Rumania ; though for very different reasons. And so also Russia came forward as a makeweight in the politics of Cavour. Neither Austria, nor even England, could favour the preponderance of France in Italy. But to that Russia was indifferent. And so, through the new intrigues of the Tuileries, the Czar was to emerge in a halo, like the moon in clouded skies between the storms. Alexander in other words, was now to be cultivated as ally.

" *Notre Empereur à nous n'ira pas voir l'autre, quoi qu'on dise,*" wrote Merimée, " *nous allons seulement voir notre*

[1] V.N.A., Prokisch-Osten to Buol, 20th February, 4th March, 1857.
[2] V.N.A., Hübner to Buol, 20th March, 1858.

bonne amie Victoria qui nous donnera probablement une bonne recette pour augmenter la famille impériale." [1] But Merimée was wrong. The Emperor did not see the Queen that summer. When asked if the Empress expected another child, he merely answered, " *Je ne crois pas.*" [2] In September, however, he met the Czar at Stuttgart. Prussia felt a little uncomfortable at this alliance between the Eastern and the Western Powers which hemmed her in, but, though there were several friendly conversations, they arrived at nothing. The Czar had proposed to sign a treaty, but Napoleon refused. " A treaty is of use," he said, " only in so far as it has a definite object." [3] But what definite object did he share with Russia? That was to be decided later, as we shall soon see.

Two months later, the young Countess Castiglione was among the guests at Compiègne . . . and wore the nightgown in which she afterwards directed that she should be buried. His Imperial Majesty was not in good spirits. He had caught a cold when one day, his pockets filled with little bits of paper, he had run away from his Court through the woods of Compiègne at a game of hare and hounds.[4]

4

It was on the evening of 18th January, 1858, that the Italian conspirators, fearing that the caresses of the Countess were insufficient to win back the old insurgent, attacked him on his way to the opera with the sharper argument of the bomb. Over a hundred and fifty persons were maimed hideously or killed ;

---

[1] Merimée : Unpublished Letter.
[2] *Cowley Papers* : Cowley to Clarendon, 9th November, 1857.
[3] V.N.A., Hübner to Buol, 15th May, 1858.
[4] *Cowley Papers* : Cowley to Clarendon, 9th November, 1857.

a splinter of glass inflamed Eugénie's eye and a stain of blood was on her skirt.[1] Though Napoleon was unharmed, he, usually so dauntless, was at once and for ever after quite unnerved. He feared neither danger nor death : but he could not face the accusation, so sharply driven home, of having been a traitor to the cause to which he had sworn allegiance in his youth, and for which his brother had died.[2] It was on this tune, the tune of "Auld Lang Syne", that Orsini, the assassin, played with Satanic skill. Orsini had with him the sympathy of Pietri, the Prefect of Police, who carried a letter to the Emperor from the prisoner's cell [3] : " Remember that, till the cause of Italian freedom is gained, the peace of Europe and your own security will be but an empty dream." [4]

Both the Emperor and the Empress made every effort to save Orsini ; but the assassin had secured so many victims that in the opinion of shrewd judges reprieve was unthinkable. The man did not plead for his life. Instead, his advocate—Jules Favre was his advocate—read at the trial the letter written to the Emperor ; and Favre read this with the Emperor's own permission. Orsini's death completed his appeal. As in the long white shirt of a regicide, his head covered with a black veil, he stepped upon the ghastly machine which in a moment was to sever his head from his body, he shouted the words " *Evviva l'Italia !* " [5]

The letters which the Emperor and Empress of Austria had sent Napoleon six weeks before to congratulate him on his escape—letters which as Hübner reminded him showed him where his true

[1] *Cowley Papers* : Cowley to Clarendon, 15th January, 1858.
[2] Hübner : *Neuf Ans*, ii, 92, 3.
[3] V.N.A., Hübner to Buol.
[4] René Arnaud : *Deuxième République et Second Empire*, p. 137.
[5] Ibid.

friends were to be found—these letters were forgotten.[1]
In July His Majesty went back to Plombières, and
there once more he found the Countess Castiglione
installed. And, no doubt, she found a way to repeat
the Emperor's secrets to her cousin, Count Cavour.
For before many days, Victor Emmanuel's Prime
Minister, with a faked passport, and under the name
of Giuseppe Benso, came to the Vosges by special
invitation [2] for an interview with the Imperial
conspirator. He was received by Napoleon at eleven
in the morning, he stayed with him the whole day.
Before he left him, he had worked out the scheme
on which the Emperor's mind no less than his own
was now set. Napoleon had promised Alexander
not to disturb King Ferdinand in Naples, and in
view of Catholic support in France, he must guarantee
Rome to the Holy Father. One must keep one's word,
of course, but men of affairs have a way of getting
what they want, even while they hold to the letter
of their engagement. If there were a revolt in the
Romagna, for instance, who had promised to put it
down? If a revolution in Naples dethroned the
King, how could the Czar hold the Emperor of the
French responsible? Cavour wanted the French
army behind him. Very well, but he must promise
to give his cause the look of injured innocence.
Driving out into the woods in the evening, Napoleon
went still further. He proposed that little Princess
Clothilde of Savoy, a girl of fifteen still in her convent,
should marry his anti-clerical cousin, the dissolute
brother of Mathilde. At that even Victor Emmanuel
and Cavour had hesitated. " *C'est une chose très
sérieuse que celle de mon mariage avec le Prince Napoléon,*"
wrote the young Princess herself, " *et qui est surtout*

---

[1] Hübner : *Neuf Ans*, ii, 98.
[2] *Carteggio Cavour Nigra.*

tout à fait contraire à mes idées." [1] It might well be. But why should the child not be happy, argued His Majesty, with a man who had already shown such excellence of heart in his relations with his mistresses? [2] And then he wrote with his own hand a note to Paris saying that he was prepared to give way to Austria and would not ask for a flag for the Principalities.[3] But before the conversations were over next morning, Napoleon received a telegram from Walewski that the police had reported from Plombières the arrival of the Sardinian in disguise. For from his Foreign Minister, who knew the ambitions of Turin and thought them highly dangerous, the whole negotiation was kept dark. The crowned conspirator was conceiving his Italian plans in secrecy and the time was not far off when he would act with promptitude.[4] His plan to involve France in war, to win Northern Italy from Austria, to turn his closest neighbour into a great power, had been developed apart from counsellors in a brain fevered by the fierce interaction of ambition, of generosity, and of fear. And yet, tortuous as were the workings of his mind, and sinister his stratagems, he could yet plead that his moves were all in the interest of progress. " When I came to my present position," he said, on 31st October, to the British Ambassador, " I saw that France wanted peace, and I determined to maintain the treaties of 1815 as long as France was respected and held her own in the Councils of Europe. But I was equally resolved, if I was forced into war, not to make peace until a better equilibrium was secured to Europe. I have no ambitious views

[1] *Carteggio Cavour Nigra,* i, 126.
[2] *Lettres de Cavour,* ii, 562-568.
[3] V.N.A., Hübner to Buol, 29th July, 1858.
[4] Paléologue : *Cavour,* p. 172.

like the First Emperor but, if other countries gain something, France must gain something also. Well, when driven into war with Russia, I thought that no peace would be satisfactory which did not resuscitate Poland, and I humoured Austria in the hope that she would assist me in this great work. She failed me, and after peace was made, I looked to the amelioration of Italy." [1]

And who can doubt that he meant what he said when he insisted that his policy was simple? Generous, friendly, sincere, such were his primal impulses. The cunning with which he developed the intricacy of his plots could not have been supported by resources more effective. "The more I see of this extraordinary man," as Lord Cowley had written two years before to Sir Henry Bulwer, "the more I respect and admire him: there is such evident intention to do well, and there is, in foreign matters at least, so much frankness in his character with those with whom he *knows* he can be frank that there is great charm in doing business with him, even when we do not agree. If he had but men about him with such honest intentions as himself, what a country they might become! Perhaps it is better for us that it is not so." [2] There is so much frankness in his character with those with whom he *knows* he can be frank. Count Cavour could echo those words (could he not?), of confidences very different to those which charmed Lord Cowley.

When Sir Henry Bulwer received this letter, he might have compared it with what his brother had written in 1839. For this man whose confidences were so winning had not ceased to be reserved and close. He was not merely dogged and daring; his

[1] *Cowley Papers*: Cowley to Clarendon, 31st October, 1858.
[2] *Cowley Papers*: Cowley to Bulwer, 1st November, 1856.

astuteness was so thorough that he had thought out all the consequences of his alliance with Cavour. If he must attack Austria, he could no longer count on England, for England had now a Tory Government with Lord Malmesbury for its Foreign Secretary. Prussia, as far as she yet counted, would be with Austria. Napoleon's only ally could be Russia, and in October he sent over Prince Napoleon to Warsaw to have a talk with the Czar. With the ground thus prepared, Napoleon pushed forward that autumn a secret treaty.[1] The diplomacy of Morny had triumphed. The man who, as the champion of the people, was to free Lombardy and Venetia from the honest cleansing control of Vienna was to do so by joining hands with the very monarch whose rule looked furthest backward into absolutism, and whose subjects of all in Christendom came nearest to being slaves. In the autumn he sent a naval officer to the Czar with two treaties. His plan was to dismember the kingdom of the Hapsburgs. Hungary, Galicia, Lombardy, and Venetia were to be cut off from Vienna, and Austria reduced to a second-rate power.[2] This particular scheme is not the least startlingly modern of the notions of Napoleon III.

5

Such in the course of a few months was the astonishing effect of Orsini's bombs. As deep calls to deep, so did the designs of the conspirator who had lost his head pass to the brain of that other conspirator who wore the eagle crown. Napoleon thus became an accessory after the fact to the designs which

---

[1] Monsieur A. Pingaud : *Un Projet d'Alliance Franco-Russe. Séances et Travaux de l'Académie des Sciences Morales et Politiques* (based on the Archives of Quai d'Orsay).
[2] Id.

had aimed at taking his own life. And while he was elaborating his conspiracies with Cavour and the Czar, he was busy with protests against the apostles of unity who were working from the base of London. There he detected with indignation the machinations of Mazzini : thither he turned to watch the trial of another desperado, Bernard. When Bernard was acquitted, the Tuileries boiled with indignation. It seemed to France a proof that England was bereft of moral sense, and the Empress poured out her whole heart to the British Ambassador in one of the most eloquent of her letters.

" In the time in which we live," she wrote, " there are such singular interpretations of the moral sense, there is so much confusion in the ideas of right and wrong, that I ask is it I who have made the mistake ? You know better than anyone how as a *woman* (for I stand apart from all questions of politics) I feel great sympathy with England. I used to admire in you the cool reasonableness, and well-known common sense, which since dispassionate balance is the pledge of justice allows you every sort of freedom. But there is one thing more to be feared than the tyranny of a single individual : it is the tyranny of the people as a whole. Ah, I must confess that what sickens my heart is not to read every day in your newspapers the silliest rumours, to see the Emperor the victim of malevolent attacks nor to have the constant fear of seeing my husband and my son struck down in my arms by one who assumes the double part of judge and executioner. No, my trust in God is too great for that. But the effect such fears fail to have upon my heart, the acquittal of Bernard does wake, I must confess : it throws me into an indescribable amazement. I have seen two men present on the same bench : one an assassin (for so in your heart and conscience you know him to be) accused by the public prosecutor, the other summoned morally before the same jury, and *he* accused by Bernard's counsel. The first has been acquitted. What am I to add, I, the wife of the second ? . . . Is it to defend the weak against the strong that juries, who are supposed to be impartial, must give this satisfaction to a crowd which gave their frenzied applause to a verdict which endorses the wretched expression : killing is no murder. It is not that I wanted to see a head fall. I asked pardon for Orsini even in the face of public opinion, so great is my horror of taking life. But what I deplore is that there has been no vindication of moral principles : as wife and mother I see the peace of my life destroyed. Before such a verdict, I feel weaker than I should be." [1]

England's sympathy with the Italian insurgents might prejudice the very existence of the Entente. " It is not my life which is in danger now," wrote the Emperor, " it is the English alliance." [2] The Queen saw the danger and planned a meeting with the Emperor and Empress at Cherbourg. There was nervousness on both sides, but the Emperor's speech was conciliatory and cordiality was for the time restored.[3] Among the many anomalies of the career of Napoleon III that was not the least extraordinary which brought him and the English to loggerheads because he was not furthering, at

[1] F. Wellesley : *The Paris Embassy*, pp. 163-4.
[2] *L'Univers*, 22nd March, 1858.
[3] Martin : *Prince Consort*, iv, 272, 273.

a moment which was in fact impossible, the project he had most at heart: the project of Italian nationalism which seems to the French of to-day his fatal mistake.

6

After the French Sovereigns had parted from the Queen, they commenced a tour in Brittany. In a day they seemed to have returned to the Middle Ages. In that impoverished province, the stronghold of fortitude, of Monarchy, and of the Church, the clergy still kept the people in the ancient ways. They venerated the Emperor as a Defender of the Faith. His presence among the peasants was like a pardon. On the Fête Napoléon, he knelt at Auray before the famous image of St. Anne, and received the Blessed Sacrament. At Rennes, the Bishop hailed him as the French Monarch who was, since St. Louis, the most devoted to his Church and to its work of progress and civilization.[1] Those good priests in Brittany did not know what had been said a month before at Plombières. They did not know that the Emperor was beginning to say, " These men in black disquiet me." [2] They did not know that all their compliments to the beauty of the Empress were beginning to irritate her husband. They did not bother about the attentions paid to Contessa Castiglione.

And yet it is a fact not to be escaped that sensualities, and in particular the sensualities of illicit passion, are always at enmity with those powerful energies which centre round the Mass. Those whose natures are the theatre of voluptuous disorder can never be at ease in the vibrating presence of the Church. They begin

[1] La Gorce, ii, 184.
[2] Paléologue : *Cavour*, p. 93.

by speaking in contempt of it : they feel it irritating and oppressive : and sooner or later they will engage against its power. And furthermore, adultery means a habit of deceit. It gave a fatal push to Napoleon's bearing towards intrigue. We do not know if his new mistress argued with him in favour of her cousin : but though she had spoken with the voice of women and of sirens, it matters nothing. When she won him over to infidelity, there was no need for more. From that moment, Cavour could have counted that the instincts of Louis Napoleon at fifty were with the disorder of his youth, and that, whatever his ideals were, they would not be compromised by scruples about defending the prestige of the Catholic faith.

Just before Christmas the Emperor wrote to the Czar that he expected war with Austria in the following May.[1] On New Year's Day, 1859, he advertised his policy at a reception at the Tuileries by speaking in a disquieting tone to the Austrian Ambassador.

7

That war, however, did not come so easily as Cavour had planned and hoped. England was on excellent terms with Austria, for under the new Tory Government she was no longer so zealous as under the guidance of the good Lord Palmerston for having men shot down in the interests of progress and democracy. On 10th January, 1859, Lord Malmesbury, in a long letter to Lord Cowley, pointed out that England's interest in the question of a change in Italy stopped short at improvements in the administration of the Papal States, a question which had been raised

[1] I owe this information to Monsieur A. Pingaud and to his paper already cited.—R. S.

as early as 1831. With Austria they could have no quarrel : and Malmesbury felt that a war with Austria would soon become a war not of nations but opinions. It would lead to a contempt for authority, inflame sentimentalism, and finally encourage anarchists.[1]

The temper of Vienna was itself reasonable : Buol was quite willing to resume conversations (for they had begun in 1857) with regard to reforms in the Papal States, and on such a subject there was every prospect of agreement with France : on the 14th February, however, the misgiving of Vienna was reawakened by a discussion in Turin parliament on the subject of a loan, a discussion in which Cavour showed that he had taken up a position from which there was no escape but war. And war might involve all Europe. It was so plain that for Sardinia to engage alone against the might of Austria could lead only to defeat and ruin, that Cavour could not dare to risk it unless confident that he could drag in France.

It was in these circumstances that Lord Cowley, as the most able of neutral diplomats, was sent on a mission of conciliation to Vienna. He at once made a great impression, and soon had a definite proposal : it was to arrange for reforms in the Papal States, to free Parma and Modena from Austria and to guarantee Piedmont as Belgium was guaranteed.[2] The Austrians were perfectly satisfied ; they felt that Cavour had been outwitted, and that in fact there would be nothing for him but to resign. Such in fact was the feeling of Walewski who had watched Cavour at the Congress of Paris, and who had come to the conclusion that he was a dangerous

[1] Quai d'Orsay (Angleterre) : Malmesbury to Cowley.
[2] Quai d'Orsay : Bonneville to Walewski, 25th and 28th February, 1859.

lunatic. Even Cowley counted that Cavour would fall.[1]

But no sooner was Cowley's mediation gratefully accepted at Paris than a suggestion emanated from St. Petersburg for a Congress of Five Powers on the subject of Italy. It was Napoleon himself who had whispered that suggestion to the Russian Ambassador in Paris.[2] And no sooner was it made than it was seen to involve every sort of difficulty. But above all it was disquieting to Cavour. He rushed to Paris, he saw the Emperor, and as he left again for Turin he declared in the coarsest current slang that Napoleon had flung him over. He came back to Turin on April Fools' Day. It was, however, very seriously that the French Ambassador noted that in the evening Turin was the scene of a demonstration, mostly of students and labourers, crying " *Viva la Guerra !* " [3]

Cavour, in fact, was not yet at the end of his sinister resources. He refused to submit the cause of his country to the Five Powers. He insisted that she should enter, and enter it on an equal footing with the others. This in the world of diplomacy was an outrage. From puny Piedmont to mighty Austria such a contention was insulting and absurd.

So it was that the young Emperor at Vienna lost his patience, he who had kept it for so long. He simply refused to allow his plenipotentiary to sit beside one from Sardinia.[4] Besides that he insisted that before Austria went into the Congress, Sardinia

---

[1] *Cowley Papers* : Cowley to Malmesbury, January, 1859.
[2] Paléologue : *Cavour*, p. 216.
[3] Quai d'Orsay : La Tour d'Auvergne to Walewski, 1st April, 1858.
[4] Quai d'Orsay : Bonneville to Walewski, 21st April. *Il motive expressement son refus sur la répugnance invincible de l'Empereur à autoriser son Plénipotentiaire à siéger à côté d'un Plénipotentiaire piémontais.* Quai d'Orsay : Malakoff to Walewski, 21st April.

should disarm. Not satisfied with the promise given by Sardinia to France and England, he pressed for one direct from Turin. His tone at once seemed menacing. If Piedmont was not careful, he burst out, he would leave his mark in Turin.[1] Even Walewski was persuaded that Austria meant war. Cowley who, feeling that Turin alone was provocative, had been wholly on the side of Austria, now laid the blame on Vienna. Franz Josef then played into the hands of Victor Emmanuel and his Minister. Turin could at last assume the guise of injured innocence. " The dice is thrown," cried Cavour. " Now we can eat our dinner."[2]

Though France made the quarrel hers, when the Austrians crossed the Ticino, neutral diplomats were deceived neither by the Emperor's tergiversations nor by the wiles of Cavour. " By violating the treaties of extradition with Austria, by fostering deserters from her army, by rallying in Piedmont the disaffected spirits of Italy, by menacing speeches against the Austrian Government, and by ostentatious declarations that she was ready to do battle as the champion of Italy against the power and influence of Austria, Sardinia invoked the storm and is deeply responsible before the nations of Europe." [3] So wrote Lord Malmesbury. He was willing that Piedmont should play a great part in reforming Italian institutions, but he argued that she should do so by her moral influence, not by bloodshed. The Queen of England expressed her anger and suspicion of the allies in the strong terms that came so easily to her. It was the judgment of England—in her official

[1] Quai d'Orsay : Malakoff to Walewski, 22nd April (midnight).
[2] La Gorce : *Second Empire*, ii, 437–440.
[3] Quai d'Orsay : Malmesbury to Cowley, 4th May, 1858.

voice—that, in spite of the last imprudent ebullition, it was Austria who was in the right. " I have no hope of peace left," Victoria wrote to Leopold. " Though it is originally the wicked folly of Russia and France that have brought about this fearful crisis, it is the madness and blindness of Austria which have brought on the war now. It has put them in the wrong, and entirely changed the feeling here, which was all that one could desire, into the most vehement sympathy for Sardinia, though we hope now again to be able to throw the blame of the war on France, who now won't hear of mediation." [1]   Behind all his shiftings and tergiversations, the moves of the French conspirator were detected. " I cannot forget," wrote Lord Cowley, " that it is the Emperor's ambiguous words and dark dealings which have brought us to this crisis." [2]

[1] *Queen Victoria's Letters*, i, bk. iii, 328–331.
[2] *Cowley Papers* : Cowley to Malmesbury, 21st April, 1859.

X

THE WAR IN ITALY

*Ahi serva Italia, di dolore ostello,
Nave senza nocchiere in gran tempesta,
Non donna di provincie, ma bordello !*
                    Purgatorio, vi, 76–8.

You behold a burnished realm of mountain and plain beneath the royal sun of Italy. In the foreground, it shines hard as the lines of an irradiated Cellini shield. Farther away, over middle ranges that are soft and clear, it melts, confusing the waters with hot rays, and the forests with darkness, to where, wavering in and out of view like flying wings, and shadowed like wings of archangels with rose and with orange and with violet, silver white Alps are seen. You might take them for mystical streaming torches on the border ground between vision and fancy. They lean as in a great flight forward upon Lombardy.
                    MEREDITH : *Vittoria,* p. 2.

I

IT was in Italy that General Bonaparte first rose to glory. The names of Marengo, Lodi, Arcola, Rivoli, rang in his nephew's ears like trumpets. He too must fight in Italy. On 10th May, after meeting a frenzy of acclamation, as he drove through the Faubourg St. Antoine, he set out from Paris for Marseilles,[1] to board his yacht, the *Reine Hortense.* On 12th May, he arrived at Genoa on one of those shining mornings when sea and shore look as though new created. Here he was greeted with joy and pageant, hailed as a hero who has already conquered : the very escapades of his youth invested him with moral splendour, conspiracy crowned him with a patriot's laurel.[2] But his work as Commander-in-Chief was yet before him. He hurried on to Alexandria, and

[1] La Gorce : *Second Empire,* ii, 448.
[2] Paléologue : *Cavour,* 227.

then marched his armies up to Novara. There the
Austrians might have attacked him in the flank :
his own plan, daring and original, was to risk that
attack, while he moved his army further to the north,
to strike in the north where he was least expected,
and thus striking turn the flank of the enemy. The
point he selected for the chief attack was that where
the railway line from Novara to Milan crosses the
stony river bed and the swift clear stream of the
Ticino flowing from the Lago Maggiore to the Ponte
San Martino, which is some four miles across the
Plain of Lombardy from the little town of Magenta.
Macmahon had already crossed the little river at
Turbigo and was fighting his way towards Magenta.
Espinasse, with the advance guard of the Emperor's
own forces, had no difficulties at the Ponte San
Martino, but, marching on towards Magenta, was
blocked by a new obstacle, a bridge over a deep
canal which was twenty yards broad and bordered
with thorny acacias and strongly defended by the
enemy. At this point, the Ponte Nuovo, Napoleon,
hearing Macmahon's cannon at Buffalora, launched
his attack at noon of 4th June. The Austrians fought
furiously ; they were driven back, only to reform and
to attack more furiously than before. Meanwhile,
another Austrian corps, thrown over the canal by
a bridge lower down, attacked the French flank.
These too were driven back. The Emperor was
waiting, baffled, even stupefied. He gave no orders.
His eyes were haggard. Of swift disposition of men
in order that they should kill, he knew nothing.
Italian reinforcements were expected, but failed to
appear. He waited, disgusted at the carnage, fearful
of failure, while his generals fought like subalterns
amidst their troops, and fell. Of Macmahon also he
could hear nothing. The general was waiting to close

up his line. But in the later afternoon he again attacked; and by evening the Emperor's generals had won him the battle. By three roads, one from Buffalora, one from the Ponte Nuovo, and thirdly by the railway line, the French forces converged upon Magenta: Macmahon, who had reappeared at such a critical moment, was greeted with effusion by his Sovereign, made a Field Marshal, made a Duke. The enemy were retiring to beyond Milan.[1]

But then came the reaction: in the evening, the next day one went over the battlefield, heard the wounded, saw the dead. The French along both road and railway line had advanced fighting every foot with rifle and bayonet. Shakos, knapsacks, muskets, shoes, cloaks, tunics, linen, all stained with blood, told the story of valour, and of valour's reward. A great change swept over the victorious army and their Emperor. The Austrians had been told that the French showed no mercy to their captives: but Napoleon's soldiers did all they could to relieve the sufferings of the wounded of both armies alike; they nursed them, said *The Times* correspondent, as mothers nurse their children. " So it's a victory ! " wrote Fleury, Napoleon's equerry. " But how many tears, how much blood ! If it was a question of beginning again, I believe the Emperor would not do it."

At Milan, " the station and the railway train," said *The Times* correspondent, " were certainly the most shocking scenes of misery one can possibly conceive. There were the wounded in all stages of agony and pain, only half clad, torn, dusty, and muddy in their own blood. . . . The priests walking

[1] This account of the battle is based on La Gorce, *Second Empire*, iii, ch. i; on René Arnaud, *Deuxième République et Second Empire*, ch. v; Fleury's *Mémoires*; and *The Times*.

about with the Viaticum to administer the Last Sacrament to the dying ; the glazed eye of death in some, showing that they had ceased to suffer, the working eyes of others and the kneeling priest before them showing that they were on the point of sighing their last : near them were others whom you would have thought dead had it not been for the imperceptible movement of the eye or the convulsive twist of a limb. . . .

"But it was above all when the wounded had to be moved to the carriages that the neighbourhood became almost intolerable. Such shrieks, such pale faces contracted by pain, such torn limbs."

These were the scenes that had wrung the Emperor's heart : anæsthetics, stretcher-bearers had not yet been brought forward to quieten the physical horror of the battlefield ; and this Emperor, who had his uncle's tenderness for his soldiers without that ruthless concentration which made him so decisive in his aims at victory, could not help noticing that the Lombard peasantry and villagers cared little for the rescue which had been effected at such a hideous price.

The morning after the battle of Magenta, Napoleon met Victor Emmanuel, whose troops had been ordered to advance and been so eagerly awaited in the uncertainty of the battle and which had not arrived. "Sire," said the Emperor to the King, "when one is to effect a junction in face of the enemy, one strictly carries out one's instructions and holds to one's engagements. I regret that Your Majesty has not done so." [1]

But men who are working in a common cause cannot afford a grievance or a grudge : on 10th June the Sovereigns rode together into Milan.

[1] Cf. Chiala : *Cavour*, iii. *Guerre d'Italie*, II, ii.

2

Nobody knew up to the last moment when the entry was to take place, and an early hour was chosen in order not to leave the people time to prepare for the reception. No troops preceded, giving notice beforehand that the moment was approaching. Here were no splendid uniforms or carriages of state. It was simply the entry of two commanders at the head of a body of their troops. They came, dirty and hot, from the last station, Bobbiette, which is about three leagues away. A small body of Cavalry and Guides preceded and closed up the rear. In the midst the two Sovereigns, the King of Sardinia in the middle of the road, and the Emperor to his right, both followed by their staff. The shortest road was chosen to pass through the town to the Villa Bonaparte which is near the Giardini Pubblici and in which Napoleon was to lodge ; but it was all in vain. The news of the Monarchs' arrival spread into the town like wildfire, and was made patent by a frantic shout of joy.

"The scene itself through which the two Sovereigns passed, it was impossible to describe," wrote *The Times* correspondent.[1] "Imagine the wildness of enthusiasm, the whole heart of a people poured out. . . . Not an eye without its tears. . . . All the outward decorations disappeared before the greetings of the people. The flowers so long prepared for the occasion were almost forgotten in the emotion of the moment, and fell often long before those had passed for whom they were intended. For the first time I saw emotion pierce through that mysterious and impenetrable countenance of the Emperor : he would have been more than a man had it been otherwise."

[1] *The Times*, 14th June, 1859.

> They call it a cold, stern face,

wrote Elizabeth Browning—

> But this is Italy
> Who rises up in her place!
> For this he fought in his youth,
> Of this he dreamed in the past,
> The lines of the resolute mouth
> Tremble a little at last.
> Cry, he has done it all.

Two days later Napoleon took the central part in another ceremony more carefully prepared. The whole infantry of the Guard, coming from the Piazza d'Armi, traversed the streets, music in front, and then formed up in line all along the Corso. As the Emperor went by flowers and laurel crowns rained through the brilliant air which rang with hurrahs and *Evvivas*. Everyone was radiant. The Emperor was received at the Duomo by the choir. He was led to the Chancel, and heard the stately Latin hymn, taken up by the tongues of the people. No matter how indifferent the peasants had been, here at last was gratitude. Rarely was there seen a thanksgiving in which so many hearts sincerely joined.[1]

Two days later the Emperor went with the King to La Scala. And as they drove away, they met some Chasseurs bringing in an Austrian standard.

Fighting was continued, and a thousand Frenchmen fell at Melegnano. The Austrian Emperor hurried from Vienna to take command of his armies. The French and Italians pursued through Bergamo and Brescia, until on 26th June their long progress over the plain, with the Alps distant on their left like a host of austere presences, was arrested by a line of hills which run from the purple heights, above the burnished surface of the Lago di Garda, and are the last incursion of the Alpine heights into the

[1] *The Times*, 16th June, 1859.

poplared plains. Running down from Desenzano those hills, crowned with villa and cypress and myrtle, and yellowing villages, were to the advancing army graven beauteously with the character of Italy. But, on them waited the army of Austria. Thus the enemies, each in command of an Emperor, met for decisive battle.

The Austrians held a magnificent position. From the Spia d'Italia, Franz Josef looked down upon the approaching enemy. He had prepared a feint in the North, and aimed at taking a lesson from Magenta and turning his enemy's right. Napoleon had, however, sent up a balloon, and saw where the real strength of the Austrians lay. Arriving on the scene, an hour after the first shot was fired, he grasped the situation instantly. He saw that the attack on the French right was possible only if the Austrians held the central heights from which Franz Josef surveyed them. Those central heights of Solferino were formidable indeed. The more the French looked at them, the less they liked them. But Napoleon III, for once Napoleonic, saw, as he stood on one of the opposing hills, that the Spy of Italy was the key of the position. "*Il faut avoir ce point-là*," he said. If it could be captured, the Austrian army could be cut in two, and would be in danger of losing one of the bridges over the Mincio. The first point was to hold the French right till this could be effected. The second was to storm the Spy of Italy. "Tell the Grenadiers of the Guard to advance," he shouted, and then remembering what they had done at Magenta, he said, "No. Send forward the first brigade of Voltigeurs." The whole brigade came forward and dashed upon the fatal declivity in the burning sun of the late June morning. The hills of Solferino grew damp with sweat and blood, but the French pressed on. " *Bravo les Voltigeurs !* " cried the Emperor. " *Bravo les Voltigeurs !* " The shout thundered from the whole army of France. While French and Austrian fought grimly beneath the tower, the weight and direction of the French artillery dislodged their enemy. At two o'clock, the French flag floated from the Spy of Italy, but not until the village was won did the cannon do its most effective work. Then the French and Italians fought the Austrians up hill and down dale from Solferino to Cavriana. The heat grew heavier, then clouds formed, as Victor Emmanuel and Macmahon pressed forward round the plain. At last the heat dissolved in thunder and storm. The rain streamed down upon the wounded and dying, and held men back from the attack. When the sky cleared at evening, the Austrians had retreated. They were not pursued, though the allied cavalry had hardly been engaged. Napoleon ate at Cavriana the dinner ordered in the morning for Franz Josef. With his head in his hands, and soaked to the skin, the Conqueror sat brooding in the house from which his adversary had fled. His staff dared not disturb him. At last he looked up and said quietly, " *La journée est terminée.*" [1]

Battle and victory : those were the words of the Emperor : he and his army could drink for a moment the sparkling wine of glory : but the next morning, his ecstasy was over : the sun, shining clearer once more after the storm, brought before his eyes the grimness of the field of slaughter. The dead, lying thickest around the Spy of Italy, told silently how hard the day was won. Sixteen hundred Frenchmen lay dead, seven hundred Italians. The allied losses were

[1] The authorities are the same as for the Battle of Magenta, and R. H. Edleston, *Napoleon III and Italy*. The main source of information is *The Times*. There are excellent maps of the battlefields in vol. iii of the *Second Empire* of M. Pierre de la Gorce.

17,000, the Austrians' 22,000. Again it was seen how few there were of bandages, of anæsthetics, even of doctors. Men died of gangrene on the very spot where they had fallen.

Such a sight could not have failed to bring to Napoleon's mind fresh questionings as to the reasons for his war.[1] He could not carry it further without leaving Lombardy and attacking Venetia, where war would be, by the very nature of the ground, more costly still. He could not wish his fleet to pour shot and shell on to the mosaics, the canvases, or the men of Venice : and yet that fleet could be now seen from the Dalmatian islands sailing up the Adriatic. But apart from these questions, he began to doubt both Cavour and his King. Massimo d'Azeglio had been on a mission to Bologna to persuade the people to declare for Piedmont. If they were to annex the Duchies, the Romagna, perhaps even the Papal States, they would begin to be a formidable neighbour.[2] He wanted the Italians free, but not Piedmont dangerous. But above all the most disquieting news came from across the Rhine. A week before Solferino, Prussia had mobilized. She had done so, wrote Schleinitz the Foreign Minister to Prince Reuss at Paris, simply as a precaution. She wanted simply to take those prudent diplomatic measures which prevent complications by foreseeing them.[3] But the news of Solferino woke in Berlin an echo from ancestral voices, and seemed a call to war. For it was the habit of diplomatists and politicians at that time to regard with a certain satisfaction the quarrels of their neighbours, unless one of those neighbours became so successful as to threaten the

[1] Dunaud : *Un Souvenir de Solferino.*
[2] *Cowley Papers* : Cowley to John Russell, 28th July, 1859.
[3] Archives du Quai d'Orsay : Prussia.

onlooker. By winning Solferino, Napoleon suddenly took the guise of a menace to the whole German-speaking world. At Berlin the Prince Regent was deeply agitated.[1] A week later it was reported by the French Ambassador at Berlin that Prussia had at her disposal half a million men, and that an army of 235,000 was concentrated between Frankfurt-am-Main and the Rhine.[2]

Walewski, who had always foreseen this complication, and who had no love for Cavour or any of his ways, did not fail to impress these views both on the Emperor, and on the Empress Regent who had always opposed war with Austria.[3] If there was one thing that Napoleon had reason to fear (was he not the Modern Emperor?) it was a combination of the German-speaking world: a combination all the more fearsome if, as he now saw, the Italians were not to be amenable as allies. Besides, he had no forces on the Rhine.[4]

And again there was England to propitiate. Queen Victoria's consort was a liaison officer of the most effective kind between his adopted and his native country. His favourite daughter was to be the Queen of Prussia. Even before Solferino, England feared that Prussia was about to join in the war. Persigny, who had replaced the Duke of Malakoff in London, wrote to Walewski that a great body of English feeling—which evidently was at one with Prussia and the Prince—saw in the Victor of Solferino a menacing reminder of the Victor of Marengo. That was the tendency of Malmesbury and the Conservatives. The Liberals, with Palmerston at

[1] Schleinitz to Prince Reuss, 17th June, 1859.
[2] Moustier to Walewski, 28th June, 1859.
[3] Moustier to Walewski, 3rd July, 1859.
[4] Randon: *Mémoires*, ii, 36.

their head, were all on the Italian side.[1] On both there was a strong suspicion that Napoleon was not fighting in Italy for nothing. " If only the Conqueror of Austria," wrote his single-hearted champion, " by some great act could prove the disinterestedness of France and the nobleness of the end he has in view, the enthusiasm and the admiration of the English people would know no bounds." [2]

Such were the arguments that began to press upon the Emperor who, like his soldiers, was put out of humour with marches and fighting by scorching days and stifling nights in the Valley of the Mincio. The time, he saw, had come for him to change his plans. He could leave Venetia to be settled later: he could insure reform in the Papal States: he had now won Lombardy: he had gone as far towards uniting Italy as he felt it discreet for a Frenchman to do. The Crimean War he had ended by making an ally of the Czar: this time he would endear himself to the other Emperor. So he could cry check both to the Queen of England and the King of Prussia by the same move, and in the end he could put through a bargain which no one so far had mentioned: he could obtain the secret *quid pro quo* which he had so astutely discussed with Cavour at Plombières. Perhaps it was not surprising that by the middle of July *The Times* spoke of him as the modern Sphinx whose very existence depended on his not being found out, or that Franz Josef waited with the remnant of his army in great uncertainty in the city of Romeo and Juliet. And so Napoleon moved forward slowly for a fortnight in the stifling valley of the Mincio, perspiring, but triumphant. To him, in the words of a great Italian historian, were due the triumphs

[1] Quai d'Orsay: Moustier to Walewski, 28th October, 1859.
[2] Quai d'Orsay: Persigny to Walewski, 6th June, 1859.

of that campaign : the swift, bold secret movement from Alexandria to Novara : to him, the stubborn resistance at the bridge over the Ticino : to him the immediate intuition of the tactics necessary at Solferino and the fury with which the Voltigeurs had been hurled forward to attack the Spy of Italy.[1]

It was on 10th July, 1859, that a French officer [2] came to the Austrian headquarters with a confidential communication. A little before 8 the next morning, Franz Josef, followed by a cavalcade, rode out from Verona on the long level road to Villafranca. Before arriving there he saw approaching a detachment of the Cent Gardes with two squadrons of Guides. At the head of them was a man in a French general's uniform, a blue tunic with aiguillettes and a collar of gold lace, and on his head a red kepi, rimmed also with gold. As soon as Franz Josef saw that figure, he spurred his horse to a gallop, and so did Napoleon. And so the two Emperors met alone and clasped hands.[3] They were a marked contrast : one, in a light blue uniform, and an undress cap, young, erect, and spare, the other fat in the face, with a large nose, and a broad moustache, and short legs which, when he walked, made his figure look heavier still.

The two Emperors, with the staffs mingling and in confusion, rode on together towards the towers and domes of Villafranca, down its high street, till on the Vallegio road they found the mean little house which Franz Josef had made his head-quarters.[4] This they entered, and for a considerable time, they were alone together. What did they say ?

[1] Panzini : *Il 1859*, p. 320.
[2] *The Times* says Kleinberg, but it was really General Fleury. See Panzini : *Il 1859*, p. 337.
[3] *Carteggio Cavour–Nigra*, p. 237.
[4] *The Times*, 21st July, 1859.

Franz Josef had ceded Lombardy, he had agreed to reform in the Romagna, he had come to an agreement as to the Pope, that he was to be the Honorary President of an Italian federation, as Gioberti had suggested in his great book of thirteen years earlier, *Il Primato*. But Napoleon could not humiliate the foe he was winning as friend. In fact when he saw the knightly figure of his young adversary he felt he could refuse him nothing.[1] To the amazement of Franz Josef, he had begun by agreeing that the Hapsburg dukes of Tuscany and Modena should be reinstated, provided they would grant a general amnesty for political offences. And Parma—where that curious aunt of Louis Napoleon had been Grand Duchess? Venetia and the fortress of Peschiera and Mantua, being unconquered, were to remain in Austrian hands.

Franz Josef pressed these terms on his shrewd old adversary who reserved a decision. "*Eh bien, Sire,*" he said, as they parted, "*je vous prie de réfléchir dans mon sens, n'est ce pas?*" At this they shook hands, and parted.[2] Once again, they had been riding together—towards Vallegio.[3]

There the Emperor met the King and related what he proposed to do. According to the Italian report, Victor Emmanuel was furious, declaring that he would carry on the war alone, and Napoleon answered: "That is as you choose, but perhaps instead of finding one enemy you will find two." At this, so the report said, the King rose, red in the face, and rode out of Vallegio, crying, "We are ruined!"[4] But Prince Napoleon tells another story. The King, he said, grateful enough, whatever

[1] V.N.A., Metternich to Rechberg.
[2] *Carteggio Cavour–Nigra*, ii, 238.
[3] *The Times*, loc. cit.   [4] Castelli: *Ricordi*, p. 237.

happened, left all decisions to the Emperor, and the Prince was sent as envoy to Verona to accept the Austrian terms. " It is a great sacrifice I make in ceding my fairest province," said the young Emperor as he signed the paper.[1] And perhaps it was not surprising that before long he was thinking Napoleon a blackguard.[2]

None had reckoned with Cavour. When he heard the news, his eyes blazed with fury, and in the words of the Italian historian he became a sight " singular and terrible to behold ".[3] Then in insulting terms he hurled his resignation at Victor Emmanuel. And the portrait of Orsini was shown in the shop windows of Turin.

But the Emperor of the French was already busy with other things. A great triumph was to be prepared for the festival of the dynasty. It was then he entered Paris in triumph, while his people flung blossoms and garlands beneath the hoofs of his charger.[4] The bells pealed, the cannon boomed. One shout rang over all : *Vive l'Empereur!* He rode on to the Tuileries where Eugénie awaited him on a balcony with the Prince Imperial. Then he turned to review the Army of Italy.

The new Napoleon had won Lombardy from Austria, enticed Austria from Prussia, and seen in England under a return to the Whigs and John Russell a country which was amazed at his moderation. Palmerston had in fact objected to Persigny that Austria should not be left with Venice. But in any case, continued Palmerston, the dispositions of the Emperor in this case do him the greatest honour.

[1] *Carteggio Cavour–Nigra*, loc. cit.
[2] *Briefe des Kaisers Franz Josef an Seine Mutter*, No. 215. *Der Kaiser Napoleon ist, und bleibt trotz allem ein Schuft.*
[3] Panzini : *Il 1859*, p. 363.
[4] Jerrold : op. cit., iv, 221. Irving : *Annals of our Time*, 554.

His readiness to recognize the authority of Europe as a whole to settle the question, the nobleness and moderation of his views were such as to give everyone the most shining vindication of his character.[1] So spoke Lord Palmerston. But all was not yet known.

4

The liberator of Lombardy (his statue still stands in the Cortile of the Palazzo del Senato at Milan) was meanwhile to turn to negotiations such as no one could expect from a conspirator. Napoleon had always been a free trader.[2] He had become more so under the influence of Michel Chevalier, a member of a family distinguished for their understanding of political economy. On 27th October Chevalier took Cobden to see the Emperor. They talked for over an hour. He himself wanted what Cobden wanted, but the majority in his Chamber were protectionist. He venerated the name of Peel. " I shall be enchanted and flattered to put through the same work in France," said His Majesty, " but the difficulties are very great. We do not make reforms in France, we only make revolutions." [3]

Nevertheless he persevered ; he believed that by this treaty, he could refasten the bonds of friendship with the Queen, and at the same time help the winegrowers : the prosperity of our labourers, he said, " has not been developed nearly as far as that of a neighbouring country." His political economy was still Adam Smith's. For a long time, he wrote, the principle has been proclaimed that the multiplication of the means of exchange increases the

[1] Quai d'Orsay : Persigny to Walewski. *Très confidentielle et reservée*, 7th July, 1859.
[2] Greville : *Reign of Queen Victoria*, viii, 291.
[3] A. L. Dunham : Anglo-French Treaty of Commerce, p. 72.

prosperity of trade; that without competition industry remains stationary and prices continue high, which prevents an increase in consumption: that without the development of capital through industrial prosperity agriculture itself will remain primitive. It follows, therefore, that, before developing our foreign trade through the exchange of goods, we must improve our agriculture and free our industry from all obstacles within the country which put it at a disadvantageous position. At the present time our large enterprises are hindered by a mass of restrictive regulations." [1] If Napoleon is not in accord with the Protectionists of to-day, perhaps he will still prove himself a modern in his political economy. Modern France will be with him to know that nothing could prevent him from mentioning wine and liqueurs as part of the arrangement. The English weighed iron against the fruit of the grape. But "upon brandy we cannot give way," wrote Gladstone. Sacred principles were involved there. "Small as the point is, we must stand to it," insisted Gladstone, "for it is a point of honour and justice." [2] But for the rest it appears that Gladstone was at one with Napoleon III. The time was to come when he was to receive Merimée at Hawarden, and Merimée was to describe him in words which might be applied to the Emperor. "*C'est un mélange très singulier de bonhomie, de science, d'ignorance du monde, de niaiseries philosophiques et je dirai presque de génie . . . Il penche vers le suffrage universel et a des idées socialistes.*" But of course at heart, as Merimée noticed, Mr. Gladstone was more of a *Conservative* than Napoleon III.[3]

[1] E. Féray: *Du Traité de Commerce de* 1860, pp. 11, 12.
[2] *Cowley Papers*: Gladstone to Cowley.
[3] Merimée: Unpublished Letters.

On 23rd January, 1860, the Treaty of Commerce was signed. The Emperor hoped that it would mean for the poor more food, more clothing, more warmth: with England, firm friendship.[1]

5

But the time was at hand when the Prince Consort's most sinister suspicions were to be confirmed, the confidence even of Palmerston and Cowley to be shaken for ever. For at last the great conspirator showed the serrated edge of the axe he had been grinding for three years. It was the sharp line of Alps from Mont Blanc to the Mediterranean. That was the secret bargain he had made with Cavour at Plombières, and which he had so insistently denied. "The man," said the Prince Consort, not unjustly, "is a walking lie." [2]

Lord Cowley took at first a milder tone. On 9th February he went with the Emperor to Rambouillet. His Majesty lamented that no one ever gave him credit for the honesty of his intentions. What could be more natural than that, if Northern and Central Italy were to be fused into one kingdom, he should desire a frontier a little better protected than France then was on the south-east. "It was unfair," he said, "to call the annexation of a small mountainous district to France by the name of conquest or aggrandisement: it would be nothing but a measure of legitimate defence."

Now it is not the function of ambassadors to accuse the sovereigns to whom they are accredited of lying, and Lord Cowley only remarked to Napoleon that it was not so much the actual annexation of Savoy

[1] A. L. Dunham: op. cit., p. 144.
[2] Maxwell: *Life of Lord Clarendon*, ii, 207.

to France which caused the distrust which had been manifested on the subject as the way in which it had been brought forward in spite of all His Majesty's declarations on going to war. It was not unnatural for Europe to apprehend that France might equally want in a short time to put other parts of her frontier which she might consider weak in a better state of defence, and might ask for instance for the frontier of the Rhine. " People who know nothing of you personally, Sire," said the Ambassador, " can only judge by Your Majesty's acts, and those acts tend to excite alarm." He then asked point blank exactly what had happened, which of the rumours were true.

" Secrets are secrets," answered the Emperor, laughing, " but nevertheless I will tell you exactly what has occurred." [1] But the facts, as now revealed, show that he did nothing of the kind.[2]

Now when people were face to face with the Emperor, his geniality and his apparent trustfulness were very hard to resist. They had made long since a profound impression on Greville.[3] And besides the French had a very good case.[4] It was true that the Emperor had said he was asking for nothing: and the bargain with Turin, though Napoleon now pretended it was only a sort of gentlemanly understanding, had not really been hidden from the British Embassy. London and Vienna alike were well warned of what was coming. But if there was one thing that unnerved the Germanies, and infuriated England, it was the thought that France should be impregnable. And, as Lord Cowley had

[1] *Cowley Papers*: Cowley to John Russell, 10th February, 1860.
[2] See *Carteggio Cavour–Nigra*, i, 123, 311.
[3] Greville: *Queen Victoria*, vii, 270.
[4] See Quai d'Orsay (Angleterre): vol. 715, pp. 251-5.

said, no one knew where this business of natural frontiers was to stop. The only thing to do was to stop it at once. " We will shame him out of it," said Palmerston.[1] But they could not shame him out of it. Once again the generosity of his intentions proved themselves the strongest resource of his diplomatic designs. He meant so well ; the thing arose so naturally. How could men say that he lied ? With infinite good humour, he would get his way in the end. Europe might sulk, but Europe would not fight him.[2] With Turin, nevertheless, there were still to be some very delicate negotiations.

6

On 20th January, 1860, Cavour was once again the head of the Government at Turin. Ten days before, Count Talleyrand had taken the place of the Prince de la Tour d'Auvergne in the French Legation, and Thouvenel at the end of the year had taken the place of Walewski at the Quai d'Orsay. For the Emperor had gone so far towards meeting the wishes of Cavour, that Walewski, who like Thiers feared a united Italy, could no longer serve him.[3] The point was that Victor Emmanuel was to sweep down to Florence taking the Romagna with Bologna and Ferrara from the Pope, and Modena, Parma, and Tuscany from the Hapsburgs. " Let the Emperor know," said the King to Talleyrand on 3rd February, " that I always have been and always will be his in everything and for everything. I am quite devoted to his service." [4] No wonder,

---

[1] Quai d'Orsay : Persigny to Thouvenel, 21st March, 1860.
[2] Maxwell : *Lord Clarendon*, ii, 207.
[3] Private information.
[4] Quai d'Orsay : Talleyrand to Thouvenel.

for he was to have a new Kingdom of twelve million people, and if in return he was to allow a few mountaineers who spoke French to opt for their own nationality, he could not complain. Cavour was equally willing to put the bargain through. To suit an accommodating benefactor like Napoleon, he said, the King of Sardinia and his Government could not but be profoundly grateful.[1]

There were still demurs—that was inevitable—but by the end of February the Emperor had insinuated his bargain. If Turin insisted on pushing its own schemes, so Thouvenel at the Emperor's orders wrote to Talleyrand, it could not count on French support. "His Majesty will not hesitate to assert his firm and irrevocable determination to take the interests of France for the only guide of his conduct." If Sardinia became a powerful State, then obviously France must safeguard her frontiers by taking Savoy and Nice up to the Alps—" a geographical necessity to ensure the safety of our frontiers." [2] The inhabitants of course were to be consulted : so also were the Great Powers. And Cavour could not but agree. The fact was that the people in question had already given their whole hearts to France. The Emperor made a formal speech to induce them to say so loudly. It created such a sensation in Savoy and Nice that the Sardinian Governor had been forced to resign. "*Le Gouvernement du Roi est devenu impraticable,*" wrote Talleyrand, "*les rouages se sont arrêtés d'eux mêmes ; la machine ne fonctionne plus.*" [3]

[1] Quai d'Orsay : Talleyrand to Thouvenel, 1st February, 1860.

[2] Quai d'Orsay : Thouvenel to Talleyrand, 24th February, 1860.

[3] Quai d'Orsay : Talleyrand to Thouvenel, 6th March, 1860.

The French, seeing that they were sure of the votes they wanted, decided to take them at once. A little later, Prince Richard Metternich, the new Austrian Ambassador, wrote to Vienna, " The Emperor has the knack, *whatever he does,* and *whatever happens* of seeming *innocent.*" [1]

Napoleon had begun his work of remodelling the map into Modern Europe. This involved still another startling anticipation of the future.

[1] V.N.A., Metternich to Rechberg, 6th October, 1860.

XI
THE CHURCH AND THE POPE

Deus, incommutabilis virtus et lumen æternum, respice propitius ad totius Ecclesiæ tuæ mirabile sacramentum, et opus salutis humanæ, perpetuæ dispositionis effectu tranquillius operare ; totusque mundus experiatur et videat dejecta erigi, inveterata renovari, et per ipsum redire omnia in integrum, a quo sumpsere principium, Dominum nostrum Jesum Christum Filium tuum, qui tecum vivit et regnat in unitate Spiritus Sancti Deus, per omnia sæcula sæculorum. Amen.
Missale Romanum : " Prophecies of Easter Even."

I

WHAT is the use and function of the Catholic Church among the nations of the world? What is the meaning and the nature of her hold upon the hearts of men? Few questions are more important in history : few are more significant in relation to the lives of any of her children : and yet none is so rarely answered. For here indeed is the power of a life which moves hidden like the waters under the earth, which streams forth sparkling to make the valley green, which pours itself into a stretching deep, is drawn up into pinnacles of cloud and dissolves again in storm and thunder. It is a phenomenon of which, though the essential is ever the same, the activity is versatile and fluid. For in each country, as in each age, Catholicism condenses with a distinct ingredient.

In France, in the middle of the Nineteenth Century, the immemorial institution was in the position of a citadel which had been besieged, invested, and restored. The Church of the Second Empire knew very little of the mystical spirituality which marks to-day the fervour of an élite : but its prestige and influence were recognized through the whole of

French society. Chateaubriand in *Le Génie du Christianisme* had revealed anew its charm and beauty: Veuillot in *L'Univers* proclaimed it unique and sacrosanct. Montalembert and Lacordaire had shown it to be one of the most powerful agencies of contemporary thought. All the people whose influence was most obvious went regularly on Sundays to Mass. There they assisted sometimes in silence for nearly an hour, sometimes to the accompaniment of song and organ and the burning of incense, at an act of worship where at the most solemn moments a bell rang, and the Sacred Host which made real in sacramental mystery to all the very Presence, the Presence in His Flesh and Blood of Him whom men had worshipped unknown in every rite of shrine, and grove, and altar, Whose coming was the theme of image and of oracle and prophet. So hour after hour in parish after parish throughout France, the Creator —as in the very womb of Mary—deigned to make Himself the thing He had created, and there, at the prayer of the believer, He gave back to the souls and bodies of the faithful as their spiritual sustenance the gift which was no other than Himself. So with a peculiar insistence the Church offered the graces of Heaven to the people of France.

Here was indeed a sacred mystery. Here the heavy eyes of the Emperor Napoleon were raised to adore. For here, especially when emotional music or the notes of a prima donna voiced to the feelings of the susceptible the mysterious pleading and worship, here where the choir sang " Glory to God in the Highest ", or implored the Lamb of God to take away the sins of the world and grant it His peace, the heart could not but be moved. When Napoleon thought of God, when he thought of doing good, when he pictured himself as the chosen agent of a universal beneficence, he found here a fresh inspiration. And how did the worship end ? As the ceremonies drew to their close the choir sang a prayer for himself. *Domine, salvum fac Imperatorem Napoleonem.* He, as a sovereign, as an agent of that sublime principle, authority, as the means of civil order, was part of the dispensation which was to work not only for the salvation of souls, but for the happiness and well-being of men on earth. " It is the duty of a sovereign to make a self examination," so he once said at Biarritz to the Bishop of Bayonne. "It is his duty above all to come to the foot of the altar to implore Divine Providence by the intercession of the ministers of religion to bless his efforts, to enlighten his conscience, and to give him strength constantly to do good and to put down evil."[1] So it was that the Emperor found in Catholicism so admirable a religion. In an hierarchical organization dispensing heavenly life in mysteries, he had never had a very warm belief : when that organization supported secular authority different from his own, and interfered with his private pleasures, he had abandoned it altogether. But if such interference were not marked, if that power gave a religious sanction to his own authority, then religion was obviously excellent ; and, provided it supported his authority and did not worry him, he had everything to gain by aiding it as the great conservative organism of the life of France.

But there were yet other reasons why Napoleon's instincts supported the Church. It was one of the best ways possible to win to himself the old classes of Royalist sympathies, the classes which believed in authority because they had in themselves the power of exercising it. Furthermore, it was from this class, more than any other, that the officers of the army

[1] *Moniteur*, 16th August, 1854.

came. The tastes and temperaments of officers are inevitably conservative. Discipline, prestige, authority: these are sacred to the army man, and their sacredness is one with the Church which consecrates them, and which keeps ever before them the reward given to valour and sacrifice. The military parade is not complete therefore until it is a Church parade. And to the Church parade on the grand scale, the military Mass at Châlons, the Emperor lent all the devices of ceremonial of which he was a master.

Close to his own tent, in front of the standard, on a mound in view of all the troops which were ranged in a circle round it, stood the altar. The sappers stood around it, their axes gleaming in the sun; then came the artillery in all the gorgeousness of their full-dress uniform, the cavalry behind them. So regiment on regiment were arrayed in a widening circle round the central glitter of the chalice of gold. Into this array the Emperor marched on foot, followed by a suite almost as numerous as a regiment. As he appeared the troops presented arms, the drums beat as for a charge, there was a flourish from bugles and trumpets. Then all the music joined to the music of the national anthem, while the cannon boomed their salute. Even the most sceptical there, as they looked upon the man, who represented France, and who in very fact had made her arbiter of Europe, were moved. A shiver passed over the army, tautening its muscles, and the eyes of not a few of the soldiers of France were moist.

So did the Emperor begin his military Mass: and, at last, as the moment of the Consecration drew near, the order *Genou terre* echoed down the troops. The Emperor and his staff fell upon their knees: Above a kneeling army, the horses' manes, the plumed helmets, the turbans and aigrettes seemed also to sink beneath the glitter of saluting swords.

Then on the stillness of this army at worship broke the thunder of the guns ; and as the white cloud arose from them, the eyes of all could see above the power and glory that they themselves figured, so arrayed, the white circle of the Sacred Host lifted up in sacrifice between the fingers of the priest.[1]

In the tension of such a moment, who could but make haste to bow their heads and adore ? Who could but believe that this was the tabernacle of God with men that He should dwell with them ? But a faith so consoling, so bracing, so complete, could not be bought by mere assistance at even the most imposing, the most significant of ceremonies. If this indeed were true, then much more was demanded. The sacrifice of the fruits of the earth, so consummated, invited, if out of mere thanksgiving, the sacrifice of the hearts of men. It invited not only the unselfish act, the forethought for the comfort of the poor and the ministering to their sick and to their aged : but it meant what the progress of his period menaced,—even while it seemed to provide,— a free and charitable community of workers living on the kindly fruits of the earth. It meant the cheer of the hearth, where love was joined to life, not only by nature but in the dispensation of grace. For, when all is said, we cannot minister to others but at the cost of our own impulses, and the hopes of our own earthly comfort. The Christian must look upward. For him the earth, even at its best, is not an end in itself, any more than his own body is an end in itself. Even while it perfects the outward world, the Church looks onward to another mode of being that is far different.

So for more than a hundred and fifty years in France, and perhaps even as far back as the

[1] General du Barail : *Mes Souvenirs*, ii, 221, 222.

Reformation that had there been strangled, the French had developed a strong tendency to look on well-being in this world as final, and the demands of the supernatural order as harsh, false, and in fact contemptible. So had come the Encyclopædia of Diderot, and the romantic sentimentalism of Rousseau. So finally had come the talk of the rights of men, and afterwards the uproar and iconoclasm of the Revolution. This movement no doubt emphasized a truth; certainly the truth was the more necessary because the organism of the Church had grown so formal. But while safeguarding this essential truth and all it promised to men's natural lives, the Bonapartes did not wish to stamp out, nor even to persecute, the Church. On the other hand, they were determined to maintain it, even while the intransigeants such as Lamoricière derided them as allying it with the Revolution, and the Faith with freemasonry.[1]

So, the clergy, even when they were sick, were paid by the State. So the army safeguarded and decorated the processions in the streets; the provinces were allowed again to hold their councils which had been forbidden since 1624; the workshops of the State were closed on Sundays; Catholicism was taught in the schools; the social principles which were centred on the family were encouraged; the religious organizations for the life of charity, of teaching, and of mystic discipline were supported; the dignitaries were greeted in Court with the most flattering attentions and the universality of the religion was recognized in the person of its universal head, the authority which was to it as the Emperor was to France the ultimate court of appeal and the strong centre of direction—the Pope in Rome.[2]

[1] Paléologue: *Cavour.*
[2] Maurain: *Politique Ecclésiastique du Second Empire*, ch. iv, vi. Thouvenel: *Secret de l'Empereur.*

2

It was in 1846 that Pius IX had been elected Pope. Comparatively young, strikingly handsome, and distinctly liberal in his sympathies, he had first appeared to promise both to Italy and to the Church, a reign of advance. But in the disorders of 1848 he had been obliged to flee from Rome and, though he returned a few months later, he did so only with the support of the French Government of which Louis Napoleon was already the head.

Pius IX was not a tall man, but the proportion of his figure and the dignity of his movements were a sufficient witness of his noble blood. His figure was made more striking by his white soutane trimmed with ermine, against which habitually stood a cross of brilliant sapphires. His features were regular and fine : but the charm of his whole person was in his expression. The lines of his mouth, although firm, suggested at the same time such a sadness, and such an utter lack of bitterness that with the extraordinarily benevolent expression of his eyes (men said they never saw eyes which shone so mildly [1]) one could not come into his presence without being at once melted by the kindness and goodness of his heart. His manner was genial, almost intimate. He excelled in friendliness. But he was none the less assured that the post, for which by an inscrutable Providence he had been chosen, was so sacred that it could admit no compromise with regard either to its own privileges or prestige, or to the principles it existed to maintain. This he, like Queen Victoria, supported with that simple shrewdness which is often more effective than all the arts of politics.

Nevertheless he had his diplomat always at hand ;

[1] F. Fernandez de Cordoba : *Mis Memorias Intimas*, iii, 146.

his Secretary of State, Cardinal Antonelli, was hardly older than himself. Slight and tall, he dressed with a taste as fine as the grace of his movements. The finest Malines lace bordered his crimson robe ; and a crimson biretta emphasized the ebony blackness of his hair. His black eyes were brilliant : his features were sharp, and his whole expression suggested the negotiator of tireless finesse.[1] His perfect manners were the shining armour of a complete control of anything which could reveal his thought : and yet, while he sat silent, they suggested a charm which invited confidence.[2] Such was the man who directed the politics of the Papal States at the time when Victor Emmanuel's ambitions, and the spirit of humanistic insurgence threatened the very existence of the temporal power.

Although the sun shone with its ancient brightness on the picturesque realm he controlled, although taxes were almost nothing and conscription unknown, although the course of the year was marked by a number of sumptuous festivals, the Cardinal was too shrewd to think that he or his régime could count on the loyalty of the people. For years a spirit of licence had been spreading amongst the youth ; for young men, taking them as a whole, are apt to revolt against singing hymns to the Madonna, avowing their faults in the confessional, and bowing to the discipline of piety. Above all, they objected to so cheap a value being put upon the instincts of virility : their admiration was not for the saint, but for the natural man, who in his very discipline witnesses his exuberance of energy. The fact that there was no army appeared to rob young men of a career, and the super-eminence of the clergy took from their horizons the lure of political power. The whole of the Papal

[1] Id., iii, 145.   [2] La Gorce : *Second Empire*, iii, 362.

States was kept in fact too much in the strict discipline of the contemporary nursery, and all over Europe there was agreement that their administration should be reformed.[1]

Whether the changes were so much for the better as the world imagined, whether the new patriotism with its taxes, its conscription, its brothels, its canaille, and its corrupt administration was really to make the people happier : that, as the Cardinal saw, was not the point.[2] Promises were made, and peoples are apt to welcome a change. The feeling of being citizens of a great country flatters them. Antonelli therefore in his policy in Italy decided only to look for support to foreign arms, and to maintain his principles, even when force was too strong for him. " Usurpation of my rights I can endure," said the Holy Father, " but I cannot recognize the usurper in coming to terms with him."[3] So the Emperor Napoleon, in view of his relations with his own clergy, was determined never to support a robbery of the Church's patrimony, and to keep his troops in Rome until he could point to a good reason for withdrawing them. He had heard somewhere that *qui mange du Pope en meurt*.

3

When the Emperor had begun his reign, he had contemplated a second coronation by the Pope in Notre-Dame. A young priest of noble birth, delightful personality and high enthusiasm, the Abbé de Ségur, had himself approached the Holy Father to urge him to give to the man whom—as a young insurgent—he had rescued twenty years before, the

[1] G. Mollat : *La Question Romaine* 301 ss. Cf. M. Minghetti : *I Miei Recordi*, iii, 336, 356, 366.
[2] M. Minghetti, op. cit., iii, 572-4.
[3] La Gorce : *Second Empire*, iii, 359.

THE IMPERIAL TOMBS AT FARNBOROUGH

"What is so edifying as a repentant sinner?"

blessing which Pius VII had given to the first Emperor. But this time the Vicar of Christ judged it expedient to summon his Emperor to Rome: Napoleon III, it was courteously suggested, could hardly take umbrage in being asked to step in the footprints of Charlemagne.

M. de Ségur returned to Paris to give this message to the Emperor. Now the Emperor had already envisaged the danger of assassination if he went back on his old alliance with the Carbonari : but, apart from that, was a coronation in St. Peter's really becoming ? " The youth I led at Rome was so unedifying," he said with his genial and disarming frankness to the young priest. " I have left there traces of such a nature, that I really hardly could appear there in a guise so different without evoking disagreeable reflections, and compromising the very nature of my consecration." That answer seemed to the Holy Father to furnish the very strongest reason why the Emperor should come. What was so edifying as a repentant sinner kneeling to abjure his sins? " If he really is not the same man," said the genial Pontiff, " well, let him come and prove it." [1] But perhaps the Emperor did not need to give that proof, for just at that moment he had taken up arms against Russia in defence of the Church of Jerusalem.

Now it was in the very course of this Holy War, that he had made his alliance with Cavour. Between being a Catholic and being a Carbonaro, Louis Napoleon had never been able to make his choice. Instead of making therefore a trenchant compromise like his uncle, he oscillated according to the pull of circumstances. But compromise nevertheless he made, and in this particular instance the compromise was the very crown of his modernity.

[1] Marquis de Ségur : *Souvenirs et Récits d'un Frère*, i, 195, 196.

4

He first sketched it in a pamphlet which above the signature of La Guerronnière was published as *Le Pape et Le Congrès*, on 22nd December, 1859, and of which Monseigneur Dupanloup said at once, " This pamphlet is hell."[1] It began by asserting the one truth that was essential to the Church : that the Pope should have temporal power in the sense that it was necessary that the head of the universal Church should not be the subject of any nationality. He must himself be recognized as sovereign, and one cannot have a sovereign without a territory. But, the pamphlet went on to say, the Pope has already been dispossessed of the Romagna : and not all the horses nor all the men of the three Emperors could put the Austrians in charge again. And was it not much better that the head of the Church should not have the function or his prestige compromised by the scandal of an unpopular civil administration ? He must have a territory to make him independent, but, the smaller it was, the better. " The more restricted his territory, the greater its sovereign. The Pope will be more powerful then in his weakness than in his strength." Let the Holy Father therefore welcome the loss of the Romagna as the first gift of a glorious freedom which would make him shine out in the Modern World as its central and loftiest adviser, because with his rights safeguarded, while his territories were limited by an international guarantee, his standpoint would be independent, and his only care the welfare and peace of men.

So—under the name of La Guerronnière—wrote Napoleon III in 1859. So he had been talking for years with Palmerston and Clarendon.[2] So in 1929

[1] R. H. Edleston : Napoleon III and Italy, i, 113.
[2] Maxwell : *Lord Clarendon*, ii, 199 ff.

spoke the Pope himself. All through the nineteen twenties, the Vatican diplomatists were insisting on the very settlement for which Napoleon III argued and manœuvred all through the eighteen sixties. For, depending as he did on diplomacy rather than decision, he sought at every turn to insinuate his compromise. No episode in his career throws more light on its significance. And it is indeed curious that in the short space of seventy years the Church should find its prophet and its counsellor in the very man whom at the time the most devout were apt to confuse with Antichrist : while the first statement of the Church's ultimate contention should be at once stigmatized by the Pope himself as a signal monument of hypocrisy, and a contemptible web of contradictions.[1]

5

And yet Pius IX was in the right. He had sworn that he would not compromise his patrimony : it was not his personal possession : it was a sacred responsibility held in trust from immemorial institution, a responsibility older and more venerable than any monarchy in Europe. Too often had the Church been despoiled : its great struggle throughout the Middle Ages had been to maintain its spiritual authority intact against the encroachment of the dominant national sovereignty in Europe : and in the nineteenth century, with all its swelling tendencies towards material civilization, towards the industrial mechanization and the consequent deadening of human life into monotony and sordidness, no sensitive spiritual organism could but instinctively recoil in suspicion against any attack upon its privilege or prestige. And neither Cavour nor Victor Emmanuel could promise a régime to edify the innocent.

[1] Papal Allocution of 1st January, 1860.

Catholic loyalties were strong on the side of the Pope: nowhere was this more obvious than in Spain, and Spaniards remembered that there was a Spaniard reigning in the Tuileries as the consort of the new arbiter of Europe. The Empress Eugénie was beginning to take a leading part in the Empire's fatal melodrama.[1] During her husband's absence in Italy, she had ruled as regent and ruled with great ability. So marked was her success that the Council of Ministers had actually asked that, after the Emperor's return, she should still be present at their sittings.[2] She had helped to bring the war to a close. And, like her Spanish friends, she felt with all the eagerness of her paladin spirit that loyalty placed her, and should place France, with the Catholic nations, as a defender of the Faith and a champion of him who ruled for Christ on earth as regent. Her old friend Salamanca acted as an envoy between her and the Holy See. For four years she carried on a diplomatic campaign with the Emperor in favour of the Pope.[3]

As for Napoleon, he was, in Lord Cowley's words, applying to Italy his old saying of Mahomet and the mountain. "If the Pope won't go to Sardinia," he whispered to himself, on his return from the war, "why, Sardinia must come to the Pope."[4] He wanted, in other words, large and liberal reforms in the Roman States but he knew that immemorial principles made a great obstacle, and it seemed perhaps easier to win the Sardinians to agreement with the Pope than vice versa. He did in fact assert his liberal principles to Rome itself. If the Pope

[1] *Cowley Papers*: Cowley to Russell, 2nd December, 1862.
[2] R. Sencourt: *Empress Eugénie*, p. 147.
[3] F. Fernandez de Cordova: *Mis Memorias Intimas*, iii, 434.
[4] Wellesley: *The Paris Embassy*, p. 188.

would secularize his government and adopt Liberal measures (so Morny wrote to Salamanca on 24th October, 1860), his interests could be more easily defended by the Emperor without giving offence to liberal susceptibilities in France. Yet political exigencies would not allow the Emperor to proceed further in this sense than within certain limits. Deploring the conduct of Piedmont, he could not for the sake of the Papacy violate the principle of non-intervention, to which he was pledged in Europe. The only compromise he could adopt in the circumstances would be to continue what he had always done, to protect the Holy Father in the Patrimony of St. Peter. But if in consequence of European intervention, he should succeed at Congress in regulating the European situation, the Emperor would defend the cause of the Holy Father in the Congress, and obtain for him a position equivalent to that he held before the recent happenings.[1]

At that time the Emperor was still anxious that the Pope should retain Umbria and the Marches. He was still working to prevent Piedmont from annexing Naples or even the Romagna.[2]

And with gratitude as one of the strongest elements of his character, he had no temptation to forget that thirty years earlier this very Pope had saved his life. " *J'aime le Saint-Père,*" he said to Metternich : " *C'est un bien brave et digne homme qui voit plus clair qu'on ne pense* ".[3] Between the Vicar of Christ and his Curia, however, the Emperor drew a distinction. " The Pope," he said " is under no illusions as to the mistakes made by the men around him. He shows

[1] F. Fernandez de Cordova : *Mis Memorias Intimas,* iii, 436.
[2] *Cowley Papers* : Cowley to John Russell, 2nd November, 1860.
[3] V.N.A., Metternich's dispatches, 15th February, 1861.

them up with just that wit, and gaiety and serenity of temper of which he has so much." [1] In fact Napoleon gave the Austrian Ambassador the impression that his hand was being forced by his Ministers. " He finds himself," wrote Metternich, " in the position of a man who is holding back from suicide, but who will do it all the same to escape the dagger of an assassin." [2] The Ambassador had forgotten that Thouvenel had been made Foreign Minister simply because his views on the Roman question were so different from Walewski's. Lord Cowley's impression of the Emperor was rather different : he felt distinctly that the chief object of Napoleon was to get his troops out of Rome. " I am convinced," wrote Lord Cowley, " that his brains are constantly on the rack to invent some plausible excuse for leaving the Pope to his fate." In fact, the Emperor hoped to persuade the Pope to accept a Sardinian garrison in Rome in place of the French. " Your Majesty," said the British Ambassador, " might as well think of jumping over the moon." [3]

Napoleon did not believe that Italian unity could be permanent : he was convinced that the old independent towns would each want their own way, and at all events, without Rome, unity would be an impossibility. The longer the French troops were in Rome, the more difficult his position became, and the more inclined he was to leave the final settlements to the Pope and the Italians. In this detail, also, his instinct was prophetic. But the votes in his Legislative Assembly in 1861 were too definitely with the Church to be ignored, for he feared that he had already lost the confidence of the clergy.[4]

[1] V.N.A., id. [2] V.N.A., Metternich's dispatches, 8th May, 1861.
[3] *Cowley Papers* : Cowley to John Russell, 11th January, 1861.
[4] *Cowley Papers.*

Thouvenel meanwhile, at the Emperor's instance, pressed on Victor Emmanuel the idea of making Rome a free town, and that with a garden and the attributes of a sovereign, and certain estates to insure his revenues, the Holy Father should have it for his residence. "Suppose the Pope were to leave Rome," said the Emperor to the Papal Nuncio, "just to show the impossibility of Italian unity!"

The Nuncio, who did not know if the Emperor was mocking him, looked flabbergasted.

"Don't be alarmed," continued Napoleon, "it is only an idea which has crossed my head. Be assured that I will do everything in my power to meet the Pope's wishes." [1]

But while the Emperor hesitated, the Empress strengthened her position. Although, like her spouse, she had a strong tendency to superstition in her nature, it is an error to suppose that there was anything of bigotry or fanaticism in the religion of this pupil of Stendhal. Her tact in managing the Roman question was praised by both Prince Metternich in 1862, by Lord Cowley in 1866, and Lord Lyons in 1867. Her object was to secure in his essential rights by international guarantee the head of the international Church against those who, in the interests of national aggrandisement, or alien religion, sought to deprive the chief pastor of the Church of rights and dignities which had been his for centuries.[2] And here she won her battle. By the autumn of 1862 she and the Emperor were at one, and so they remained till the end. "He will exhaust every effort at conciliation," said the Protestant Fould to the Protestant Cowley, "in order to show the world that he has done his best to save

[1] *Cowley Papers.*
[2] V.N.A., Hübner to Rechberg, 9th June, 1862.

the Pope; but he is excessively irritated at the attitude taken by both Italy and England, who, he thinks, want him to act dishonourably, and care not for the consequences to him."

"If Rome is to be evacuated," continued Fould, " and we shall arrive at it by degrees, it must be done by degrees, thro' appeals to the Emperor's sense of justice, and not by irritating him. Nothing irritates him so much as being told that by right Rome belongs to Italy. He will never be a party to recognizing the rights of a Government of eight days to what has existed in another form for nearly as many centuries. If Rome is to be evacuated, it must be without prejudice to the Pope's position." [1]

So, to his honour, did Napoleon leave the question of Church politics. So it still was at his fall. So, in its essentials, it stands to-day, the most striking witness of all to the Modernness of Napoleon III.

6

With the Catholic Empress, it is another story. Hers, it is true, was a spirit of progress, and she was often mesmerized by the thought of her husband as the emancipator of the people, as he in his conversations both with the Austrian Ambassadors, and Madame de Mercy-Argenteau, repeatedly emphasized his duties as a Catholic sovereign, his love of authority, and even his distrust of popular movements. For the reactions of the Emperor and the Empress on one another were complex and profound: each had double elements in their natures, which in their married life made the subtlest interplay. But as the Empress had, at the root of her excitability and her changes of mood, an immaculate honour, and an unswerving

[1] *Cowley Papers*: Cowley to Russell, 3rd October, 1862.

faith, so, beside her husband's intricate conspiracies, she maintained not only a standard, but also a policy which was consistent. In European politics that meant not only, and not even chiefly, the Holy See: above all, it meant Austria, as it included England. From early in 1861 it is not difficult to trace Eugénie as a leading influence in French policy, working frankly with her devoted friends, Prince and Princess Metternich. All through, their object was an alliance —alliance of England, France, and Austria against the attack of Prussia which Eugénie felt in her bones to be inevitable: this alliance was to keep the balance of Europe on the side of traditional civilization, It must not be laid to the blame of Eugénie, or of Napoleon, or of Richard Metternich, if, after doing all they could in this wise plan, their offers were rejected in both London and Vienna. But in those critical years, the early sixties, Rechberg, then at the Ballplatz, could not rid himself of the idea that Austria's only danger was from Napoleon III.[1] So the chief Catholic powers of Europe were divided against themselves. And Prussia, which in Napoleon's plan was to have a wide field for her ambitions, began in her own interests to make the rearrangements which Napoleon had once dreamed should be in those of Europe. This henceforward was to be the tragic drama of the Second Empire. It was not, we must repeat, Napoleon's mistake. It came from divided counsels in London, and a fatal error of judgment in Vienna. Napoleon's own plan he summed up to Metternich in one of his memorable phrases. "The marriage of reason which holds the two Western powers together in all the questions which arise,"

[1] Rofhe: *Kapital und Konjunctur*, p. 47. Friedjung: *Der Kampf um die Vorherrschaft in Deutschland*, 1859–1866, Anhang ii, Band ii. Mittheilungen des Grafen Rechberg. Steefel: *The Schleswig-Holstein Question*. Engels-Janosi: *Rechberg, passim*.

he said, " does not prevent the two greatest powers of the Continent from engaging in a close and passionate liaison." [1]

7

In the beginning of the close and passionate liaison thus defined, there was a charming interlude of comedy. It was staged at the moment the clock struck, twelve on New Year's Eve of 1859. Two guests and two alone had spent the evening at the Tuileries, the Prince and Princess Metternich, and they had been entertained with that ease and intimacy in which the Emperor and Empress, like their guests from Vienna, showed their consummate social powers. As the year came to its end, Napoleon offered his arm to his Empress and danced her into 1860 with the Ambassador at the piano playing a Viennese waltz.

" I could not help laughing inwardly at the scene," wrote Metternich to his Minister. " The Austrian Ambassador making the French Emperor dance in the New Year struck me as at least a very original idea. I could not help playing the Radetzky march, and our national anthem as soon as the Emperor and Empress had stopped their dance.

"Last year, on New Year's Day, at the Tuileries, no one was expecting that a year later the Austrian Ambassador would be playing them tunes so little in accord with their tradition." [2]

[1] V.N.A., Metternich to Rechberg, 26th February, 1863. Napoleon urged the idea of a combination with Vienna to settle the German question : *Vous ne comprenez pas votre intérêt comme moi ; eh bien, je vous le répète—je l'ai dit dernièrement à M. de Hübner— je crois que notre entente peut être maintenue sur les bases les plus pacifiques . . . Je ne doute pas que si le malheur voulait que nous nous séparions, la Prusse chercherait à se placer dans le joint : mais tant que nous aurons l'air d'être unis, je défie bien la Prusse de lever la soupape à son ambition.* V.N.A., Metternich to Rechberg, Fontainebleau, 12th June, 1863.

[2] V.N.A., Metternich to Rechberg, 3rd January, 1860.

XII

THE QUESTION OF THE MAP

> *Tu me crois peut-être*
> *Un homme comme sont tous les autres, un être*
> *Intelligent, qui court droit au but qu'il rêva.*
> *Détrompe-toi. Je suis une force qui va !*
> *Agent aveugle et sourd de mystères funèbres !*
> *Une âme de malheur faite avec des ténèbres !*
> *Où vais-je ? Je ne sais, mais je me sens poussé*
> *D'un souffle impétueux, d'un destin insensé.*
> *Je descends, je descends, et jamais ne m'arrête.*
> *Si parfois, haletant, j'ose tourner la tête,*
> *Une voix me dit : Marche ! et l'abîme est profond*
> *Et de flamme ou de sang je le vois rouge au fond.*
>   VICTOR HUGO : *Hernani*, iii, 4.

I

IT was not only in the matter of the Papacy that the campaign in Italy showed itself to be the turning point of the Second Empire. What there was of greatness in the soul of Napoleon III was that his phenomenal susceptibility of brain and sense made him in his hopes and fears an organ for the prophetic soul of the wide world dreaming on things to come. For he not less than his predecessor was a man of European destiny, even while he pledged the forfeits of his dynastic doom. In France it was his function to apply to the world of spreading industrialism the great sanities of the system worked out by the First Emperor: in Europe it was to conjure with the map till the ancient sovereignties walled in by the Congress of Vienna should be dissolved so that we should, for better or for worse, make ready for the Europe of to-day. For, after the pact of Villafranca and the absorption of Savoy, he was felt, in spite of all his hesitations and his subterfuges, to be indeed the arbiter of Europe.

At once he began his game of forfeits on the map : the game which held him captive as the turf and gaming table hold the inveterate gambler. His two great preoccupations were Italy and Prussia. In 1860, therefore, he decided that they should each increase but not beyond their bounds. Piedmont should have Venetia, Parma, Modena, the Romagna ; the Pope in exchange should take the Abruzzi from Naples ; Naples should find compensation in the regency of Tunis. The Duke of Parma should have Sicily. So much for the South of Europe. In the North there was a still more sweeping plan. Prussia should absorb Hanover, Mecklenburg, Hesse, Waldeck, Anhalt, Lippe, ceding in exchange to Belgium or to Holland the left bank of the Rhine. Austria, ceding Venetia to Piedmont and Galicia to Russia, should take in return Serbia, Bosnia, and Egypt ; the King of Hanover should acquire Roumelia with the title of King of Constantinople, and the Duke of Mecklenburg, Bulgaria, Wallachia, and Moldavia. Russia was thus to gain Galicia, and England was to be propitiated with Cyprus and the Euphrates. Such were the happy combinations which would be gained by wiping out of the map ungrateful Turkey who for three centuries had usurped great tracts of the Mediterranean coast-line and put Christendom in Europe to shame.[1]

[1] This map was printed by Edward Stanford in 1860. See F. Fernandez de Cordoba : *Mis Memorias Íntimas*, iii, 439, 440. *Este mapa se habia impreso y formado bajo la inspiracion de Napoleon III y se referia a el en sus cartas por contener todo el plan de las transformaciones europeas imaginadas por el que entonces se suponia árbitro de todo, y era indudablemente el soberano que más pesaba en los destinos del mundo. España me decia que este proyecto era el rasgo más caracteristico de la fisonomia moral del Emperador.*

If we are to understand the complete revulsion of the Emperor on the subject of Turkey, we must remember first that England, the traditional protector of Islam, had been very difficult in her attitude towards Rome. The English Liberals had taken umbrage at Napoleon sending troops to Rome and vessels to Gaëta.[1] And besides, the Empress, whose religious and ancestral pride had been Spain's conquest of the Moor, delighted in the discomfiture of Moslem power. She had been persuading the Emperor that above all he was a defender of the Faith. The idea of thousands of men on their knees before a consecrated sovereign : that was the sort of picture which now began to fascinate him.[2] He now saw himself as the champion of oppressed Christians, and how, he asked, could he countenance a Moorish monarchy in Europe, a monarchy at whose head was " a sovereign plunged in debauchery, half mad, and whose most striking exercise of his prerogatives was to promote his dentist to the post of Field-Marshal."[3]

It was not only that the championship of the Sultan left the French victor cold. He had been in relation with the Rumanian patriot, Prince Cuza—as we have seen—and already in 1859, his vision of a national Rumania was solidifying beyond the now accomplished reality of a national Italy. This was modifying his notions of what should be done in those interesting regions of mixed races and clashing interests between Hungary and the Black Sea : Napoleon III was greatly preoccupied with the whole question of the Balkans fifty years before they became the bone of contention between Russia and Middle

[1] V.N.A., Metternich to Rechberg (Telegram), 3rd November, 1860.
[2] V.N.A., Hübner to Rechberg, 10th May, 1862.
[3] V.N.A., Metternich to Rechberg, 8th January, 1863.

Europe. There too his schemes and dreams were prophetic of things to come.

And his liaison with Russia was over. " That great country was," he said now, " in a condition as deplorable as France before the Revolution. " Its aristocracy is cancered from top to bottom and things are taking a very nasty turn." [1] This view—and it was also prophetic—was one with his new interest in Poland : the Poles rose in insurrection against the Czar in 1863, and, in spite of all his approaches to the Czar, the Liberal instincts of the Emperor could not restrain him from the line of his old ambition. As he had himself written long before : " *On revient toujours à ses premiers amours.*" [2] Here was a way to appease at once the Liberals and the Catholics, to persuade the Empress and the Pope that he was at heart a great Catholic sovereign, while at the same time he could show Prince Napoleon, with his attendant republicans and anti-clericals, that he was the champion of democracy against the tyrant.

2

Through his secret service he learnt in 1862 that Mazzini had been combining with Polish conspirators and during the winter of that year, he obtained possession of papers which made the whole plan clear. He was anxious, naturally, that the Polish cause should not be surrendered to Mazzini who in his eyes was little better than an assassin : but, on the other hand, he could not put pressure on the Czar. What did he expect at the time ? That was the question which Metternich put to the Empress on 1st March, 1863.

" A Poland all but undefended under a Grand Duke," she answered.

[1] V.N.A., Metternich to Rechberg, 30th June, 1862.
[2] Jerrold : *Napoleon III*, ii, 417.

THE EMPEROR IN HIS LAST EXILE
From a photograph in the Duke of Alba's collection.

"His schemes and dreams were prophetic of things to come."

"And what," he asked, "do you mean to give in return?"

"We shall take broad views on all questions touching the East."

But a month later, the Emperor's fancy was running wild. Austria had joined England and France in protest, but the Austrians were always vague. Now, wild as the Emperor's plans were, it was his ambition to be precise. He sometimes asked himself whether it might not be possible to take possession of some port or island in the Baltic and tell Russia that it would be held till she had given complete independence to Poland. He hardly seemed to realize that so to seize an island was an act of war.[1]

For at heart the Emperor was determined to avoid war. "Let us come to an agreement like the honest fellows we really are," he said, "and not like thieves who want to cheat each other."[2] He wanted to settle matters by a Congress. It was indeed the one hope for Europe. That the map should remain for ever as it had been marked out in 1815, he already knew—and history since has fully proved—to be impossible. Nationalities had been recognized by the First Emperor as one of Europe's instincts, not to be stifled. Cavour had made it possible for Italy to be a nation. Bismarck had brought to Prussia the strength and resource of his genius in the hope of dominating from Berlin the innumerable States which the Congress of Vienna had left between France on one side and on the other Russia, Prussia, and Austria. It was the Modern Emperor's plan to humour and combine the developing nationalities, and then combine them into the United States of Europe: and in this sense he made his great

[1] *Cowley Papers.*
[2] Maxwell: *Lord Clarendon*, ii, 217, 218.

pronouncement to the Senate on 21st November, 1863.

"With all my heart," he said, "I long for the time when the great questions which divide Governments and peoples can be settled peacefully by European arbitration. This is what the head of my family desired when he cried at St. Helena : 'It is civil war to fight in Europe.' This great thought, once Utopian, couldn't it become to-morrow a reality?

"However that may be, it is always an honour to proclaim a principle which tends to wipe out the prejudices of another age. Let us unite our efforts towards this noble end. Let our only thought of obstacles be to overcome them, and of incredulity to confound it." [1]

3

Such was the central ambition of Napoleon III during the last seven years of his reign : he wanted, it is true, to strengthen the frontiers of France against the rise of Prussia, as he had strengthened them against the rise of Italy. At times he lent his ear to those who wanted the Rhine as frontier : but that was rarely. He did feel the necessity of a buffer State between himself and Prussia. But just as in the earlier years of his reign, he had emphasized the idea of authority, now it was the doctrines of popular government which romped, handsome roysterers, through his now ramshackle mind. The habit of intrigue continued master, and widened the distrust which men had always felt of Napoleon III. They grew as suspicious of the integrity of his heart as of the capacities of his brain : but they should have looked lower down for the cause of trouble : the

[1] *Archives diplomatiques*, 1864, i, 82.

organism of the Emperor of the French was being slowly poisoned from his kidneys.[1]

Always emotional, always voluptuous, always the victim of his nervous instability, the sovereign from this time on was liable to crises of exhaustion, which were the more apt to paralyse him the more he needed to have the power of decision. He could still conceive with secrecy, but no longer act with promptitude. He had always been inclined to wait and see: he now could do nothing else. "He has certain ideas and desires floating in his mind," wrote Lord Cowley, "which turn up as circumstances seem favourable, but a man of less decision of character, of more indolent disposition, or more inclined to wait upon events instead of creating them I never came across." [2] It was therefore by an instinctive necessity that he turned to the people and their leaders for the power to govern which the slow poison of uremia was strangling in his blood. Spasms of exhausting torment, the tearing and straining of sensitive tissues by the stone in his bladder, and an embarrassing derangement of one of the simplest processes of nature worked havoc in the arbiter of Europe, and troubled with deeper and more disquieted surmise those who had long racked their brains to solve his riddle. And yet, if the truth was known, the new mystification could be quite simply explained: it was that the malady and the symptoms were not of a nature then customary to discuss. And even now, it would be unbecoming to be too precise.

But although one cannot insist too strongly that the Emperor's strength poured from him in his conflict with disease and torture, this itself was not

[1] See Salomon: *Ambassade de Richard Metternich*, 140, 141, 145, 146.
[2] *The Paris Embassy*, p. 237.

the major complication of his historic case. Poland signified greater things. Poland explains why he irritated the Czar : the reason why the Czar's irritation with him became at that moment fatal must be sought elsewhere—in a field sharp with menace and contention, as nasty to traverse even to-day as stubble to bare feet. For the national hero of Germany is the national villain of France. Nothing is of more significance in the career of Napoleon III than that the year which followed the death of Cavour in Florence should see Bismarck appointed First Minister of Prussia. Bismarck dominates the last ten years of the Second Empire, as in turn Palmerston and Cavour had led the Emperor to the summit of his power. The old genial crowned conspirator was to pit his skill against a new conspirator uncrowned, merciless, and far more able because his ambition was set on a nearer and narrower end.

4

Bismarck is the Napoleon of Prussian bureaucracy. His mind was as concrete as that of the First Emperor. Born in 1815, and trained as a diplomat, he attempted a compromise between his heritage as a squire in Pomerania and the high politics of the great powers of Europe. Like all great men, he knew that individual capacity is independent of the privileges of primogeniture. He was prepared to allow a parliament provided it did not interfere with government or army. He set before himself one object, one object which he held sacred, the supremacy of Prussia in Germany—Prussia, the State whose strength was in her soldiers ; Prussia, stronghold and birthplace of the Lutheran religion, of co-ordinated labour, of loyalty and discipline, and all the solid virtues which go with the maintenance of cleanliness and comfort, of honest work and kindness. For such an end he knew no scruples as to the means. To it he devoted his genius with a thoroughness that stuck at nothing. The strength of Prussia lying in her army, his whole object was so to alternate his supreme qualities of ruthlessness and finesse in his dealings with his neighbours that at the chosen moment his army could strike at his weakest or his strongest neighbour with the same deadly certainty as when a cobra coils and springs upon a rabbit.

Poland gave him the first opportunity to show his powers. While Austria, France, and England combined to irritate the Czar, Bismarck sent his lieutenant Alversleben to St. Petersburg to arrive at an undertaking with Gortschakoff. The result was that while Poland was left perforce to the tender mercies of the Czar—who in his interview with Napoleon III could not conceal his irritation on the subject—Bismarck made friends with the huge embattled power which hung on his Eastern horizon. He was thus left free to give his patriotism full play elsewhere.

Almost immediately, the death of Frederick VII of Denmark invited his attention to possibilities in Schleswig-Holstein. There was a movement in the Duchies to free themselves from Danish control and assume independence under the sovereignty of the Prince of Augustenburg. The idea, of course, appealed to the French Emperor. " I believe," he wrote to the Prince on 3rd January, 1864, " there is no greater honour than to be the representative of a cause based upon the independence and the nationality of a people ; and in this regard you can rely on my sympathy : for my conduct will always follow a certain line. If I have fought for the independence of Italy, if I have raised my voice for the national cause in Poland, I cannot in Germany have other sentiments, nor obey other principles." [1]

But in reality there was no real question of making the Prince of Augustenburg an independent sovereign. Bismarck was afterwards to boast that his aim was to annex the Duchies himself: in his way towards that stood the qualms of his King, for William was an honourable man. He was at the head of a great army, but neither he nor his people thought of using it for unjust wars. Bismarck had therefore brought forward Augustenburg as he might hitch an ox to a steam plough to pull it over rough ground: but once the plough ran itself, he unhitched the ox.[2] He had now drawn in Austria, who came forward with Prussia as champion of German nationalism. They declared war on Denmark together.

Palmerston, then in charge of the Foreign Office, realized that the danger to Europe was great. The Prince of Wales had just married a Danish bride, and he was already suspicious of Prussian ambition. His mother's sympathies were drawn by her daughter's marriage and her husband's memory on to the Prussian side. "My heart and sympathies are all German," she wrote.[3] Palmerston made an impulsive and characteristic gesture in favour of war, and hurried over an inquiry as to whether the Emperor would act with him: an inquiry pressed home by Morny.

Napoleon's answer was that he could not run the risk of war with Germany in order to save half a province for the King of Denmark. Morny suggested that from a war against Prussia, it might be possible to pluck a solid advantage, but the Emperor's answer was:—

[1] *Archives diplomatiques*, 1864, i, 135.
[2] Ernst Vogt: *Die Hessische Politik*, p. 212.
[3] *Letters of Queen Victoria*, Second Series, i.

THE QUESTION OF THE MAP 259

"I am satisfied with what I have, I do not want more. Nor does France. She prefers peace and tranquility to an increase of territory."[1] "If I engage in war," so four months before he had expressed himself to Cowley, "one of two things must happen. It must be successful or the reverse. If successful, France will not be satisfied to have squandered men and money for the maintenance of Denmark. She will want something substantial for herself." And that he knew was the last thing that England wanted: a France wider or more secure. "But if I am beaten," concluded the Emperor, "who will come to my assistance or even pity me?"[2]

In his heart of hearts, he still believed that the cause of that vague fascinating thing, Liberalism, was the strength of Prussia. "Prussia's influence," was Bismarck's comment, "rests upon her army."[3]

The following year, the great Prussian Minister boasted to the Austrian Beust, with the candour peculiar to him, how he had set to work. He had offered the Danes conditions which he knew that they could not possibly accept. At the same time he had encouraged them towards war by sending secret agents who gulled them with hopes of assistance from England. But he knew that England could not fight, for he had already felt assured that the Emperor could not take up arms in favour of Denmark.

As to Austria, and the cleverness of her policy, Bismarck merely smiled.[4] He had as yet only begun to set to work. But enough has been said to show that

---

[1] *Cowley Papers*: Cowley to Russell, 13th June, 1864.
[2] *Cowley Papers*: Cowley to Russell, 23rd February, 1864.
[3] Oncken: *Rheinpolitik*, pp. 17–21.
[4] Ernst Vogt: *Die Hessische Politik*, p. 212 ff. This is quoted in L. D. Steefel's masterful work, *The Schleswig Holstein Question*, which states the evidence available in all the archives, and leads to the inevitable pertinent conclusions.

Prussia had now at her head a giant and concrete brain, intent on one great object, that of unifying the countless States of Germany under the hegemony of Prussia. Such a power, so united, could not but be a danger to France. The conquest of Schleswig-Holstein was but a beginning : but for the Emperor it was the beginning of the end. Of that he guessed nothing. In the one place where the protection of small nations and independent peoples would have saved him, he held back in the end from applying his darling principle. And so in the very instance where foresight was vital to the sovereign of France, the Father of Lights withheld it from him.

This mistake, which was to be made more fatal by another and a greater one made three years later, was not all the Emperor's. The persons who are most to blame were Queen Victoria's Prime Minister and Rechberg at Vienna. Lord Russell (for Lord John had just been made an Earl) had refused the Congress before the Danish question arose, and had withheld in this new crisis the help he should have given to one whom he had no real cause to distrust. " England wishes to forget that the Emperor has been her faithful ally," so wrote the Queen of Holland to Lord Clarendon, " that he helped her in the Trent affair, that he fed your people in the Commercial Treaty.

" You answer him with scorn. You deeply move and insult public feeling in France, always ready to turn against you ; and your present proposal of conferences in the Danish question proves the ultimate necessity of settling the disturbed state of Europe. The Germans are wrong in their violent pretensions ; but it is no easy matter to make a *people* who wish to become a *nation* understand that whatever they claim or urge is wrong and folly.

"If the Congress had been a Tower of Babel, at least it would have taught lurking democracy the sincere desire of the governments to do something to settle claims and wrongs which are growing daily more clamorous." [1]

Such was the judgment of Queen Sophia, and it was a sane one. It is an apt reminder how difficult it is to pass judgment on the policy of Napoleon III, and how seldom even after his health began to fail he was responsible for what almost all have combined to despise as his mistakes.

5

It is true, nevertheless, that the Emperor's conviction that he was in Europe to be the agent of its perfected federation : the weakening of his system through uric poison : the clouding and drugging of his mind through his incessant smoking of cigarettes : and above all his increasing belief in Liberalism, made him a man of straw as against the audacity, the ruses, and the self-control of Prussia's patriot. For to canker all, Napoleon, though he could not but feel the force, and therefore the menace of the Prussian's ambition, believed that the man of the age belonged to times gone by.

"Bismarck, like Cavour," he said to Metternich, "is a most interesting man. He has not the Liberal and revolutionary movement behind him, and so probably will lack the power to accomplish great things. Happily, he cannot control the devices which Cavour put to such effective use : for, if he could, we should long since have had to busy ourselves with the fire that he has lit on the hearth of Germany." [2]

That was in 1865. The truth was that the Emperor

[1] Maxwell : *Lord Clarendon*, ii, 286.
[2] Salomon : *Ambassade de Richard Metternich*, p. 113.

was so busy with his hounds in the long hunt of years that he did not see the ditch being dug on the other side of the hedge which he thought he could take so easily. And, besides, he had just obtained two trusty mounts—or so he thought. Those mounts were M. Rouher and Julius Cæsar.

6

Eugene Rouher was born at Riom in the Auvergne in 1814. He was thus a year older than Bismarck. He had early caught the attention of Morny by his immense capacity for work and the ease with which he could see all sides of a question. The Emperor had drawn to him over the railways and the roads. To his efficiency he added a warm and expansive nature. Largely built, with a tendency towards stoutness which gave him, as he grew older, the paunch of Falstaff, he never looked distinguished. But at the same time, in spite of the remains of a provincial accent, he could speak impressively, and there was in his flowing speech something so genial that his adversaries did not at first notice that he had neglected to give any precise answer to the questions which they had pressed hardest.[1]

At first his task was easy. It was summed up in a parody of Chateaubriand :—

> *Alors je n'avais qu'à paraître*
> *A la tribune, pour soumettre*
> *La chambre, qui, folle de moi,*
>   *Son maître,*
> *Votait, sans demander pourquoi,*
>   *Ma loi.*[2]

In him, according to Michel Chevalier, the Empire

---
[1] Maupas : *Mémoires*, ii, 217.
[2] Petit Homme Rouge : *The Court of the Tuileries*, p. 389.

found a barrister to plead its cause, not a statesman to direct it.[1]

But by degrees, Rouher lost the public confidence. He combined with the imperiousness of a strong ruler an almost servile attitude in the Court. He sought not to advise the Emperor but to flatter him, and studied his master's tastes with the same care as he sought to pick the fruit of occasion in his political policy. If Napoleon was anxious, Rouher always found a means to calm and reassure him. He played in fact, according to Maupas, the part of the doctor, who, by tactful words and a cheerful demeanour at the bedside, succeeds in hiding from the patient the gravity of a disease which is hurrying him to the grave.[2]

So the gifted and busy Rouher was, in spite of his loyalty to his master, a fatal servant. The very success which first greeted his playing for popularity was the cause of his later failure. For he lived for the hour. The skill with which he seized opportunities cheated him of the statesman's instinct of working on stable principles to gain an end which years endorse. And he began to lose power as an orator as he got the reputation of being a pleader for bad causes.[3] The parodist now sketched a different picture of Rouher's adventures in the Palais Bourbon :—

> Aujourd'hui la Chambre indocile,
> A ma voix n'est plus si facile ;
> Son dévouement, par contre-coup,
>   Vacille.
> Je n'en viens presque plus du tout
>   A bout.[4]

[1] M. Chevalier : *Journal Intime.*
[2] *Mémoires,* ii, 218.
[3] Du Barail : *Mémoires,* iii, 109.
[4] Petit Homme Rouge, loc. cit.

Rouher's fatal error, as we shall see, was to fall under the spell of Bismarck. Matched with that giant force, the brain in the great head above his swelling body was a pigmy's.

Meanwhile the Emperor looked back to Cæsar for defence and inspiration. It was a long way to look. But as early as 1861, he had begun to look back on the founder of the Imperial dynasty of Rome as one who offered him inspiration, and claimed his allegiance. His *Life of Cæsar*, written, mostly by himself, but with the help of scholars, was to be the offering of his reign to classic learning : and to it he dedicated the surplus of his energies.

The enterprise was hardly worth his while. Few men of learning praised this book. It furnished Sainte Beuve, as we have seen, with an occasion for a piercing criticism of Napoleon III, the most piercing ever made. His chief aid was a young German scholar, Froehner, who has left us a record of his patron's generosity, perseverance, and evenness of temper. He found the Emperor a man who loved a joke, and an amusing story, and who wore beneath his shirt front not a corslet of mail, but underclothes of pink silk.[1] And his picture of the scholar beside the lamp is an interesting, a piquant contrast to those left by others of the man in the three-cornered hat and hunting dress of the time of Louis XIV burning his spirit lamp to heat a cordial in the woods [2] : or of the Prince de Chimay coming from a November excursion in the forest of Fontainebleau to tell his children how he had seen the Emperor leave his uniformed suite to play hide and seek in the hole of a tree.[3] For the Emperor did not spend by any

[1] *Revue des Deux Mondes*, 1st April, 1931.
[2] Madame Octave Feuillet : *Quelques Années de ma Vie*.
[3] *Revue de Paris*, 15th February, 1933.

means all of his time in discussions with Ministers, in managing Ambassadors, or in courtesies to Kings and Queens. His study was ever open to the inventor. And his old friends kept returning to him, and being welcomed to the stateliest functions of the Tuileries with the ease and distinction of their perfect host. Conneau, Madame Cornu, Thélin : the people of Arenenberg : the people of Ham : the friends of London. These were always sure of welcome and attention in the Court of Paris ; to its splendours they had the entrée. There they saw as many as four thousand courtiers dance in the presence of their Majesties, in the brilliant light of the chandeliers which bathed the scene in a Turneresque haze, and through it moved white shoulders, fluttering gauzes, diamonds, stars, uniforms embroidered in gold, Court dresses of violet, stockings of black silk, embroideries, crinolines : the actors in this scene were men who had their names famous and women who were the most beautiful of their time. It was on such a scene as this that inner doors would open, and a chamberlain cry " *L'Empereur* ". Then the scene was all reverences, answered by the famous curtsy of the Empress, who to one after another as they were brought forward would address her gracious words.

" You will tell me the name of your dressmaker," said Her Majesty to one young lady being presented.

" Madame, it is a man : an Englishman."

" Ah ! And his name ? "

" Worth, Madame. He has just come to Paris."

" As for her," so the narrative proceeds, " that evening she was a goddess descended from Olympus : she wore a robe of white tulle sown with knots of black velvet attached by diamond buckles. On her head was an aigrette of diamonds : on her superb

neck sparkled all the diamonds of the crown. . . .
One would have said it was a King's daughter issuing
from a palace of the Arabian Nights, and bringing
in her train all the marvels of Babylon." [1]

7

This was she whom once the Emperor had pursued
with such impassioned ardour, and to whom throughout his life he offered his courtesies, his service, and
his respect. "He yields to her in all," [2] so said the
Queen of Holland in 1867. Her tone to him became
almost that of a mistress to her pupil; but Emperor
and Empress were no longer united by the central
realities of marriage. In 1864 her feeling was disgust
when the object of his attentions was Marguerite
Bellanger, whom he had found no one knew where,
a vulgar woman, who was, as Lord Clarendon
guessed, a coquine.[3] It was with this woman that he
went to Algeria in the following year. And in his
absence Eugénie was again regent. "As one saw her
during her first Regency," wrote Madame Baroche
during her second in 1865, "so she appears again
to-day, mastering all discussions by the loftiness of
her views, by her knowledge of men and things,
by the ease of her language, astonishing even those
who before they saw her at work set the highest
value on her political capacities. No one can deny
that she grows greater according as the responsibilities
of her position become heavier." [4]

[1] *Revue des Deux Mondes*, 15th January, 1933, quoting and slightly altering Madame Octave Feuillet: *Quelques Années de ma Vie*, p. 207.
[2] Maxwell: *Lord Clarendon*, 4th November, 1867.
[3] F. Wellesley: *Paris Embassy*.
[4] Baroche: *Notes et Souvenirs*, pp. 281, 282.

THE EMPRESS EUGÉNIE
From the bust by Carpeaux at Malmaison.

"A King's daughter issuing from a palace of the Arabian Nights and bringing in her train all the marvels of Babylon."

So it was that she was able to cope with Prince Napoleon, who during the Emperor's absence, made a sensational speech at Ajaccio.

But with all her gifts, she could make great errors of judgment: already she had initiated with the Emperor the one fatal venture of her politics, one which was not forgotten, though some thought it the greatest idea of the reign.

XIII

THE NEW WORLD

The statesmen of the past would no more have thought of altering the fundamental social and moral relations than of interfering with the course of the seasons. But on the contrary the change which is taking place in the modern world leaves no aspect of moral or social life unaffected. Civilization is being uprooted from its foundations in nature and tradition and is being reconstituted in a new organization which is as artificial and mechanical as a modern factory.

In Western Europe, however, the traditions of the older culture, although greatly weakened, are still strong enough to prevent the full development of the process. It is in the outlying territories of our civilization, in Russia on the one hand, and in North America on the other, that its success can be most easily studied. In Russia the change is being carried through consciously and deliberately by the power of the government in the face of the passive resistance of a society which still rests largely on the foundations of a primitive peasant culture. In America, on the other hand, it is the unfettered development of the new economic forces which has produced the change, and public opinion and social authority still attempt to preserve as far as possible the rural and social traditions of the older culture. But in spite of this important difference, there is a curious similarity between the two societies. In both cases there is the same cult of the machine, and the same tendency to subordinate every other side of life to economic activity. In both the individual is subjected to a ruthless pressure which produces a standardized type of mass civilization. And finally we see, in both societies, the breaking down of the family as a fixed social unit.

CHRISTOPHER DAWSON : *Christianity and Sex.*

I

THE more we know of the Modern Napoleon, the more clearly we see how the Europe of to-day is preoccupied with just those internal problems which occupied his scheming. But even in the wrench and grind of running, while they are still badly adjusted, the devices which were so dear to his inventive mind, Europe is disturbed and harassed by threatening outgrowths from its civilization, which threaten not only its ideals but its means of life. One of these is, of course, Russia. Now, as then, it is a country where liberty is unknown, where power is absolute, and a bureaucracy is all. Then, as now, it was a country which was feared by European civilization as a whole, which looked without sympathy on the individual freedom and enterprise of the English-speaking world, which shared no centre with the Catholic countries, and which found its one possible opportunity in Prussia. Over the noon of Liberalism in Europe, Russia hung already like a thunder-cloud.

There were some who discerned on the other side of their Continent another threat to the ways of life which were as dear to them almost as life itself. The United States of North America had been sweeping over their continent since the days when Louis Napoleon was among them. In 1848 and 1853, they had taken over great tracts, each as large as France itself, from Mexico. Their tone was already boisterous, sometimes aggressive. Even when among them, Louis Napoleon had felt misgivings with regard to their temper. It is possible that he sensed that their tendencies already menaced both authority and family life through adapting their social institutions to the impulses of sex as an end in themselves. That tendency, which can be traced back to the encyclopædists, Diderot and La Mettrie, is now strong everywhere : in North America and in Russia, however, it undermines the social system of Christendom. In each country, a systematized industrial organization has overborne the great humanist tradition and left the State without either religion or the graciousness of consecrated leisure. But if Napoleon III felt this, he felt it dimly. What he definitely wrote of the United States was that their aims and tendencies were too materialistic : and that the mob menaced individual freedom. Moreover, he had a strong notion that Catholic civilization had also its part to play in the New World : and this sentiment was supported by the Empress Eugénie's fire and energy. Impulsive, ambitious, excitable, and zealous for both authority and reform, she had felt from the beginning that she was to use her great position to do some signal service to Spain. " The ardent love," wrote Hübner, " which the Empress has kept for the country which gave her birth, is equalled by her hatred for the nation which threatens to rob the Crown of Spain of its finest jewel. ' Europe,' she said, ' must form a league against the United States.' " [1]

It was as early as 1857 that the first of an active body of Conservatives from Mexico had begun to persuade her to champion their cause. Hers for seven years was the motive power which steadily influenced the French Government in the noble but quixotic project of giving Mexico what the Second Empire had given to France, a Liberal and Progressive centre of stable government. To these fevered and forceful counsels, the Emperor gave a willing ear. He had long been interested in Central America : it appeared to him the most gratifying extension of his reorganizing influence, and gradually the complex possibilities of the scheme twisted like the branches of a tropic creeper among the tortuous growths and branches of his mind, and mingled, unobtrusively but inextricably, with his irresistible inclination towards conspiracy.

[1] V.N.A., Hübner to Buol, 20th November, 1853.

NAPOLEON III ON THE TERRACE OF THE VILLA EUGÉNIE
From a contemporary painting. By courtesy of Dr. Mercier des Rochettes.

" He had an irresistible inclination towards conspiracy."

2

At first he saw no opening. But it was always his habit to wait and see. His chief obstacle was the Monroe doctrine. The Government at Washington had long since determined that, though it might not be able to force Canada out of the British Empire, no other European power should enter the Americas to dispute with the States of the North their hegemony of the two continents. Furthermore, the tendency of the United States fought hard against all that was either Catholic or Conservative: and they had watched with great impatience an attempt at imperial government in Mexico.

That attempt had broken down long since. The Church was corrupt; the prelates avaricious; and there was a strong tendency among the lower classes, the classes of Indian blood, to react not only against the Church but against all that remained of the great colonial traditions of Spain. This revolt was headed by a man who had been brought up in such poor circumstances that, at the age of twelve, he knew no Spanish, and could neither read nor write. Born in 1806, Benito Juarez was of unmixed Indian blood. He was endowed with a mind of amazing capacity and energy, a lust for power, and an ambition ruthless to the point of cruelty. His face and figure were both repulsive. He was squat and small: his broad flat head was covered with lank black hair: his coarse Mongolian features were disfigured by a scar which was suffused with blood; his eyes were small and ferrety. His every feature spoke a brutal and sensual force.

Here was the man who was the head of the rebel party, the champion of popular rights, and the darling of Washington.

With the United States behind this man, the Emperor of the French could do nothing in Mexico. But in 1861, it will be remembered, the United States began a civil war; and in the meantime, the Emperor of the French had found the man whom he wanted to make Emperor in Mexico. Brother of the Austrian Emperor, he would be a means to cement peace with Vienna. And he had married a beautiful Princess, daughter of King Leopold of Belgium, a cousin therefore of the Orleans Princes as well as of the Queen of England.

"There is no need for me," so wrote Napoleon to Flahault, who was then his Ambassador at St. James's, "to enlarge upon the common interest which we in Europe have in seeing Mexico pacified and endowed with a stable government. Not only has that country, which enjoys every natural advantage, attracted much of our capital, and many of our fellow-countrymen, whose existence is subject to continual menace, but, if it were regenerated, it would form an impassable barrier to the encroachments of North America, it would afford an important opening for English, Spanish, and French trade, while exploiting its own wealth, and lastly it would render great service to our manufactures by extending the cultivation of cotton.

"The consideration of its various advantages, as well as the spectacle of one of the finest countries in the world given over to disaster and threatened by impending ruin, such are the motives which have always given me a keen interest in the fate of Mexico." [1]

That the Emperor was extraordinarily interested in Mexico had long been noticed: and men even went so far as to say that the Empress accepted him as a husband only on condition that he would do

[1] Corti: *Maximilian and Charlotte in Mexico*, i, app. 1.

something for the country.[1] That no doubt went further than the truth : but the Empress had always had her ambitions, and was now beginning to take an ever more important rôle in the drama of politics. " She now mixes up," wrote Lord Cowley at the end of 1862, " in every political question that arises." [2]

3

It was not merely Mexico that drew the eyes of the French sovereigns towards the Americas. Their sympathies were with the Southern States at war. The Emperor even hinted that England might join forces with him in active assistance to the South, so strongly did he resent what he called the " overbearing insolence of the United States Government in its days of prosperity ".[3] He wondered that the British Government did not recognize the Southern States as an independent nation.[4] He heard later that New York was continuing her trade with the Southern States, and argued that the Washington Government had no right to interfere with European trade with the South.[5] When he heard that at Washington they were contemplating an invasion of Canada, he determined to ally himself with England.[6] But none the less clearly he had to admit that he could not actively engage on the side of the Confederate armies.

And meanwhile he had launched his scheme in

[1] *Cowley Papers* : Cowley to Russell, 9th December, 1861.
[2] *Cowley Papers* : Cowley to Russell, 2nd December, 1862.
[3] *Cowley Papers* : Cowley to John Russell, 2nd July, 1861.
[4] *Cowley Papers* : Cowley to John Russell, 10th April, 1863.
[5] *Cowley Papers* : Cowley to John Russell, 18th December, 1864.
[6] V.N.A., Metternich's dispatches, 2nd December, 22nd December, 1861.

Mexico. Irritated at the expedition which the Spanish Government had sent there, and above all at the way in which Prim had conducted the campaign—there were many who thought Prim wanted to make himself Emperor of the country he invaded—Napoleon and Eugénie had worked out their plan.

They had sent an expedition to Mexico under Admiral Jurien de la Gravière and Bazaine. The Emperor saw the danger of compromising with Juarez while resistance was organized, and gave orders to his forces to capture Mexico City as soon as possible. Only then, said Napoleon, could one tackle and solve the question of political reorganization.[1] Meanwhile, in spite of violent opposition from the French Government, from the Austrian Court, and from the British Minister in Mexico, Napoleon and Eugénie had persuaded Franz Josef's brother, Maximilian, and his wife, Charlotte (King Leopold's daughter), to accept the Aztec crown; and in May, 1864, the new Emperor and Empress, supported by the army of Bazaine, assumed the government of their wide Empire, an Empire which Maximilian was soon dreaming of extending over the whole of Central America and even to the confines of Colombia and Peru.

The fact was that to rule Mexico itself was far beyond his powers. A more gracious and intelligent prince seldom reigned : but what alone could have brought a calm to Mexico was not high ideals, finely applied. It was the strong hand employed ruthlessly in a thorough system of efficiency. The genius, the resource, the centuries of patience, the trained army, the tireless police, the powerful administrators,

[1] Quai d'Orsay (Mexico) : Thouvenel to Jurien, 21st February, 1862.

the firm tax-collectors with which England consolidated her Indian Empire — Maximilian could command none of these. In a short time, he found that his financial resources were exhausted. He had difficulties with Bazaine. And before many months the French Emperor saw that the great scheme launched by him and his Empress was not going well. He was justly irritated by the demand for a further loan which he knew it would be by that time imprudent even to suggest. And he began to realize that Maximilian's talents, fine as they were, were not equal to the task. The Emperor of Mexico was, in short, a disappointment to the Emperor of the French, and even between the Empresses some rather acrid letters passed.

Painful scenes were to follow : but in 1865, Maximilian's reign in Mexico was manifestly doomed. It was not only that he was harassed by a lack of money and by the ineffectiveness of Bazaine's army. He had now to fear American intervention, because the Civil War had come to an end. Lincoln was assassinated, but with the experienced and chauvinistic Seward as Secretary of State and Andrew Johnson as President, there was no question of Washington forgetting the Monroe doctrine.

4

Johnson like Juarez had risen from the lowest class. At the age of twenty he could neither read nor write. It was in fact his wife who taught him to do so. A tailor in Tennessee, he owed his rise to the fact that he had been a Federal in a Confederate State. When Tennessee was reconquered, he had been sent there as military governor to enforce the wishes of the North.[1] He was a heavy drinker. And when

[1] Quai d'Orsay : Geoffroy to Drouyn, 17th April, 1865.

he was elected Vice-President, his official address of thanks had been so contemptible that it was thought more charitable to state that his condition was such that he could not make a speech.[1] Such a man was a natural ally of Juarez, and it was natural also that the Federal soldiers, finding their own war at an end, should be ready to join Juarez's armed bands in Mexico.

Napoleon III had made to Washington protestations of friendship as profuse and as emphatic as the most exacting could require. He had sent over as Minister the Marquis de Montholon, the grandson of the writer of the famous *Memorial of St. Helena*. In vain Montholon at once observed that in the *Washington Chronicle*, which was almost an official organ, the references to France were less than courteous.[2] Seward reinforced this impression by a definite protest against the Mexican monarchy.[3] In the autumn Johnson appointed his personal friend, General Logan, to represent Washington in Mexico. It was to Juarez that Logan was ordered to present his credentials.[4]

Montholon had already seen that, for France and for Mexico, the attitude of Washington was definitely menacing. He argued that Paris must make her definite choice in the dilemma. She must either speak firmly to Washington, pointing out that Europe as a whole had recognized Maximilian and that Europe as a whole had acted against Juarez because he deliberately cheated in the matter of the loan, or

---

[1] *New York Herald*, 6th March, 1865.
[2] Quai d'Orsay : Montholon to Drouyn.
[3] Quai d'Orsay : Montholon to Drouyn, 6th September, 1865.
[4] Quai d'Orsay : Montholon to Drouyn, 20th November, 1865.

else, said Montholon, Paris must make up her mind not to irritate American opinion.[1]

Meanwhile Leopold had written to Eugénie that, the Civil War in the now reunited States being over, there was no time to lose.[2] Misled by Monarchist agents who had long lost touch with the country, they had fatally under-estimated the power and influence of Juarez. He could have been overcome only by a chain of powerful garrisons, with a field army much stronger than France could have sent out of Europe. The task which had been given to Bazaine was in fact beyond his power.

Even in his attitude towards the Americas, therefore, Napoleon was taking his prophetic place in history. " It is the great fault of the Emperor," wrote Lord Cowley, " that when he wants to do something, he will not believe that all the difficulties cannot be made to vanish." [3] The task he essayed in Mexico proved a failure—how tragic we shall see. But in his resentment at the overbearing attitude of the United States towards France, in his fear of their financial domination over Spanish America, and in his distrust of their material civilization, he resembled the France of to-day, whose reactions are so trenchantly expressed by M. Duhamel in his *Scènes de la Vie Future*. Between the ideals of British America and Spanish America, there is now conflict and not adjustment. And if it had been possible for the Modern Napoleon to have successfully intervened in the Americas, it would have saved as much trouble as if the system of the First Napoleon had taken root in Spain. An

---

[1] Quai d'Orsay (Etats Unis) : Montholon to Drouyn, 8th August, 1865.
[2] Duke of Alba's Archives : Leopold to Eugénie, 1865. Cf. R. Sencourt : *Empress Eugénie*, p. 189, n. 3.
[3] *Cowley Papers* : Cowley to Clarendon, 1st December, 1865.

English-speaking country was as hostile to that adjustment in Mexico in the sixties as England had been to a similar adjustment in Spain itself fifty years earlier. In each case the speakers of English defeated their Napoleon : in each case that defeat set back the clock of history.

XIV

THE MENACE OF DISASTER

> These quicksands, Lepidus,
> Keep off them, for you sink.
> *Antony and Cleopatra*, ii, 7.

I

" THINGS will be in a fine mess when Lord Palmerston can no longer go and sleep at the House of Commons." [1] That was Merimée's idea when he was in England in the summer of 1865. The old man was already eighty-one, and weakening daily. " His health is excellent, in fact," said Lady Palmerston, " but I don't know what's the matter." [2] Others wondered what was the matter with Queen Victoria : some said she was going mad. Albert was gone four years, and now, with " Old Pilgerstein ", King Leopold was going too ; and before the end of the year Napoleon saw that, of his chief supporters in the Mexican scheme, not one was left.

For Morny too had died. That consummate man of affairs, who had with so much judgment and success supported the throne of the half-brother whom he had placed upon it, had worn himself out before his time. Not one of the devices at the command of his speculative genius, not all the pills of Dr. Joliffe could save him. He had died at the beginning of March, and they had emptied his brains out of his skull and weighed them on the scales. His lovely Russian wife had cut off her curls to lay them with the body that had embraced hers, and it was noticed how, as the flakes of snow fell on the coffin, she had stretched over it, and covered it with her velvet

[1] Merimée : Unpublished Letters.
[2] Ibid.

cloak. The light of her life had gone out; but in time she found consolation, marrying that very Duke of Sesto to whom the Empress Eugénie had offered years of chaste devotion. The Emperor, however, found no one to replace Morny. Count Walewski could not do so, and he, too, was soon to die. Prince Napoleon, never a strong support, had on 15th May at Ajaccio made a speech so violently Republican and anti-clerical that the Emperor had had to compel him to resign.

A new force in Europe, the force of Bismarck, invaded the French Court in its retreat at Biarritz. The affair of Denmark had been settled, but Bismarck had inserted in the Austro-Prussian Alliance certain clauses which the Austrians might find irritating. " There are some dogs," he said, " who remain quiet and inoffensive as long as they are free. You need only put a chain on them to make them bark and snarl."[1] He dared not provoke Austria, however, unless he thought that he was safe on Prussia's western frontier. In October of 1865, he came, as he had come already in 1862, to Gascony, and breathed once more the golden autumn air. That last visit had been a failure. " *M. de Bismarck,*" Drouyn de Lhuys had said, " *est venu m'offrir tout ce que ne lui appartient pas.*"[2] But the patriot who knew no scruple shrewdly guessed that, if he sounded Napoleon III a little more delicately, he would not be too late to reap the harvest of occasion.

When Bismarck returned to Biarritz, October was already ending. The air was sharp, and there was no one on the sand. His gigantic figure with the great head, the protruding eyes, was seen walking in sight of the waves and seaweed, sometimes with Prince

---

[1] G. Rothan : *Politique française en '66*, p. 33.
[2] G. Rothan, op. cit., p. 42.

Orloff, sometimes alone, and thoughtful : in the Villa Eugénie, his sarcasms delighted the wits, and his gallantries made such an impression on the ladies that one evening they carved out his silhouette and placed it in the bed of Madame Latour-Maubourg as a little surprise for her when she went to her room.[1] While the Court amused itself with such games as these, the Emperor busied himself once more with his project of draining and settling the Landes, but his grip on affairs was loosening. After seven years of kidney trouble, his violent amours with a vulgar woman had failed to provide a cordial for his poisoned blood. Affairs were becoming too difficult for him : he was growing tired of administration : tired of men : tired even of conspiracy.[2] He was becoming what Bismarck called " a great unrecognized incapacity ".

So when Bismarck was received by him at Biarritz, he was totally incapable of dealing with a conspirator whom at the best of times he must have found much abler than himself at his own game. Many ideas they shared. It is significant that one of the things which he pressed hardest on Bismarck was that the great Powers should combine to prevent the spread of cholera, and other infectious diseases in Europe, and act in concert to preserve the Continent from dangers attendant on the pilgrimage to Mecca. But what Bismarck had first assured his King was that the Emperor was full of sympathy with Prussia —and that of all countries in Europe those of Prussia and France were the most interdependent. Bismarck admitted that he had gone a step further : he had developed the thesis that the strengthening of Prussia's power in Schleswig-Holstein demanded French sympathy : because with that sympathy, Prussia

---

[1] Barthez : *La Famille Impériale*, pp. 258-9.
[2] G. Rothan, op. cit.

would grow in friendship to France. Without it, Prussia would be forced to seek for defensive alliances elsewhere.¹

Such was the account which Bismarck, as Chancellor, sent to his King. And it has long been asked if Napoleon would have accepted it as correct. We are now, through the private correspondence of Lord Cowley, able to throw further light on this great crisis in French history.

" Bismarck's object," said the Emperor, " seemed to be to ascertain what France would do in the event of the Duchies (of Schleswig-Holstein) being absorbed by Prussia, and if a war between Prussia and Austria ensued. Napoleon gave Bismarck to understand that such a *dénouement* would not be pleasing to the French nation, and that, if war were to be the consequence of it, his desire would be to observe strict neutrality. His abstention from war in defence of Bismarck was not to be considered approval of the proceedings of Germany, but a dislike to involve France in hostilities which in that case would have become general. With regard to the Rhine provinces he had no wish or intention of disturbing their present position." This account of the conversation was endorsed by the Prussian Minister.²

It is not difficult to follow the course of the conversation or of Bismarck's conclusions from it. Behind his earnest eyes, his Bible-reading, his flashing phrases, and his roar of a laugh, he wanted really to know only one thing : would he be safe in attacking Austria in the following summer ? Napoleon, whose trustfulness too often weakened his judgment,³ and

¹ Oncken : *Rheinpolitik*, ii, 72, 73. This was first published in Sybel : *Begründung des Reichs*, iv, 215-224.
² *Cowley Papers* : Cowley to Clarendon, 2nd December, 1865.
³ Persigny : *Mémoires*, p. 345.

who believed, as we have seen, that Bismarck was too conservative to be one of the powers of the age, had given him an answer which showed him that the road up the Elbe was clear. From that moment France and her Empire were on the edge of doom : though, even so, there was still an opportunity to draw back.

2

Until the end of the spring of 1866, men still hoped for peace : and among the shrewd observers who were sure of it was the British Ambassador in Paris. What Napoleon believed was that Austria was the stronger, and that he need not prepare his army. " The fact is "—such is the crushing indictment of Lord Cowley—" that he originally encouraged the quarrel between Austria and Prussia and made Italy join the latter in the hope that they would all be weakened and leave him strong." [1] This was his fatal mistake. So he threw away his last chance. So he slid over the edge of the cliff.

Bismarck, confident in the Prussian Army and its needle-gun, pursued his ruthless plan. " Not a day passes," wrote the Crown Princess in Berlin, " that the wicked man does not with the greatest ability counteract and thwart what is good, and drive on towards war, turning and twisting everything to his own purpose . . . and the King, in spite of all his reluctance, gets more and more entangled without perceiving it." [2] Napoleon III had his faults and his abilities. Bismarck had like faults and like abilities, developed infinitely further. Goethe has said that, " The great man is he who knows how to seize

[1] *Lady Burghclere's Papers* : Lord Cowley to Lady Derby, 12th October, 1871. But it must not be forgotten that Lord Cowley himself advised neutrality.
[2] *Letters of Empress Frederick*, p. 59.

his opportunity."[1] Bismarck by these standards can be measured. Not only did he seize his opportunities: he had made a fine art of manufacturing them. And furthermore he had introduced a new artifice into diplomacy. It was to say quite loudly what he intended to do, and so awaken the ambitions of those who otherwise would have been bound to foil his plots. He was one of those talkers whom it is a joy to meet. A sneer, a sarcasm so pointed as to be repeated everywhere, would give a new turn to all the projects and prejudices of nations, and then echo through Europe like the warning of a prophet. In his strange mixture of finesse with brutality, of religion with unscrupulousness, of patriotism with treachery, of fascination with ugliness, of ruthlessness with nervous sensibility, of downright Lutheranism with what is called Jesuitry, he, like a fierce and masterly caricature of Napoleon III, was pursuing the treacherous policy which he had already conceived when he persuaded Rechberg to make Austria his ally: the policy of making Austria frantic the moment he was ready to seize for himself what he shared with her as the result of this alliance.

Before 1866, it was the fond idea of both Paris and Vienna that they were defending Southern Germany against Prussia. The course of affairs at the Diet of Frankfurt might well have encouraged both in this idea. It was Prussia, and above all the Prussia of Bismarck, which the other States of Germany then regarded as their danger. It was naturally to Vienna that the Catholics looked for help. "But the truth," said *The Times*, "is that Austria is not Germany and will not be Germany. She will not allow Prussia to be Germany—why should she, of course?—or even Germany to be

[1] Rothan, op. cit., p. 42.

Germany. She wishes to divide and reign by dividing : Prussia to unite, and reign by that unity." That was the fact which Bismarck understood, with such a searchlight power of mind and will that it makes his countrymen still blind to all his faults. " It is an old saying," went on *The Times*, " that an army of sheep commanded by a lion will beat an army of lions commanded by a sheep. It is an army of sheep that Prussia is addressing, and she must prove herself a lion, an animal that sees far, decides quickly, can make a terrible spring and, when once it grasps, never leaves hold."

It was Bismarck rather than Prussia which was the lion. He declared war with Austria on 19th June. " I consider the war a mistake," wrote the shrewd Crown Princess, " caused by the uncontrolled powers of an unprincipled man." [1] But however wrong, the Germans quickly conquered. The campaign was already decided on 3rd July, at the villages of Königgrätz and Sadowa, by one of the most fateful battles in history.

We have seen why there had not long been an alliance between Paris and Vienna. It was because the gullible Rechberg, with his blind trust in Bismarck, had turned with scorn from the shrewd proposals of Napoleon and Eugénie. In those fateful days of this short war, the Empress fought desperately to carry her project through.[2] But it was now too late. Behind her was a failure in Mexico, and the Emperor could not rely on carrying France with him. He had gone wrong in all his calculations. He could not

[1] *Empress Frederick's Letters*, p. 64.
[2] The fearful drama of the scenes in the councils and Eugénie's proposal that she should force the Emperor to abdicate and assume the regency, the author has told already in the *Empress Eugénie*.

mobilize in less than two months, and Reuss came with a warning from Bismarck that any attempt at mobilization would be answered with an immediate declaration of war. He had been convinced that Austria was the stronger, and that, at the last moment, he could intervene as conqueror, winning Venice for Italy, and supremacy for France while Austria regained Silesia.[1] " What the Emperor really wants," wrote Lord Cowley before the war began, " is the settlement of the Venetian question. He feels that, if it is not settled before his death, he leaves his son seated, as he himself expresses it, on a barrel of gunpowder, and he is determined, or I am much mistaken, that it shall be settled now." [2]

Venice, indeed, he got, and Paris celebrated the armistice as a victory. But in the evening of the day chosen for this festival, a storm changed the triumphal banners into sodden rags. And a terrible presentiment fell upon the heart of the wretched man, who, tortured and paralysed by the pain and poison in his bladder, had seen the Empress Charlotte become a raving lunatic in his very presence, because she thought he had betrayed her when he, with the fateful message of Reuss fresh in his ears, was powerless to give more help.[3] Then, as he listened to her, the tears had run down his cheeks. Now, in the moment when through his own official journal he had been declared the arbiter of Europe, he saw the spectre

[1] *Cowley Papers* : Cowley to Clarendon, 4th June, 1866.
[2] *Cowley Papers* : Cowley to Clarendon, 7th May, 1866.
[3] Record Office : Cowley to Stanley, 12th July, 1866. Prince Metternich wanted him to place an army of observation on the Prussian frontier, but His Majesty felt that flushed with their successes, proud of their army, and driven on by popular excitement, the Prussian Government might demand explanations, which might lead to irritating discussions and eventually to war.

of his doom advance and stare him in the face. "Never," wrote Prince Metternich, "since I have known the Emperor, have I seen him so utterly prostrate. Fallen from the high position in which the declaration in the *Moniteur* had placed him, the reaction which the Emperor has suffered is quite extraordinary. The ravings and stormings of Prince Napoleon, the news of an Italian attack on Borgoforte, the sorrows of the Minister of War who declares that nothing is ready, in fact the consciousness of the immense responsibility which the honour of the nation imposes on him—all burst upon him in the evening of the day before yesterday, while the towns and faubourgs were glorifying his triumph." [1]

For he had declared to the British Ambassador that there was only one thing which could induce him to abandon this reality, and that was the supremacy of either Austria or Prussia demanding the complete control of Southern Germany. Bismarck, whose genius never blazed more brightly than in the discreet advantage he took of his victories, contented himself for the present with consolidating Prussia. Had he gone further, he could not but have infuriated a France that was still powerful; while England, which had made exactly the same fatal error of judgment as Napoleon III, might at once have allied herself with France, as finally the expansion of Prussia did compel her to do. But neither Queen nor Government would support the Prince of Wales's proposals, or the Princess Frederick's warnings, against the power of Bismarck. And Napoleon, who had at last won the support of England in favour of a Congress, found himself face to face with a man who was henceforward secure against the vicissitudes of fate. The Prussian lion had seen far, decided

[1] V.N.A., Metternich to Mensdorff, 7th July, 1866.

quickly, made a terrible spring, grasped, and was never to leave hold.

For years Napoleon, as well as Eugénie, had foreseen that fatal eventuality. It had been his dream to give France a strong natural frontier : that had been the spur that pricked on his ambition for his country. Foreseeing Italian unity not only as a move towards Liberal progress in Europe, but as an inevitable necessity, he had made friends with the future, and established both a claim to gratitude from the new nation, and a frontier which made her, however strong, almost innocuous to France.

He had tried to do the same on the North-East : and Bismarck at Biarritz had promised that he should succeed. At times, Napoleon had thought that as France, at the advent of the first Napoleon, had the Rhine as a frontier, so she should have it again. But that was only one of many ideas which welled up from the depths of his endless cogitations. His policy thoughout had been to help Prussia, as he had helped Italy, to be a great and united nation ; but she was to be a nation fundamentally at peace with France, and from which in all changes of weather, the serenity, the vineyards and harvests, the mines and machinery, the farms and villages of France would be secure. Once free from the will of Cavour, Napoleon's one intention, formally expressed, was " to evade war by every possible means ".[1] In 1860 he had tried to see the Crown Prince of Prussia and to persuade him that the Alpine frontier did not also mean the Rhine. " Unless I were attacked," he said, " I did not want to go beyond my frontiers." [2] " The day when I have

[1] V.N.A., Metternich to Rechberg, underlined, 20th March, 1863.
[2] V.N.A., Metternich to Rechberg, 25th June, 1860.

Savoy and Nice in the South and sufficient fortresses in the North, my mission will be accomplished." [1]

His great object, he insisted to Metternich, was to have such frontiers that he could disarm, and above all that he should not need to maintain an army as large as that of Prussia.[2] And what he maintained to Metternich, he confided with equal consistency to Cowley. It was, said Cowley, as early as 1860 an idea familiar to the Emperor's friends that France should be given a frontier *that would enable her to disarm.* " We must be prepared," wrote the British Ambassador, " for hints given to Prussia that she may extend her territories in the North provided that France obtains compensations on the Rhine." [3] As the Empire became more democratic, the Emperor, who always believed in lowering taxes, was especially anxious to reduce his army, but how could he reduce it if he had a close neighbour which had already made two wars of aggrandisement, and still maintained an army out of all proportion to her population? If Prussia had 600,000 men under arms, how was France to do with less? That was the plain question which the Emperor had to ask himself. The vast increase of armaments which was central in Bismarck's policy had meant a general rivalry in Europe : and the fact that Napoleon III had to face it is yet another reason why we must think of him as a man of to-day.

In spite of Napoleon's capital error of judgment in 1866, his whole policy was pursued with more ability than, since his death, Frenchmen or others have been wont to allow him. It is too often forgotten that, in

---

[1] V.N.A., Metternich to Rechberg, 26th November, 1859.
[2] V.N.A., Metternich to Rechberg, *très secret*, 26th November, 1859. Cf. Maxwell : *Lord Clarendon*, ii, 241.
[3] *Cowley Papers* : Cowley to John Russell, 2nd May, 1860.

two great and critical wars, Italy refrained at critical moments from attacking France and, though she may not be an altogether comfortable neighbour, it is possible to imagine a worse. In any case, the Italian frontier of Napoleon III is almost impregnable. As for the rearrangement of Europe, succeeding years have shown that to be inevitable, and if a Congress had been held when Napoleon III urged, it would have prevented not only three wars, two of them hideous, but would have saved Europe at least many of the anomalies of to-day. For no sooner was Sadowa won than, as England's veteran diplomat insisted, Prussia became a danger not only to France but to England herself. From that moment the events not only of 1870 but of 1914, if not inevitable, were perils to be feared.

As for the struggle of Napoleon III with Prussia, he and Bismarck were both conspirators : and in that domain he was far inferior to Bismarck. But so, it must be confessed, was everyone else, not only in France, but also in Austria, in Russia, and in England. And if, as a conspirator, he was quite outclassed, it is no small credit to him that as a man he was less ambitious, more unselfish, and more honourable. In a word, he really had what Bismarck found in him, a heart that felt for Europe. And, in spite of the Emperor's failure, it is still possible to ask whether in the long run his work will not prove to be the more beneficent of the two. For Bismarck with his mighty genius, and mighty success, had at the base of his religion and his wit such ruthlessness and unscrupulousness as made him of all in history the most outstanding example of Dr. Johnson's famous phrase that patriotism is the last refuge of a scoundrel. He thus undermined at its basis the structure of German unity which has within itself so many dear and precious elements of virtue and of glory. And in later years, he was to show his short-sightedness in attempting to weaken if not to eliminate from this new unity in Germany, the noblest traditions which the people had inherited from the Holy Roman Empire of the German nation. Of such crudities and superficialities no one can accuse Napoleon III.

3

In Paris and Biarritz, in Fontainebleau and Compèigne, in the autumn of 1866, the weak, saddened, sick man, with his head leaning to the right, still rolled his thick form on his short legs with something more than the name and additions of majesty. His grip on his own towns was weakening, but in the country he was still secure. France had not ceased to grow in wealth. The railways and telegraphs were completed, and still the industries of France marched forward. The coal production had increased from 72,257,605 quintals in 1856 to 113,000,000 in 1865.[1] The comfort and prosperity of Paris in the sixties were a splendid contrast to the hunger and unemployment of 1851.[2] The Emperor could claim in 1862 that the telegraph had been completed; that apart from the three milliards of francs spent in completing 6,553 kilometres of railway line, 622 million francs had been given to other works of public utility: the fleet had been transformed, churches and public monuments rebuilt, soldiers and civil servants all had increased pay. And after all the country was happy. "Have you not seen towns change their appearance, and the farms grow rich by the progress of agriculture?" asked the Emperor as he opened the

[1] *The Times*, 13th March, 1866. [2] Mels, *Wilhelmshöhe*.

legislative Session of 1862, " and the exterior trade rise from 2,600,000,000 to 5,800,000,000 ? " Paris, a city transformed, reminded them every day as they drove from the Tuileries, how much had been accomplished. Even in the sphere of foreign policy, there had been much that looked like triumph : the Northern Courts had been divided, the influence of Russia eliminated from Central Europe. Germany and Italy were free, and England had been for thirty years the friend and ally of France.[1]

And now the greatness of France and the splendour of the Empire were to glow with a new and exotic ripeness. Paris was to be the scene of yet another exhibition, which was inaugurated in the summer of 1867. To the intoxicating heterogeneousness of its surprises came Czar and Sultan, the King of Holland, the King of Wurttemberg, the King of Spain, the King of Portugal, the Prince of Wales. In outward seeming the transformed Paris seemed at the zenith of her glory. But even in the royal processions, and the glittering parades, the warnings of disaster rumbled nearer, threatening the time when the lightning would strike merciless upon the city and the throne in which the civilization of the Western world was centred. For, though the King of Prussia came, he insisted on bringing Bismarck with him. Napoleon was furious, but he could not refuse.[2] And even as he drove back from the military parade with the Czar on one side and the Prussian King on the other, a Polish rebel, Berezowski, fired a pistol at the Czar ; and what was worse, the Radicals applauded. It was in vain that the Emperor remarked that the Czar and he had been comrades in arms,

[1] Record Office, London : Cowley to Clarendon, 2nd September, 1866.
[2] *Cowley Papers* : Cowley to Clarendon.

together under fire.[1] The Emperor Alexander was not to be appeased. And it was at one of the chief fêtes of the exhibition that Napoleon and Eugénie heard that their protégé, Maximilian, had been shot at Queretaro at the order of Juarez. That was heartrending. " I have seen them weeping," wrote Metternich, " in their grief at a tragedy for which they are to a certain extent responsible." [2] And then Napoleon's whole policy of friendship with Italy had been disturbed by a freebooter. He had at last withdrawn his troops from Rome, and left to Victor Emmanuel the protection of the Holy Father. Pius IX might not feel very confident : he might have recalled

> There was once a young lady of Riga
> Who went for a ride on a tiger.

But this tiger, called a *Galante uomo*, had given his word of honour. However, there was in an island off the Tuscan coast, a man who wore a red shirt, attacked the clergy in noisy and unreasoned speeches, had a gift for guerilla warfare, and was endowed with power over the hearts of Italian as well as English sentimentalists. Garibaldi took ship from Caprera, and at the head of a marauding band invaded what was left of the States of the Church. It was a disgraceful affair, and the Emperor, once more to his honour, came to the defence of the venerable Sovereign who had once saved his own life. At the battle of Mentana, the soldiers of France, armed with the new chassepot rifle, fought back the marauders : and the Father of the faithful dubbed Napoleon a knight of the Order of Christ. But such was the mood of the time that what was called Italy took umbrage at this defence of the Primate of Italy

[1] R. R. Baroche : *Souvenirs*.
[2] Metternich to Beust, 2nd July, 1867.

by the very man who had won for Victor Emmanuel Lombardy and gained him Venice—at the exorbitant cost of awakening distrust in Austria.

Austria was friendly now. In spite of the horrors of Queretaro, and the tragic ravings of Charlotte at Miramar, Franz Josef and Elizabeth, held back by their mourning from the exhibition, received Napoleon and Eugénie at Salzburg. It was a quiet meeting in the dear old town, beneath the walls and towers of the Burg, sheltered by the hill where Mozart as a child had been haunted by the melodies which give such a smooth voice to the passion of the heart. These royal persons were accomplished in all the arts of courtesy, and they were persuaded that not only their own crowns but the welfare of their people depended on their uniting against the new lion of the North. But they did not go far enough. The close and passionate liaison with Vienna which Napoleon had urged so long, he had it now, now when it was already too late. " *Quand la vertueuse Autriche,*" said a cynical observer, " *se décida à accorder ses faveurs à Napoléon III, elle trouva un Abélard après l'opération.*" [1]

4

On the 23rd October, 1867, Franz Josef returned the visit. Elizabeth, expecting yet another blessing on her marriage, had been advised by her doctor not to risk the journey. But for her Emperor, the French sovereigns prepared, with an *empressement* sobered by their memories, all the honours of their capital. There was no Bismarck now to cause disquiet to French patriots, no Berezowski to fire his sinister

[1] Vitzthum : *Denkwurdigkeiten*, iii, quoted in Salomon : *Ambassade*, p. 192.

pistol. A hunt at Compiègne, a gala at the Opera, receptions at the Tuileries, at St. Cloud, at the Austrian Embassy—these filled the glittering hours. At a great dinner at the Hôtel de Ville, in the presence of three hundred and fifty people, the three Sovereigns were joined by two others, King Louis of Bavaria, and Queen Sophia from The Hague. " You know," shouted the King, who was so deaf as not to be able to manage his voice, " I used to know your father very well, King Louis, when he was at the Hague." The Emperor, who had the Queen of Holland on his right, felt it an unsuitable moment to be reminded that his own father had been the King of Holland. But the good Bavarian overrode such unnecessary sensitiveness. " No need to trouble," he shouted across the Emperor to the Queen. " One nail knocks another out." [1]

5

And yet in this very year of 1867, secret negotiations were being pushed on between the decrepit conspirator of Paris, and the triumphant conspirator of Berlin. Bismarck held out Luxemburg, and even Belgium as baits.[2] No sooner had Napoleon grasped at Luxemburg than Bismarck said it was impossible and threatened war.[3] In the matter of Belgium he was astuter still. He obtained in the handwriting of the French Ambassador in Berlin a set of propositions which England, if she saw them, must regard as treachery. These no doubt meant nothing, but they looked nasty. And Bismarck reserved his publication for the moment when he had picked his quarrel with France.

[1] Princess Pauline Metternich : *My Years in Paris*, ch. ix.
[2] Maxwell : *Lord Clarendon*, ii, 4th November, 1867.
[3] Salomon : *Ambassade de R. Metternich*, pp. 199, 200.

XV

THE CONFIDENCE OF MILLIONS

> We cannot expect to give very many hours to pleasure. Circumstances are like clouds, continually gathering and bursting. While we are laughing, the seed of some trouble is put into the wide arable land of events; while we are sleeping, it sprouts, it grows, and suddenly bears a poison fruit, which we must pluck.
>
> KEATS : *Letters of 14th February*, 1819.

I

THE Emperor was touching sixty, a sixty which licence and disease had turned almost to decrepitude. He felt, and those around him knew, that he had not long to live. For twenty years he had held the reins in his own hand, with the result that we have seen. Among all the recoils and alternations of his temperament, the constant reactions between activity and exhaustion, between a French and a European policy, between loyalty to his wife and infidelity, between compromises with Liberalism and the assertion of sovereign power, his influence had been at work in interpreting the trends of his time, but in ways so contradictory, so complex and so curious that, like a kindly sphinx, he seemed to defy the most astute to solve the riddle of his heavy and impassive face. What was his essential character? What his objects? What his ability? These questions seemed to become more insistent than ever. After twenty years, the leaders in Paris had a new preoccupation: What really was their Emperor?

For sixteen of those twenty years, the shrewdest and most experienced of English diplomats had watched him. And Lord Cowley's conclusion was that the Emperor, in spite of all his opportunism, knew what he was about. "*Nous vivons au jour le jour.*" [1] That had been the Emperor's own confession. He liked to keep several doors open so that at the most convenient moment, he might walk down the most convenient corridor.[2] But after all he had some objects clear, the maintenance of his dynasty, the security of France, seasoned, as Hübner noted long since, with a little glory, and beyond these, such changes in the map of Europe as would suit more liberal minds than that of Clement Metternich. Well, in twenty years, most of them had been obtained ; only in the last few years the Emperor, who had done so much, had overreached himself, not so much by his own incapacity (though at the critical moment, he had failed to follow the heroic lead of Eugénie) as by the fact that no one in Europe could cope with the diplomatic lion of the North.

But even Bismarck seemed secondary. The failing man must prepare for sweeping changes so that, in a constitutional government, his son and the regent would be secure. For that and for every reason, the long promised Liberalism was at last to put the pinnacle on the solid edifice of the Empire. And what was Liberalism? It was " a harmony between institutions and morals, a steady tendency in all those who had power in their hands to replace force by persuasion, and menace by goodwill : in short a régime which proclaims both in its law and in its acts the sovereignty of public opinion, and so

[1] *Lady Burghclere's Papers* : Lord Cowley to Lady Derby : " He has his own way of doing business but you may depend he is not in that uncertainty which it is the fashion to attribute to him."—11th January, 1869. *Cowley Papers.*
[2] V.N.A., Metternich.

even tenders homage to the truth which is the base of every democratic State and every free society: that governments are made by and for the people, and not the people for the governments." [1] Such was the system over which his young son was to preside.

The Prince Imperial at ten years old had become central in his father's heart. The old roué felt that all his relations with women were not to be counted in comparison with the purer gold of those affections he had felt for his mother and his son. Perhaps Napoleon never felt a sharper twinge of anguish than when he began to fear that the little boy was already the victim of a malignant growth. The trouble was an abscess in his hip: but it was obstinate. It might be—what? In those anxious moments, the Emperor felt his heart was broken.[2] Ah! if there were to be no son to succeed, what was there to hope for? He was so discouraged that what was left to him of decision in the paroxysms of his pain was paralysed. So he had felt even as he opened his Exhibition. But as then, so afterwards, the pageant of Empire could not be less splendid because, either within or without, it was in danger of annihilation. For, as those knew who best could judge, the situation with regard to Bismarck was becoming more and more critical.

"France," wrote the Austrian agent, Klindworth, to Vienna, on the 6th June, 1868, "is irritated at Prussia and alarmed at her increases in territory. Louis Napoleon is not, in himself, too eager for war. He is not a military commander, as he willingly admits himself, and, besides, his state of health could hardly stand the fatigues of a campaign. The country

[1] Abbé Bauer: *L'Europe en* 1867.
[2] V.N.A., Metternich to Beust.

has ceased to be a simple spectator of events from outside, and passes a severe judgment on them. It insists on the policy being national and absolutely French. Furthermore, it is in a nasty temper with Prussia, a nation whose own feelings are themselves eminently hostile to us. At the Tuileries, they regard Russia as the rearguard of a future Prussian coalition against France. And, therefore, it is that Rouher has told me that we should put our military forces on a footing that would enable us, if need arose, to confront Russia and Prussia at once." [1]

2

In the preparation for a Parliamentary government, two things were necessary—to make friends with the Liberals and give licence to the Press. For through all those twenty years, and never more than now, Thiers had pursued his implacable hostility. The time of revenge, so long awaited, seemed at last to be drawing near. How fierce and how insistent, the tireless orator could make his warnings against that folly of allowing the neighbours to be strong! " *M. Thiers sait tout, tranche tout, parle de tout*," said Sainte-Beuve. He was beginning to frighten Napoleon : so many acute minds took up the tale : so much anxiety was felt from year to year at the thought of what Bismarck was about. " From that time," said Napoleon after the fall, " events followed with a swiftness which of itself was irresistible and fatal." [2]

While foreign politics disturbed the patriots, a new

[1] V.N.A., Klindworth to Beust. Why does Professor Oncken omit this passage when noting so many others of this date, and on this subject from the Vienna archives ?
[2] Baron Mayendorff's Papers.

generation had arisen with feelings as Republican and anti-clerical as Prince Napoleon's. To these the Catholic Empress was anathema. " I was shocked by her unpopularity," wrote Queen Sophia, " even among the Court people. I like her, with her grace, her beauty, her sweetness." [1] All that was shrewdest in her instincts, or noblest in her character were taken as new headings in vile indictments of her. And in the lampoons of the more vulgar papers, she, who was as chaste as ice, as white as snow, had to see the lowest mock her greatness under the name, and in the posture, of a whore.[2] Not all the injustices of the newly licensed press were so gross. Earnest men recalled the *coup d'État*, and pointed to the absurdity of it as an exordium to what was supposed to be popular government. With indignation, which was sincere, they recalled the casualties in the street fighting and believed them to be worse than they really were. Rochefort in his *Lanterne* indulged in quips that were too witty to forget. He was an imperialist, he said : he had his Bonaparte ideal, but it was Napoleon II. " What a reign ! " he wrote, " what a reign, my friends ! Not a tax ; no useless wars with their weight of debt ; none of those far expeditions where one spends six hundred millions to get back fifteen francs, no devouring civil lists, no Ministers accumulating five or six different portfolios at a hundred thousand francs each. That is the sort of monarch I understand. Oh yes, Napoleon II. Unreservedly I love him and admire him." [3]

[1] Maxwell : *Lord Clarendon.*
[2] F. A. Simpson : *Rise of Louis Napoleon.* See also *La Femme de César* and the Archives of Hippolyte Mayen : *Les Nuits de St. Cloud, Les femmes galantes de César, Le Pilori.*
[3] Guedalla : *Second Empire*, 2nd ed., p. 304.

An accident brought new fuel to those whose primary passion was to deride the name of Bonaparte. When the Emperor had been in New York in 1836, it will be remembered, his reputation had suffered from a confusion with his cousin, Antoine. Just such another was Pierre, the son of Lucien. This young man had in his stormy youth killed a Papal gendarme and been condemned to death. But the sentence had been commuted to imprisonment in the Castle of St. Angelo. And the Prince, finally set at liberty, had after his adventures in New York and elsewhere, came to France at the rise of Louis Napoleon and established himself in Auteuil, though never given the entrée to the Tuileries. In the beginning of 1870, two comrades of Rochefort, both armed, entered his house and a certain Victor Noir had stabbed him in the face; he had answered with a shot from his revolver which, as it happened, went through his assailant's heart. Next morning Rochefort's papers had in black headlines notice of the "*Murder of Noir by Prince Pierre Napoleon Bonaparte.*" Not only Pierre was the subject of insulting references, but all the Bonapartes, including the reigning Emperor, were attacked. "I was weak enough," wrote Rochefort, "to think that a Bonaparte could be anything else than an assassin . . . It is now eighteen years that France has been in the blood-stained hands of these cut-throats who, not content with turning the machine-gun on to the Republicans in the streets, draw them into their filthy traps to do them to death in private houses." [1] The Courts declared the Prince not guilty; but the incident had a nasty effect. It was all part of that undercurrent of rebellion which, despite the acquiescence and loyalty of the immense mass of the people, was growing

[1] La Gorce: *Histoire du Second Empire*, vi, 16.

so disquieting. And even when the Empire seemed most solid, there was much that was hollow and rotten at its heart; this was as it were the counterpart of the obstinate tendency to immorality in the Emperor's own private life.[1]

3

And now in his decrepitude, Napoleon III engaged in an affair with yet another lady. It is from her that we get the most intimate portrait of him at this period of his life. The Countess de Mercy-Argenteau was born a Princess de Caraman-Chimay of the great Belgian family. Her husband, once an Austrian, had transferred his allegiance to Napoleon. " The Emperor's step was slow," said this lady, " his head stooping slightly to the right. But his manner was at once both bright and kindly; his voice was pleasant and his eyes irresistibly charming. It was the heavy dominant nose which gave the air of boldness to his features. Behind it he seemed often to be sick of everything and tired."

Madame de Mercy-Argenteau claims that Persigny employed her to counteract the influence of the Empress.[2] Making use of the secret passage through which, in the old days of the Presidency, Louis Napoleon had walked from his palace to a house in the Rue de l'Elysée, Persigny led her into the sacristy of the disused chapel.[3] Here, in the dying perfumes of incense, the Empress and the Belgian beauty met. She described the first time they came together

---

[1] La Gorce: *Second Empire*, v, 373-435.
[2] But this is not supported by Persigny himself, who in his *Mémoires* declaims against the *injustice revoltante* which accused the Empress of being a sinister influence in French politics. Persigny: *Mémoires*, p. 393.
[3] Mercy-Argenteau: *Last Love*, p. 108.

through the underground passage. How she sat in her own room, "wavering, irresolute." "Suddenly something seemed to move; frightened, I uttered a feeble cry— It was not an hallucination— The door was opened, and the Emperor appeared, holding out his arms to me." [1]

"It has been often said," she continues, "that I was his last love. Without any misconceived pride, I may admit that this is true. But his mistress I have never been." [2] This is the lady's statement: no evidence can be adduced against it. We must leave it as it stands, with the implication that the health of Napoleon III was no longer what it had been.

To her he spoke not only of love but of politics. "The nation," he said, "is a slave which has to be induced to believe that it is on the throne." "A king," he said again, "should always know what his people want for they do not know themselves." "Why have the plebiscite?" he asked finally, turning to the well-worn metaphor. "Because I need to know the whims of France. Louis Philippe was her husband. I am her lover." [3]

Madame de Mercy-Argenteau never tires of trying to depreciate the Empress. That in the circumstances was not surprising. It was, after all, Eugénie who counted.

4

In 1869, the Empress was charged with a high political mission in the Mediterranean. It was her object at once to propitiate the Sultan at Constantinople, and to open the Suez Canal which

[1] Mercy-Argenteau: *Last Love*, p. 111.
[2] Mercy-Argenteau, op. cit., p. 112.
[3] Op. cit., pp. 125, 126.

at last her cousin Ferdinand de Lesseps, after innumerable difficulties and conflicts, had succeeded in completing. A sense of triumph was in the air. Marseilles was to become the gateway to the Far East : the shortening of weeks of voyage for men and merchandise was to mean closer relations of life and thought between India and England. European civilization was to find itself closer to a new task, the absorption into its own swiftness of a life so conservative, so desirous of quiet, so convinced of unseen realities, that the passage of the centuries found the lives of its millions unchanged. Here through the Canal, Europe was to send her traffics and discoveries into the silent gorgeousness of the walled city and the bazaar, to draw from the jungle the means of cushioned speed, while she gave the means to hurry over the arid spaces in the intense light of moon and sun. If Napoleon thought of this great task being given to his Spanish consort—Spain as a country had been for centuries the Canal between the Eastern and the Western world—he saw it, no doubt, through the haze of Moslem languor :

> Down the Horn Constantinople fades and flashes in the blue,
> Rose of cities dropping with the heavy summer's burning dew,
> Fading now as falls the orient evening round the sky and you.

He spent the weeks of her absence at Compiègne. For more than a month the Château saw no guests but shooting parties ; but at last in the middle of November, the fading woods were lit by the gleam of Parisian ladies' presences : Princess Mathilde was installed as hostess. The Duchesse de Mouchy, Madame de Pourtalès, the charming Mademoiselle

Pillé came to pay their court to the most gallant of Sovereigns; in hunts, rides, plays, balls, the ladies found how well their host had planned their pleasure. Ministers and ladies, young and old, were compelled by His Majesty to join with him on Sunday evening in the Carillon de Dunkerque. In a swift whirl, the dancers chased the flying hours, and the musicians had given out before the flying feet found rest. The heart and soul of it all was the Emperor, who had forgotten how ill he had been in August. "*Il a étonné et charmé ses invités,*" wrote Madame Baroche, "*par sa gaieté et son entrain.*" But these hot hours, so suddenly improvised, woke a craving for food and drink. Napoleon commanded a supper, only to find that all that had been left from dinner had been eaten by the servants. The cupboards were locked up, the cooks had gone. A sudden requisition was made from the barracks. "Ladies," said the Emperor gaily, "we shall do as they do in war: we shall eat our ration of bread." And with the appetites of harvesters, his Parisian ladies devoured their ration, washed down by a little champagne and water: and never had the guests taken the cheer of Compèigne in such a gamesome mood. Such was the Sunday evening. There was a half-hour on the Tuesday afternoon between luncheon and the train. The party spent it in a waltz which lasted till the carriages were at the doors, and so the ladies passed out of sight as they had come, in music. On the 20th of November Napoleon returned to Paris for the elections.[1]

5

The Empress was at that moment in Egypt, and, though she had by no means welcomed the Emperor's policy of handing over his sovereign power to a Parlia-

[1] Baroche: *Notes et Souvenirs,* p. 549.

ment, yet she had encouraged him in the line he had taken. "It is right," she wrote on 27th October, 1869, " to keep faith in the Concessions that have been granted. I hope that your speech will be in this spirit. The more strength may be wanted in the future, the more important it is to prove to the country that we have ideas, and not only expedients. I speak thus far away, and very ignorant of what is happening to talk in this way, but I am deeply convinced that the only real force is to follow a consistent plan. I do not like violent measures, and I am sure that one does not carry off two *coups d'État* in the same reign. I am talking upside down, for I am speaking to one converted who has known about it longer than I do : but I really must say something, were it only to show that my heart is with you both, and if in the days of calm my wandering thoughts love to run out through space, it is with you both that I love to be in the days of care and anxiety." [1]

When the Empress returned, she found Rouher on the point of resigning, and the Liberal Empire about to be inaugurated. The Emperor, in opening the new Chamber, made one of the most striking and the most successful of his speeches. France, he said, desires order and liberty. "As for order, I answer for that." There was a great burst of cheering, and the Emperor repeated the words, but not more loudly than before [2] : "As for order, I answer for that. Help me, gentlemen, to save freedom."

It was not without a sigh that Napoleon surrendered the sovereign power : but if he compared himself to a lion, who was allowed to keep only his mane, it was with the steady confidence that he had willingly

[1] *Papiers et Correspondance de la Famille Impériale*, i, 221, 222.
[2] Jerrold : *Napoleon III.*

encouraged the policy which would make all easy for his son. Ollivier became President of the Ministry in the last week of the year; when he announced his new Cabinet on 2nd January, 1870, he seemed competent to give the needed aid in safeguarding freedom, even though it was the same week which saw the fracas between Pierre Bonaparte and Victor Noir. Ollivier was a gifted man and a brilliant personality: and there was something singularly winning in his way of speaking. He had not only the most melodious of voices, but a charm and fervour that persuaded his fiercest opponents.[1] " Ollivier has two qualities," said His Majesty, " which always make me forget his faults. He has faith in myself, and voices my mind eloquently, above all when I let him think it his own." [2]

The advent of the Liberal Empire seemed to refresh France with a great hope, as with a wind of warm air from the southern sea. The old Parliamentarians, with Guizot at their head, rallied to the Emperor and the reconciliation of the older politicians coincided with a new enthusiasm in the younger men. So powerful was Ollivier's government that on the 22nd February, Jules Favre, having called for a division, found that the Opposition could not command more than eighteen votes.[3]

It was in fact not France, still less Germany, but Rome which held the interest of the French in the earlier months of 1870. It was well over twenty years since Pius IX had assumed the tiara, and in the tension of new scepticisms, new fervours, and new miracles, he had decided to call together an Œcumenical Council to discuss the great verities

[1] Du Barail: *Memoirs*, iii, 109.
[2] Oncken: *Rheinpolitik*, iii, 350.
[3] La Gorce: *Second Empire*, vi, 32.

of the Christian religion, and their relation to his own function as the teacher and father of the faithful.

The Emperor had doubted which policy he should pursue on this great occasion. He said that he expected " a work of progress and conciliation " from the Council,[1] without making any suggestions as to whether his notions of progress and conciliation would or would not coincide with those of the Vatican. It was Guizot himself who warned Napoleon to go no further.[2] After making great pronouncements on the Dogmatic Constitution of the Faith, the Council proceeded to define the doctrine of Infallibility, but in terms so moderate and careful that few could decide where they were cogent. To France the definition was of less interest than the date. It was on the 18th July, 1870, that the Bishops held their final sitting. And by that date, the Bishops of France and of Germany, and in fact of Europe, were being forced to think of other and sterner things.

For the world was to be taken by surprise. Society was being hurried unseeing to its execution, as lightheartedly as in a game of Blind Man's Buff. In consultation with Ollivier, the Emperor prepared a new plebiscite, which was to enable him, if not his dynasty, to reign secure until the end. The words of the Spartans were jestingly recalled : " If Alexander wishes to be God, let him be God." [3]

On 20th March, 1870, Napoleon had advised Ollivier to submit a *senatus consultum* to the Chamber ; and on 8th May he referred the question of the Government of the new Liberal Empire to the country in a plebiscite. The question that was asked was in the form of an approval of the Empire as

[1] Jerrold : *Life*, iv.
[2] La Gorce : *Second Empire*, vi, 70.
[3] *Journal des Débats*, 21st April, 1870.

reconstituted. But what was meant, and what was answered, was to test the feeling for the dynasty. The first answers came from the towns, and they were not favourable. The Empress was irritated, the Prince Imperial exasperated, and the Court indignant.[1] But Napoleon did not allow his confidence to be disturbed, and when the final result was announced the figures were 7,207,379 in favour of Empire, as then reformed; 1,530,000 against it: a majority no longer of 100 to 3, but still of 5 to 1. The North, the West, the South-West were solid for the Empire. It was in Hérault, down the Rhone, and in the Var that the majority was unfavourable; and it was there that the Socialists had risen against the Empire at its advent. What the vote showed was that few had changed their minds. Where the Empire had been welcomed it was still supported; where it had found enemies, it found them still.[2] Of the seven millions favourable, wrote Metternich, there were at most 500,000 or 600,000 who approved of the *Senatus Consultum*: the rest voted for the Emperor and his dynasty. Of the million and a half who said "No," there were 300,000 or 400,000 who found the terms too liberal; the rest were hostile to Napoleon, and hoped for a revolution.[3]

The Emperor was struck by the difficulty of finding efficient Ministers: but he spoke with more confidence than he felt in making his formal announcement of this result. He sketched a sweeping policy: "To rally round the constitution which had been sanctioned by the country for the honourable men of all parties: to maintain the public peace: to calm party passions: to preserve social interests

---

[1] La Gorce: *Second Empire*, vi, 114.
[2] La Gorce: op. cit., vi, 115.
[3] Oncken: *Rheinpolitik*, iii, 349.

from the contagion of false doctrines : to enlist the highest intellects in the promotion of the greatness and prosperity of France : to spread education : to simplify the administrative machinery : to transfer activity from the centre where it is superabundant to remote places where it is deficient : to introduce into our codes of law, which are national monuments, the improvements made known to us by experience : to increase the means of production and wealth : to promote agriculture and the development of public works ; and finally to devote our labours to the alleviation of the burden of the tax-payer—such is our policy . . . Who indeed can be opposed to the forward march of a dynasty founded by a great people in the midst of political disturbance, and fortified by liberty." [1]

" More than ever," said the Emperor, " we should regard the future with fearless eyes."

Those words were spoken on the 21st May by a man whose physical condition showed that his whole system was poisoned ; day by day, the forces of disruption in that soft heavy body accumulated quantities of purulent matter.[2] The effects had been very clearly stated by the new British Ambassador. " His energy and decision of character," wrote Lord Lyons to Lord Clarendon at the end of 1869, " wane rapidly with advancing years," and the Ambassador was repeating a warning he had already given in August of that year.[3] But nevertheless, in the month of June, while the Emperor's specialist was noting all the symptoms of decay, the season was particularly bright. At St. Cloud the life of the

[1] Jerrold : *Napoleon III*, iv.
[2] *Papiers de la Famille Impériale.* Report of Dr. Germain Sée.
[3] Record Office, London : Lyons to Clarendon, 27th August and 21st December, 1869.

Court seemed as happy as the sky itself was cloudless. And though in weather so hot and dry the peasants were a little nervous as to the results of their harvest, Europe and France took their omens from the splendour of the summer. It was on the 30th June that the new Premier spoke in the Palais Bourbon of his impressions. He said that the Government had no anxieties whatever. " In whatever direction one looks," he added, " one can see no sign of any troublesome question and never in history was the maintenance of peace in Europe so certainly assured." [1]

That was on a Thursday. On the Sunday evening a telegram reached Paris which made Ollivier himself thrill with excitement at the thought of war. War, and war only, was to be henceforth the thought of Europe. When the Bishops returned from their long Congress at the feet of the Servant of the servants of God, they found all questions both of faith and morals absorbed and overmastered by the unsearchable dominance of war—war between the two nations most powerful in the Christian Continent of Europe.

[1] La Gorce : *Second Empire*, vi.

PART III

TRAGEDY

XVI

THE ROAD TO RUIN

> Our eyes do yet fail in looking for our vain help.
> In our watching we have watched for a nation that could not save.
> They hunt our steps that we cannot go in our streets :
> Our end is near, our days are fulfilled, for our end is come.
> Our pursuers were swifter than the eagles of the heaven ;
> They chased us upon the mountain ; they laid wait for us in the wilderness.
> The breath of our nostrils, the anointed of the Lord, was taken in their pits ;
> Of whom we said : Under his shadow we shall live among the nations.
> *Lamentations*, iv.

I

THERE was hardly a man in France who did not take the bright summer days as a presage of peace. The very sense of well-being beguiled the men in power into a confidence which was soon to be translated into carelessness. But the one statesman on whom all hopes of peace depended, though none knew it, was going out of reach : Lord Clarendon died on 2nd July. " Never was I more glad of anything than I was to hear of your father's death," said Bismarck to his daughter, Lady Emily Russell, a year or two later. Lady Emily looked aghast.

"Ach, dear lady, you must not take it like that," answered Bismarck. " I mean that if your father had lived, he would have prevented the war."[1]

That Bismarck deliberately envisaged war when he sent a secret messenger to Madrid about placing a Hohenzollern Prince on the vacant throne of Spain, we can no longer doubt.[2] The secret of the intrigue was revealed by his secretary : though it must not be forgotten that when this confession leaked out in England, it was suppressed both in France and Germany.[3] But the negotiation which would have hemmed in France between the Hohenzollern Princes, when one of these Princes was already her chief cause of disquiet, Paris was bound by every principle of diplomacy to prevent.

And yet this candidature was not only mentioned. It was brought forward a second time and rejected. On 3rd July, 1870, when Clarendon's body was hardly cold, a sensational message from the French Ambassador in Madrid hurled it before men's attention yet a third time : and this time it struck, not only Paris, but London and Vienna, as peculiarly pregnant in its implications.[4]

Napoleon was not behind his contemporaries in

[1] Maxwell : *Lord Clarendon*, ii, 366.
[2] C. Grant Robertson : *Bismarck*. M. Busch : *Tagebuchblätter*, 238, 239, 330, 331.
[3] Busch : *Bismarck—Some Secret Pages*. " He denied his letter to Prim until I reminded him that I myself handed it to the General in Madrid. The whole Hohenzollern candidacy was represented as a private affair of the Court and he was obliged to confess that it was discussed at a session of the Council of Ministers." This is the passage which is *suppressed* in both the German edition of Busch's *Tagebuch* and the French. It need hardly be pointed out that it is of capital importance.
[4] V.N.A., Beust to Metternich, 5th July, 1870. Oncken : *Rheinpolitik*, iii, 396, 400, 401, 403.

obtaining information either by espionage, or by directer means, and when he and Eugénie both referred to Bismarck's negotiations with Prim, they were not talking idly.[1] Not merely imagination, not even political instinct, could have brought them to speak with such precision. From that moment the Empress, with the blood of warrior ancestors hot within her and her fiery temperament ablaze, saw through the wiles of her adversary, and envisaged the possibility of war. There is no proof that she worked for it; and once at least she spoke in favour of a neutral arbitration [2]: but the honour of France was uppermost in her mind. When war is in question, as we have already noted, no quality is so fatal as sensitiveness on questions of honour. The heart of the Empress was beating in unison with the patriots of France, who believed that their chance had come.

There can be no question that Napoleon also believed that this third candidature could be managed to French advantage.[3] The common feeling was that a quarrel must inevitably come, and that, if it came on such a question as the Spanish succession, it would draw Europe to the side of France, and give no reason to the Southern States of Germany to side with Prussia. The Emperor, therefore, like his Minister, Ollivier, was on the 8th July in the highest spirits: he seemed enchanted.[4] He believed that England and Russia, and he hoped that Austria would support him. The Empress herself, under the tragic delusion that Bismarck had been caught

---

[1] Pierre de la Gorce: *Second Empire*, vii; founded on the Archives of the Quai d'Orsay: Mercies to Gramont, June and July, 1870.
[2] G. Rothan: *Allemagne et Italie*, p. 388.
[3] Oncken: *Rheinpolitik*, 400, 401.
[4] Oncken: loc. cit.

in a trap, looked ten years younger.[1] Many of the Paris papers, though not all, took a chauvinistic tone. But all was concentrated so far on one end : it was to instruct the French Ambassador, Benedetti, to obtain from the King of Prussia, then taking a cure at the little watering-place of Bad Ems on the Lahn, a promise that he would not allow the candidature and that it should not be renewed.

King William was distinctly embarrassed by such a question. Bismarck had consistently left him in the dark as to the intrigues which had war for their object, and it was not easy for him to give a peremptory command to distant members of his family on what seemed a purely formal matter. Least of all could he do so if it seemed that the French were giving him the order : but he was as courteous as he could be, and was undeniably delighted, when he heard on 12th July, that his cousins, father and son, had withdrawn the candidature. He naturally believed that the question had been settled. Paris might too have been delighted, for the French had gained a diplomatic victory and there, according to every dictate of human or heavenly wisdom, they should have been both thankful and content. Bismarck, had they known it, was so furious that he was on the point of resigning the Chancellorship.[2] By one of those circumstances, however, which seem accidental, but are strong with the momentum of high tides of hurtling patriotism, the French Minister for Foreign Affairs had already thrown away the immense advantage he had gained. After consulting the Emperor, as well as Ollivier, he had asked the Prussian Ambassador at Paris and the French Ambassador at Ems to press for a promise from the

[1] Oncken : loc. cit.
[2] Bismarck : *Reminiscences*, ch. xxvi.

King that the candidature should never be renewed. From support of this fatal foolishness of Gramont's, one can exonerate neither the Emperor nor the Empress, though Ollivier had pushed Gramont to it before them.[1]

When the news had reached Paris, Napoleon's joyous excitement had been followed by one of his temperamental reactions, and he was horrified at the thought of war.[2] On the 12th July when the withdrawal became known, he was undoubtedly relieved. Anxious to make the most out of the victory, he had written to Ollivier to see that the King of Prussia was associated with the refusal, saying that otherwise the country would be disappointed. But as he drove to St. Cloud, he said to his A.D.C. : " It means peace. War would be unnecessary, absurd. Suppose an island rose in the Mediterranean near the French coast. Germany wants to take possession of it : I oppose her. But while we are talking, the island disappears. Neither Germany nor France would be mad enough to fight for an island that had disappeared."[3] Both countries were madder than Napoleon realized.

Arriving at St. Cloud he at once met, according to Ollivier, another mentality. According to this authority, the A.D.C. in whom the Emperor had confided leapt on to the billiard table, drew his sword,

[1] Gramont : *La France et la Prusse*, p. 126. Paléologue : *Entretiens*, pp. 148, 149. Gramont and Ollivier had agreed on 12th July in asking the Prussian Ambassador to insist on exactly the same step. R. H. Lord : *Origin of the War of 1870*, Document No. 150 from German Archives. This shows that in the one point where the influence of the Empress was said to be decisive, she had been anticipated by Ollivier, and that her avowed support made no difference to the situation.

[2] Ollivier : *Empire Libéral*, xiv, 239.

[3] d'Eichthal : *Le Général Bourbaki*, p. 47.

and said : " Henceforth I refuse to serve." The Empress, according to the same report, cried : " It is shameful. The Empire will tumble to pieces." [1] But the first of these statements is not easy to reconcile with the record left by the A.D.C.[2] : and the Empress, excitable as she was, must have lost the common sense which was one of her dominant qualities. And though Gramont arrived shortly afterwards, he said that " the Emperor and his counsellors were looking only for a peaceful solution ".[3] The British Ambassador was convinced that he was thoroughly averse to war.[4] In view of this statement, Ollivier is wrong in the phrase which, on hearsay, he attributed to the Empress. It is easy to see how, at the time, it seemed that the only way of closing an incident which, for the third time, had faced France with the prospect of war, would be to ask for a declaration from King William. " Prudence," wrote Gramont, " commanded that before we had dropped this affair, we should have a positive assurance against the return of the peril which had so suddenly surprised us." [5] But whoever is responsible for the decision, however and whatever its intention, we —wise after the event—can only say now that it proved a capital mistake in the end.

William answered as best he could the representation of the French Ambassador, but as King he was

[1] Ollivier : *Empire Libéral*, viii.
[2] d'Eichthal : loc. cit.
[3] Gramont : *La France et la Prusse*, p. 131.
[4] Lord Newton : *Life of Lord Lyons*, i, 296. Both Werther and Gramont contradict Ollivier as to the innocence he claimed as to his part in pressing for withdrawal. See P. Muret : Ollivier et Gramont, *Revue d'Histoire Moderne*, xiii, pp. 305-328 ; xiv, pp. 178-213, 1911, which proves that Ollivier was far from being a reliable witness.
[5] Oncken : *Rheinpolitik*, iii, 438.

not accustomed to be pressed, and he felt that it was not becoming to give a promise in the dark as to an eventuality that was hardly his affair.[1] He telegraphed his views to Bismarck in Berlin.

From that moment all hope of peace was gone. Bismarck's only fear was that his Sovereign should be too conciliatory. He himself admits that he had decided on war.[2] With the war lords at his right hand, he did not need to make many changes in the telegram to give it an insulting tone, and then published it in the newspapers.[3] So published it was—in Bismarck's own words, as a red rag to a bull: deliberately it was meant to sting the French into a war for which they were not ready, and to give them in all Europe the air of bullies. Not avowed until long afterwards, this, the most notorious of Bismarck's *tours de main*, at once deceived Europe and maddened the French.

Gladstone in London, and Beust in Vienna, in spite of their full cognizance of their entente with France, had decided that, in view of what looked so very like aggression, they could neither of them bring their country into war on the side of France. Gladstone, for his part, decided, without evidence, that the Empress was most to blame.[4] Napoleon with more reason complained of the incapacity of

---

[1] R. H. Lord: *Origin of the War of 1870*, Document No. 262, quoting *Festschrift der Kaiser Wilhelm Gesellschaft zur Forderung der Wissenschaften*. Berlin, 1921, pp. 273–4.

[2] Loftus to Granville, 13th July, 1870. *Bismarck Reminiscences*, i, 274, 276.

[3] The manipulations made were not of such nature that they justify the word *forgery*, or *falsification*. See R. H. Lord: *Origin of the War of 1870*, Documents 163, 184.

[4] Oncken: *Rheinpolitik*, iii, 421–7, 434, 438. Personal Papers of Lord Rendel, p. 64.

Ollivier.[1] For, when a war is imminent, nothing is so fatal as instability and indecision. And Ollivier had both of these faults. At one time he was sharing the excitement of the Palais Bourbon ; at another moment, he was compromising ; at no time was he master either of himself or of the situation. And yet his system had taken responsibility from the hands of the Emperor. His seventeen volumes of apology cannot disprove the fact that it was his loose constitution which had enabled Gramont to take the fatal step without being really responsible to anybody.[2] But we could not expect Gladstone to blame a Liberal Minister, when there was a Catholic Empress within reach of attack. And she was made everywhere the scapegoat of Liberals, Republicans, Royalists, atheists, and Prussians.[3]

[1] Vitzthum : *Denkwürdigkeiten*, p. 184.
[2] This argument is developed at length by the last French authority to write on this subject, M. Henri Salomon in *L'Incident Hohenzollern*.
[3] For the question of the Empress's responsibility, see my *Empress Eugénie*, pp. 238-244, and my correspondence in *The Times Literary Supplement, 1931*, pp. 165, 199, 252, 271, 288, 307, 327, with Professor Harold Temperley. The evidence he adduced is of the greatest value. But I have taken this opportunity to amplify my original statements, which remained finally unshaken : (1) That the Empress was in the excited state of a patriot on the verge of war ; (2) There is no evidence that she took, or could have taken, any decisive step.
Since then, M. Henri Salomon has added to the books on this question : *L'Incident Hohenzollern*. He does not exonerate the Empress, but adduces no new evidence against her.
The legend of her guilt, against which she protested to the end of her life, can be explained by the fact that a sinister influence was felt to be working for war, but no one could say where or how. It was felt that it must be Eugénie. Only after Ollivier had published his seventeen volumes, did Busch publish Bismarck's confession to him, and Sir Herbert Maxwell his *Life of Lord Clarendon*. The sinister influence was then seen not to be at St. Cloud but at Berlin.

When one considers the chain of events, however, it is impossible to point to any particular one which was so very different from the rest. All who have undergone calamity, and perceive how in reacting on one another they knitted character with fate, see a hundred ways in which they might have acted differently. On the French side, no doubt, mistake was heaped upon mistake. The Emperor in his bad judgment, the Empress with her misguided honour, Gramont who tried to make assurance doubly sure, Ollivier in his inexperience and indecision, Le Boeuf in his false security, Benedetti in following instructions, Thiers in criticism, Cassagnac and Girardin in chauvinistic journalism, deputies, officers, newspapers, people—all excitable—are involved together: and the generals in their incompetence follow after them. But *is there one of these who played a decisive part, without whom things would have been much different?* It was a holocaust of national folly, driven headlong by national pride. For years, however, all had been shaping for war. And since no one was prepared for a Congress, the War could not have been escaped.

On Bismarck's side, however, there were no mistakes: for there was no defeat. When one has gained a sweeping victory, all that led up to it, however crooked, however rash, is swallowed up in approbation.

2

By the time that Bismarck's studied insult had goaded the French excitement into uproar, the Emperor was appalled. He tried to recall the order for calling up the reserves, and Le Boeuf supported him. "What!" cried the Empress. "You also approve of this cowardice. If you wish to stain your own honour, do not stain the Emperor's."

"Oh!" cried Napoleon, "how can you speak like that to a man who has given so many proofs of his loyalty?" Eugénie at once saw that she had been carried away, and with all the generosity of her nature begged the Marshal's pardon. But her judgment, thought Ollivier, was right. The Emperor's order would have given an impression of weakness in a country which could no longer save herself from war.[1]

That evening there was a meeting of the Cabinet, which the Empress attended for the first time since the appointment of Ollivier; but she did not speak at it. Only as she left it did she approve the suggestion of arbitration. But no sooner was the meeting held than the newspapers published Bismarck's insulting communiqué. Paris greeted it with a mad roar of fury. A compact crowd filled the boulevards, shouting for war. A shiver of pride and vengeance thrilled in an hour through the crowds on that summer night.

Next morning, Friday, the 15th July, the Ministers met again at St. Cloud at nine. Even the most pacific had changed their tone, when Ollivier said they had been forced into hostilities. Napoleon, clapping his hands, voted with the rest for war. Only Eugénie desisted and said nothing.[2] Ollivier hurried to the Palais Bourbon and found his request for war credits supported by 245 votes against 10. A country could hardly be more unanimous. But that evening, the Empress, now fully aware of all that was involved, walked sadly in the park, speaking of the fearful price that even victory would exact, and foreseeing, not for herself or even her son, but for France, the ruin of defeat.[3] Never, she said later,

[1] Ollivier: *Empire Libéral*, xiv, 270, 271.
[2] Ibid., pp. 391-3.
[3] Carette: *Souvenirs Intimes*, ii, 100, 101.

had she seen a war begin with such a tightening of the heart.[1] The Emperor, too, was now weighed down with apprehensions. He, too, knew that for him defeat meant fall and ruin. When he spoke to his courtiers it was to foretell a long and arduous war. Neither he nor anyone around him had any certain plan. He saw that he could expect no help from his allies, and that Le Boeuf's bold words about readiness covered a muddle that was soon to prove murderous. An agony of premonition, a weight of care and disappointment clouded over his mind with a torment that nothing could allay, and, before a shot was fired, he was ready to make peace. But there was no peace. One morning he went to see his cousin Mathilde. She saw a man whose eyes were dead, whose eyelids were puffed, whose face was the colour of clay, whose very legs trembled beneath him.[2] The words of " Partant pour la Syrie ", which his mother had composed à propos of Flahault were running in her head.

" Cousin," she said, " you hardly remind me of the ' beau et jeune Dunois ' who before setting out for Syria appealed to the Virgin to give her blessing to the exploits. You are more like le pauvre Malbrouk who went off to war."

The Emperor took these words in good part. He gazed out sadly into space. Donna Laura Oldoini who was with them felt that he had lost faith in his star, and felt already that disaster was upon him.[3]

He felt bound to take command of the armies and leave the Empress Regent. And at last on the morning of 29th July, with the Prince Imperial in his suite, he drove down with the Empress to the little station

[1] R. Sencourt : *Empress Eugénie*, p. 244.
[2] Paléologue : *Entretiens*, p. 157.
[3] Von Bülow : *Memoirs*, Eng. ed., iv, 1849–1897.

in the Park of St. Cloud to take the train for the front. The sky had clouded, the light had faded, and an autumnal air was already stripping from the branches the summer leaves. A mournfulness fell on all gathered there as they searched for politenesses to fill the dragging minutes and said their farewells, meant to be cheerful, but melancholy in spite of themselves, to him who with such charm, such simplicity, such kindness, had lived among them for twenty years as host and master, and in whose presence majesty had joined to magnetism to invite them to revere him. Sad, quiet, affectionate, the Emperor's eye wandered among his courtiers. The words he said were vague and few. Had he said good-bye to all? There was still one left, Dumanoir. And then the signal was given, the train started.[1]

So the Emperor travelled round his capital, the city he had made so rich, so splendid and so fresh—and which had wished to give him a last ovation, for responding to its wishes. But that he could not face. "The journey," he wrote that evening to Eugénie from Metz, "had been very fatiguing, for at every station there were fervent demonstrations; but when one has very serious things on one's mind, shouts and exaggerations are wearying. Things are not so well forward as I thought."[2]

3

The Emperor's letter was certainly not an overstatement. Before he left St. Cloud he had learnt in one telegram after another, how badly his Army was prepared. Care and anxiety weighed deeper with every day. For while he saw his resources

[1] La Gorce: *Second Empire*, vi, 359.
[2] *Revue des Deux Mondes*, 1st October, 1929.

dwindling, he learnt that Southern Germany had allied with Prussia, and that the enemy was therefore far stronger than he had ever imagined. At the same time he learnt that Austria could not help him. All these things alone had been enough to make him wretched before he arrived at Metz ; and at Metz, he found telegrams all asking with the same desperate monotony for men, for horses, for provisions : he found also a pile of anonymous letters denouncing his various generals as incompetent.

Nor did he find anyone capable of advising him. Bazaine was there, but sulky, for he had expected something more than the command of an army corps. The Emperor could not plan what to do : from him the only decision of which we have a record is a telegram to the Empress asking her to send a bracelet for his hostess.[1]

On Sunday, 31st July the people of Metz (there were some German spies among them) saw him walk with the Prince Imperial to hear Mass in the Cathedral. And then another day passed. But in the meantime he had arrived at a little plan of action.

It was to attack the small frontier town of Saarbrücken. At nine in the morning of 2nd August he left Metz : two hours later he was on the field of battle : at two all was over. The Prince Imperial came under fire, and bore himself well. The engagement (it was hardly more than a skirmish) finished with French troops on German soil. That, however, meant nothing : The gigantic German armies were massing elsewhere. But there was one incident of profound significance : as the engagement was closing and the Emperor rode round to review his troops,

[1] *Derniers Télégrammes de l'Empire*, 30th July, 1870.

his features were suddenly convulsed, and he dismounted. In the arms of a General, he fell almost in a faint.

" Your Majesty seems to be ill," said the General.

" I am terribly ill," said the Emperor.

" Would it not be better to order the carriage for Your Majesty to enter it here ? "

" No, I would rather walk a little." [1]

Silently, though in torture, he walked on. The jolt of his ride had moved the stone in his bladder, and he was undergoing one of those paroxysms of torment which are among the worst the nerves and flesh of man can endure. When the excruciating bouts of pain are over, the patient is a wreck : the torture is so fierce that it can kill. Such was the state of the Commander-in-Chief of the French army : and all that he heard showed that a comparable torment was soon to gripe his army and his people.

4

The next day he could do nothing. But, on the 4th August, the news that Macmahon was defeated at Weissenburg warned him to prepare for the invasion of Alsace. Two days later he heard that Macmahon had again been defeated at Reichshofen, and Bazaine at Forbach. The enemy were sweeping on in enormous force and already cutting off his retreat. On the 8th he wired to the Empress that it was too dangerous to retreat to Châlons where he might have found the army of Macmahon. " I can be useful if I remain at Metz with a hundred thousand men reorganized. Canrobert must return to Paris to make the nucleus of a new army. So there will be

---

[1] La Gorce : *Second Empire*, vi, 366.

two great centres, Paris and Metz."[1] Beyond that neither he, nor his generals, could decide what to do. A clamour arose from the army, and from the country, that he should hand over the command to another.

Fierce altercations took place among his generals. Only on one thing were all agreed: that he must relinquish his command. Even his faithful Pietri insisted that the Sovereign had not the strength to face an active campaign, to pass his days on horseback and his nights in the bivouac.[2] Napoleon could not but agree. Would it not be better for him to hand over the command to some commander who would be responsible for the next reverse while he, the Emperor, went back to organize the resistance in Paris? But to give up the command the Emperor found one of the hardest things of his life. His men were there, more than a hundred thousand of them, aflame with ardour: and yet he was incapable of leading them. His advance towards German soil had been followed by the invasion of France: and against himself in Lorraine were advancing three German armies, each stronger than his own. Both his own men, and the people behind him, had lost confidence in him. But who was to take his place? His generals argued, pursuing their jealousies and their recriminations. At the end of a stormy council, His Majesty waited—his face hidden in his hands—while they debated who should succeed him. At last the voice of Changarnier dominated, persuading them to accept Bazaine.[3] On the 13th of August, therefore, Napoleon handed over to Bazaine the last remnants of his authority, and prepared to return towards Paris. The next morning he drove out of Metz on

[1] *Derniers Télégrammes*, 7th August, 1870.
[2] Ibid., 8th August, 1890.
[3] *Œuvres Posthumes*, p. 48.

the road to Verdun ; but only a few miles down the road—at Longeville—whether on account of doubt or of exhaustion, he halted his equipage, and there he stopped the night. Hearing that Bazaine had checked the enemy at Borny, he complimented him. " You have broken the charm," he said. But before long he knew that he had spoken too soon. In the evening, he went out to witness the scene of the defeat, and found the bodies of dead men piled a metre high, and throwing a sinister shadow in the moonlight.[1]

The next morning—the *Fête Napoléon*—the Emperor awoke before dawn to find that several officers of his escort had been killed during the night by the enemy's bombardment. He set out therefore at four in the morning with two regiments of household cavalry. Finding the main road impossible to traverse, the Emperor travelled on by-ways. The enemy were so near that shells crashed among his escort. He himself, with his carriage and pair, was driven on in fresh physical tortures : for depression or anxiety were of themselves enough to renew his throes, and to the mental anguish was added the aggravation of movement. All could see that he was very ill, and he seemed like an old man. At his side in the carriage drove a boy, in the uniform of a sub-lieutenant of the grenadier guards, a boy, tired and strained too, holding back his tears, not understanding what the wild events about him meant. This boy had dreamed a fortnight before of victory and triumph : now he had found that war meant anxiety on anxiety, and a drive back into the unknown. That evening, dusty, dirty, and unrecognizable, the Emperor's cortège stopped at Gravelotte. In the distance they could

[1] Verly : *Etapes Douloureuses*, p. 35.

hear the boom of cannon, the sharp regularity of the machine-gun, and the desultory bangs of rifle fire.[1] The young Prince, pale but keen, looking but for the Legion of Honour on his tunic like a schoolboy in a college uniform, kept asking questions of the officers, and tried to read their thoughts. But none knew of the dire events that were about to happen. And as it was the date of a festival, they brought the Emperor flowers as tokens of affection, with their good wishes for better luck.

The night was quiet, but the Emperor dared not tarry. At early dawn, his carriages were at his door. As he took his seat, he could not disguise his exhaustion. Bazaine came up to take farewell. " I leave in your hands," said Napoleon, " the last army of France : think of the Prince Imperial." [2]

Then he drove out once more, through the hills and dales which separate the valley of the Moselle from the valley of the Meuse. They had thought to take the nearest route to Verdun, through Mars-la-Tour, but at the instance of the Marshals, who knew the Germans to be already there, they went through Corflans to Etain. Here they were soon out of reach of fire, and all that they saw of battle were a few Uhlans, who, being on reconnaissance, disappeared as soon as they were seen.

Perhaps it was this sight of the enemy disappearing that deceived the young Prince, perhaps it was the lovely summer weather : for he wired from Etain to his mother : " It is all going better and better." [3]

Those words were a shocking contrast to the truth. On the day that they were sent, the army of Metz fought and lost yet another of those battles which

[1] Verly : *Etapes Douloureuses*, pp. 36–8
[2] La Gorce : *Second Empire*, vii, 58, 59.
[3] *Derniers Télégrammes*, 16th August, 1870.

THE PRINCE IMPERIAL
From the bust by Carpeaux at Malmaison.

"Think of the Prince Imperial."

decided the fate of France. For the Germans, superbly generalled by Moltke, had almost completed the encircling movement which isolated the city of Metz. That long day, as they engaged at Vionville, at Rezonville, Gravelotte, and Mars-la-Tour, along the very road the Emperor was to have taken, the French were fighting not to hold back invaders, but to regain their own country. They had Paris before them, not behind them. Fighting therefore desperately, they had on that day superiority in numbers. For several hours they held the advantage, and as night fell at Mars-la-Tour, their commander, Ladmirault, was victorious. But in that he was alone. Everywhere else along the line, the French, although they fought with all their gallantry, and although their new rifles did deadly work, were at last driven back. Bazaine disposed them badly, and failed to use his cavalry. But though the French losses were nearly 14,000, those of the Germans were higher still. And there was still hope that they might be defeated, as they moved northward to cut off Metz. Bazaine therefore established his divisions on the line of hills which extended some twelve miles from Rozérieulles to St. Privat. There on the 18th of August, another epic battle was fought. But once again, the Commander threw the chance away. Holding the heights, he refused to attack the Germans on their flank as they moved northward. In this final battle of the Army of Metz, twelve thousand Frenchmen and nearly twenty thousand Germans fell. As an occasion of heroic courage, it was a day splendid alike in the military annals of either nation. But the strategic object was lost by the French, and gained by the Germans: and at last as, on the 18th August, the sun set in splendour over the burning houses of that hillside in Lorraine, the invading army found themselves masters of St. Privat, masters of Jerusalem. Metz the inviolate, long vaunted as the most formidable fortress in Europe, was about to be beleaguered by an army that could afford to wait till the besieged army was starved into submission.[1]

Such was the news, pregnant in glory and in affliction, which greeted the Emperor and his staff, when having taken the train at Verdun they joined the army of recruits, assembling under General Trochu at Mourmelon. Napoleon, deeply moved, thought of the occasions that he had missed.[2]

5

At the Camp de Châlons, he found himself one of four actors in a new and distinct drama. The morning after him, the Duke of Magenta had returned from Alsace with the remnant of his army. Two questions arose: what was Macmahon to do, what was to be done with Napoleon himself—questions which were the subject of incessant debate not only between the Emperor and the Duke. For there was another general there: an able and popular man, eager for reform, and ready with his words. Behind his rather lumpy features and his squint (for it was General Trochu) this man had an immense confidence in himself. The fourth actor had joined the Emperor some time before, and accompanied him, though generally in a separate carriage, from Metz. This was Prince Napoleon, whose feeling at the reverses was tempered with something other than dismay. From early youth he had had the temper of a rebel, at

---

[1] La Gorce : *Second Empire*, vii, 61–154.
[2] *Œuvres Posthumes*, p. 102.

any prospect of contradiction his heart distended in its strength. And since he regarded the war as the work of the Conservatives, with the Empress at their head, he was prepared to meet any reverse with the equivalent of " I told you so ! " Coming as he did from Metz, he was well able to plead that the presence of the Emperor with the Army was, as had been found at Mourmelon, an insupportable addition to the responsibilities of a commander. " Why," he said, " you might just as well be sent into battle with a plate of soup on your head, and the order not to let a drop of it be spilt." [1]

The homely comparison was not inept. The Emperor had become a side issue, and his rank a tragic absurdity. " Sire," said one of the generals, " it is our duty to hide nothing from Your Majesty. We are in an extremely serious situation. The Emperor neither commands the army, nor occupies the throne. It is a position unworthy of a sovereign of France. The Emperor must be at the head either of his troops or of his government." Napoleon's only answer was to say, in a weak voice : " It is true. I seem to have abdicated."

For at heart the Emperor did not want to face either his Capital or the Empress. " Do not worry about Paris," she had telegraphed to Metz. " I answer for that." [2] And when Pietri had wired from Metz that the Emperor was unable to hold the command, she had answered : " Have you thought of all the consequences which would follow your return to Paris after two reverses ? For my own part, I cannot take the responsibility of advising you. But if you do decide on it, the step must be put before the country as provisional—the Emperor returning to Paris to

[1] La Gorce : *Second Empire*, vii, 165.
[2] *Derniers Télégrammes*, 8th August.

reorganize the second army, and provisionally confiding the chief command of the Rhine army to Bazaine." [1]

Among all the doubts, perplexities, and arguments of Metz and Mourmelon, that voice of decision alone had been clear. What had happened since it made its argument more final, its resolution more imperative. That voice, which for so many years now, had dictated to him what he should do ; that energy which had replaced his dying magnetism, insisted on one point : " You can't come back, beaten, before a battle." To the man, whose name was Napoleon, that was clear.

His cousin thought otherwise. He wanted the Emperor to return with Trochu, who was popular with the Republicans and hateful to the Empress. So one might deal her three blows at once. He had soon to see that Eugénie had made up her mind. Trochu was sent back to Paris, but the Emperor remained with Macmahon. As for Prince Napoleon, he was three days later on his way to Florence to see what diplomatic pressure his father-in-law, Victor Emmanuel, might bring to bear.[2]

As for Macmahon, the Government at Paris made a decision for him also. It told him to lead his army out and join that of Bazaine. There are many who think that this was the most fatal decision of the whole war. Napoleon himself described it as a move contrary to all the principles of strategy and to common sense.[3] And in this march, in the footsteps of Macmahon, he was to be made the victim of sufferings more tragic than any he had yet endured.

[1] *Derniers Télégrammes*, undated.
[2] Prince Napoléon : *La Vérité à mes Calomniateurs.* Daumois : *Notes pour servir à l'histoire de la guerre*, pp. 194–211.
[3] *Revue des Deux Mondes*, 1st October, 1929.

6

When Macmahon began his march from Mourmelon, the decision as to his movements was not final. The troops were directed toward Rheims and they were to continue towards the north-east. But that evening Rouher arrived from Paris to insist that Macmahon should join Bazaine.[1] Macmahon did not agree. The next day, however, hearing that Bazaine was taking the offensive, he freely and deliberatey changed his plan and marched northwards through Champagne. Napoleon then gave up his last thoughts of a return to Paris, and decided to remain with the army. In his own words, " he felt himself before everything a soldier," and if he could not command, he thought he should share his army's sacrifice and danger.[2] On the 23rd, he left the environs of Rheims : on the 24th the headquarters were at Rethel, on the 26th at Tourteron. At Tourteron the Prince Imperial took leave of his father who insisted that the boy should leave for Mezières, which is within an hour of Belgium.[3] So, says M. de la Gorce, do they send his children away from the sick man's bed when they see that he is about to die.

For as the Emperor went on with that long march, he saw that no good could come of it. The weather had changed, and the soldiers tramped on in the wet. The roads were terribly congested. The provisioning became worse and the men were often exhausted for lack of food.[4] In these circumstances, who can wonder if they thought less of fighting than

---

[1] *Enquête Parlementaire*, Depositions, Rouher, i, 30.
[2] Granier de Cassagnac : *Souvenirs du Second Empire*, iii, 239, containing Napoleon's own corrections.
[3] Filon : *Prince Impérial*.
[4] Palat : *Guerre de 1870*, vi, 300.

of their night's shelter and a decent meal? Who can wonder if the Emperor's equipage, the gold braid of his staff, and the shining breastplates of the *Cent Gardes* seemed to mock their miseries? And when they caught sight of the Sovereign himself, with his eyes half closed, as though in dream, they thought he cared nothing for their fate. They did not know that behind that vacant gaze, and within that loose and heavy form, suffering had worn out the will. They did not know that every jolt of his carriage dragged from his stoic calm a groan. They did not know that to mount his horse was sweat squeezed out in torment. They did not know that his surgeon was always within call, and that each morning as soon as he awoke, every evening as he finished his stage, this surgeon with a racking instrument released the poisoned matter of his excretions. Once, he had been forced to leave his carriage, and lean his head against a tree, so insufferable were his spasms. Once, at table, his body had been shaken by violent shivers, while the tears poured down his hollow and livid cheeks. His hair grew white, his skin turned grey; his haggard features were those of an old man, grievously ill.[1] So he arrived at Raucourt on the 29th. The next morning he did not leave his lodgings. Walking up and down in them, and dragging at his lank whiskers, he would stop from time to time to place his feverish forehead against the windows. As the troops filed by, hungry, exhausted, out-of-hand, they did not salute the corpse-like face, and haggard eyes that watched them, almost unseeing. When the peasants asked them whither they were going they answered fiercely: " A la boucherie ! "[2]

" A la boucherie," repeated the Emperor. The

[1] Paléologue : *Entretiens avec l'Impératrice Eugénie*, pp. 218, 219.
[2] Verly : *Etapes Douloureuses*, p. 73.

curtain dropped from his fingers, and tears coursed down over his sagging cheeks, unheeded. "*Le dîner de Sa Majesté,*" cried a servant at the end of the morning. With a gesture of despair, he only answered : " What's the good ? " And again he was alone, and there was silence. Then hiding his face in his hands, he thought of his soldiers and he wept.[1]

7

So it was that he passed with his army out of the rolling scenery of Champagne into the broad valley of the Meuse. Macmahon hardly knew where he was. Neither he nor one of his generals had a map of the country—only maps of Germany ! On the 30th of August the Emperor left Raucourt at eleven in the morning, with wagons and an escort. There were a few cries of " *Vive l'Empereur !* " The woman who had done his washing was in the market square. " *Mon Dieu, mon Dieu !* " she said. " *Ce n'est possible, c'est l'Empereur cet homme qui a l'air si malade, c'est impossible !* "

At Beaumont, as the village church chimed out the Angelus, and the army of Macmahon rested, the first German shells fell among them. For Moltke, having heard of Macmahon's manœuvre, which at first he thought incredible, had sent great forces to bar his way.

The Emperor meanwhile was proceeding up the Meuse from Raucourt to Mouzon. Woods now came down to the road, brooks flowed sparkling through them, and as the weary Sovereign passed, the birds were singing their songs. Before arriving at Mouzon, he stopped at Ponçay Mill ; and from there, to see the battle which Macmahon had engaged at

[1] Verly : *Etapes Douloureuses,* p. 73.

Beaumont, he climbed to the Baybel farm between Mouzon and Carignan. There lunch was served but the Emperor could eat nothing. At four in the afternoon he left Baybel for Carignan,[1] where he arrived at five. Between seven-thirty and eight in the evening, General Ducrôt arrived with the news that at Beaumont Macmahon had been again defeated. " *Mais c'est impossible,*" said the Emperor, " *nos positions étaient magnifiques. Quelle fatalité! Mon Dieu! Quelle fatalité! Quelle implacable fatalité!* " [2]

At a quarter to ten that evening (it was still the 30th August) [3] the Emperor left Carignan in an old train in which they could not light a lamp. All that could be seen was his cigarette showing its fiery tip against the dark. Towards midnight, when the rumbling carriages arrived at their destination, the engine-driver opened the door.

" Sire, we are at Sedan," he said. " Does Your Majesty wish to get out or go on further? "

" But where do you want me to go? "

" Sire, the line is still open : we can get as far as Mezières. There Your Majesty will be out of danger."

" No, what's the good? " he answered. " I want to share the fate of the army, whatever it is. The army is coming back to Sedan. Let us rest at Sedan." [4]

The Emperor set out on foot with a railwayman for the Porte de Paris. There in his cloak he was not at first recognized, but, at last being allowed to pass, he reached the Préfecture at half-past eleven, to hear how his son had been a guest there a few days before.

---

[1] Verly : *Etapes Douloureuses*, p. 74.
[2] P. de Massa : *Impressions et Souvenirs*, p. 310. Ducrôt : *Bazeilles Sedan*, p. 10.
[3] Verly : *Etapes Douloureuses*, pp. 88, 89.
[4] Verly : *Etapes Douloureuses*, pp. 90, 91. Palat : *Guerre de 1870*, vi, 445.

8

The Emperor found himself in a little old grey fortified town deep in the valley of the Meuse, which there flows leisured and full, of a width equal to that of the Thames at Goring. The waters of the river, curving slowly, washed the very ramparts of Sedan. Around in a rough oval were the heights and woods which, if he could have discerned them, would have shown him at once the charm of the view, and the strategic quality of the situation. For on each of them a skilful commander could station cannon which would shoot death and ruin either up the valley, or into the little town, and this the more so because its streets were narrow, and its grim houses were wedged tight one against another. There was an old walled castle in Sedan, but hardly an open space. And it was into this crowded and ill-provided town, made for 15,000 people, that Macmahon, under the impression that it might still serve as a fortress,[1] led back from Beaumont his shattered and demoralized army of 90,000 men to prepare to make another stand against the advancing enemy. Napoleon, thankful to rest, waited quietly in the Sous-Préfecture until the evening. He dictated a proclamation: "God," it concluded, "will not abandon our country if each man will do his duty."[2] Then he walked out to see what provisions there were in the shops. He soon found that there was nothing. A few women cried "*Vive l'Empereur!*" With a sad gesture, Napoleon entreated them to be silent. At four o'clock on the morning of 1st September, Macmahon had joined battle.

But it was already too late. The only hope for the

---

[1] Macmahon: *Souvenirs Inédits* (*Revue d'Histoire*, 1906, i, 592).
[2] Verly: *Etapes Douloureuses*, p. 101.

French lay in strongly holding the surrounding heights with artillery. And it was not Macmahon who had done this, but the Prussians. The strategy of Moltke was fixed on one great principle. It was to encircle his enemy, and cut off the retreat. During the night and day of the 31st August, while Macmahon gave his retiring troops a rest, and tried to provide them with food and ammunition, the armies of Moltke were moving rapidly forward. With him there was no lack of maps or of spies, or of cavalrymen on reconnaissance. Even a subaltern cannot spend an hour in that neighbourhood without seeing that Moltke's plan was masterly, and that Macmahon was making every possible mistake. The position which his forces had taken up was fatal.[1]

While the German artillery was being dragged on to the southern heights, which commanded Sedan, the main divisions were advancing down the Meuse. Some two miles out of the town, they collided with the French at the village of Bazeilles. Macmahon had ridden out at dawn. An hour or two later, when the Emperor rose, one of his orderly officers announced that the Marshal was being brought back, put out of action by a shell which had wounded him from behind in the thigh. When he heard this, Napoleon looked yet sicklier than before, and large tears poured from his faded eyes.[2] Although he was no longer responsible for the command, and no one consulted him, he decided to ride out with his staff on to the field of battle, and taking the road to Bazeilles, he remained first at Balan and then rode round into the valley of Givonne, on the banks of which the larger French divisions were posted. There he met the man who had assumed the command,

[1] Prince Hohenlohe : *Lettres sur la Stratégie*, ii, 284.
[2] Melchior de Vogüé : *Heures d'Histoire*, p. 254.

General de Wimpffen.[1] This man was so full of confidence and understood so little the cleverness of the German tactics, that he believed he had won the day, when he saw the Bavarians driven out of Bazeilles. " Your Majesty has no need to worry," he said. " In the morning I shall have thrown the enemy in the Meuse." Having so spoken he rode away, while a mocking voice answered, " Please God we shall not be thrown into it ourselves." [2]

For the Emperor was under few illusions. In that moment, he had but one wish : to find the release and refuge of death. For—

> Death cannot appal
> One, who past doubtings all
> Waits in unhope.

It was in the knowledge that that day was to involve him, and all for which he stood, in irreparable mischance, that he looked for the only escape his dignity would allow. And, as in a burning house those who have been paralysed for years will arise and escape, so great over their weakness is the power of the occasion, so in the face of his disaster, anguish gave this man a power to ignore his physical martyrdom. For hours he sat his horse ; for hours he rode over rough ground. On his way out, he met Macmahon being carried in. He rode on to Balan, and himself worked with a machine-gun, and skirting Bazeilles moved round into the wooded valley of Givonne, while from the attacking Bavarians, and from the cannon across the Meuse, the German shells crashed round him. Once he rode out on to a spur of the hill, and there against the grey sky, his heavy form stood out on his black horse, the most obvious

[1] Napoleon III, *Œuvres Posthumes.*
[2] *Moniteur,* 22nd July, 1871.

of marks.[1] Not far from him, one of his orderly officers had been killed. But no ball struck the Emperor. His hour had not yet come. There was still much for him to do, and to endure.

It was almost noon before, swept back in the flood of retreating soldiers,[2] he returned to his quarters. By that time, after a desperate defence, Bazeilles had fallen. Everywhere the French troops had been crushed back within the walls of Sedan and far down the Meuse the emplacement of the German artillery cut off the one hope of retreat that Napoleon fondly imagined might remain. After a short rest, he attempted to ride out once more. This time an escape was impossible.[3] The last hopes were already leaving the French army. The spectre of disaster came nearer and stared them in the face. Then it was that, as wild lightnings can burst out of the clouds of storm and darkness, and throw into distinctness outlines which in better weather would be hidden, so in the stress and horror of his sufferings, Napoleon saw that, with the bombardment crashing down upon his trapped soldiers in the invested city, there was no alternative between massacre and surrender. For himself he had desired only death: his demeanour that morning was proof enough of his readiness: but he could not allow the thousands of his men to perish for a vanity. Moving for so long as a troublesome encumbrance to his army, deprived of all authority, he then, arbitrarily reassuming it, took it upon himself to give a decisive order. It was to hoist the white flag on the Citadel. But the bombardment was so furious that in a few minutes the flag was shot down. For hours that afternoon

---

[1] Verly: *Etapes Douloureuses*, p. 96.
[2] Microt: *La Journée de Sedan*, pp. 32, 33.
[3] Wimpffen: *Sedan*, pp. 308, 9.

he waited for an answer from Wimpffen, who, filled with the elation of his last fight, believed that he could yet pierce the Prussian lines, and march on to Metz. Meanwhile shot and shell stormed down into Sedan, smashing the walls, setting the houses on fire, maiming those who, whether simple inhabitants or soldiers, were shut up inside, killing those whom solicitude still hoped to save.

Napoleon has left his own record of the murderous scene. " I never thought," he wrote to his wife, " that a calamity could be so dreadful. Imagine an army surrounding a fortified city and itself surrounded on every side by forces far superior. After several hours' fighting, our troops broke and tried to re-enter the town. The gates were closed. They climbed over them. Then the town was full of a compact crowd, mingled with vehicles of every description, and on this agglomeration of human heads the shells hailed from every side, killing the people in the streets, tearing off the roofs, setting the houses on fire. In this extremity, the generals came and told me that resistance was impossible. There were no more organized forces, no more munitions, no more provisions. They tried to pierce their way through, but could not manage it." [1] Then he went on to say how Macmahon was wounded ; how the officers of his staff also had been hit. He might have added that his starving troops were in an uproar : and that he could not find a general to take the responsibility for stopping the carnage. But on one point he was clear : that this was no time to speak of honour or to fear what men might say of him. For what remained to him of life, his enemies were never to let him, a Bonaparte, forget the word

[1] *Revue des Deux Mondes*, 1st October, 1929. Cf. Ducròt : *Journée de Sedan*, pp. 43–7.

coward. But there is no greater courage than to face that accusation and persevere. And never did this Napoleon show himself worthier of his name than when, assuming once more his sovereign authority, he took it finally upon himself to appeal to the King of Prussia. "They claim," he said afterwards, "that in burying ourselves under the ruins of Sedan, we should have done better service to my name and my dynasty. Perhaps we should. But to hold the lives of thousands of men in my hands and not to make a movement to save them was something beyond my powers. To honours so sinister my heart says 'No'."[1] And so, in a moment, when each general shirked responsibility, he assumed it: and before abandoning his empire for ever, he became once more the master that he might save the lives of men.

On the evening of that bloody day, the sun shone through the clouds, and the sky itself, above the smoke and fire of Sedan, itself took on the colours of fire and blood. It lit up the brick red of the *Sous-Préfecture* with the same lurid hue.[2] Then it was that the white flag flew once more, and this time it was not shot down, for German officers came under it with a summons to surrender. Napoleon answered them with a letter to the King, saying that, as he had failed to find death at the head of his troops, all that remained to him was to place his sword in the hands of the King. Such was the fateful message with which the Prussian officers, now accompanied by General Reille,[3] climbed up through the woods of the Croix Piot, the height on the south-west of Sedan, where King William and his staff were waiting.

Napoleon, as the autumn fell on Sedan, had the

[1] La Gorce: *Second Empire*, vii, 368.
[2] Verly: *Etapes Douloureuses*.
[3] E. Picard: *Sedan*, 160, 161.

satisfaction of seeing the firing cease, and knew that the rest of his soldiers were spared. Three thousand had been killed, fourteen thousand had been wounded: but there was still eighty-three thousand whose lives had hung on his decision.[1] But he could not rid his mind of the knowledge—and perhaps in all the experiences of life there is none more bitter—the knowledge that all for which he had worked, all for which he cared, was brought to ruin. It was but a short hour before the German envoys arrived that one of the most gallant of his officers, General Margueritte, had been brought into Sedan on an ambulance. The Emperor had laid aside his own cares for a moment to share the sufferings of the wounded General, and to say how he hoped for quick healing of the wound. The General could not speak. He took a pencil and wrote thoughts that were both his Emperor's and his own : " *Sire, moi ce n'est rien ; mais la France, la France !* " [2]

[1] These figures are taken from a letter written by Colonel Beauchamp Walker, Military Attaché in Berlin, to Lord Augustus Paget, on 3rd September, 1870. The letter was placed at my disposal by the courtesy of Sir Victor Wellesley.
[2] La Gorce : *Second Empire*, vii, 353.

XVII

THE EMPEROR A PRISONER

> I have had those earthly visions
> And noble aspirations in my youth,
> To make my own the mind of other men,
> The enlightener of nations ; and to rise
> I knew not whither—it might be to fall ;
> But fall, even as the mountain cataract,
> Which having leapt from its more dazzling height,
> Even in the foaming strength of its abyss
> (Which casts up misty columns that become
> Clouds raining from the re-ascended skies),
> Lies low but mighty still.
> BYRON : *Manfred III*, i.
>
> The nobleness of love is in love's woe.
> MASEFIELD : *The Daffodil Fields.*

I

THE next morning—it was the fatal Friday of the 2nd of September—the same gloom of cloud and mist hung heavy over the scene where the last hopes had been shattered. It was at six o'clock in the morning that the Emperor, after a night of sleeplessness and misery, was driven out, wearing his red velvet kepi, a hooded cape lined with red, and white kid gloves,[1] in a carriage and pair from his lodgment in Sedan to meet those who stood between him and his capital. At the gateway the Zouaves on guard cried " *Vive l'Empereur !* " and he who took the salute realized that he would never hear that greeting again. The few who in that early hour caught sight of him through the mist saw that the poor man, though pale and tired, was calm.[2] Some, seeing that his cigarette was

[1] Busch : *Bismarck*, i, 150. Kaiser Friedrich's Tagebuch, p. 112.
[2] P. Guériot : *La Captivité de Napoléon III*, p. 36.

at his lips, taunted him with the thought that its mechanical solace meant a lack of gravity.[1] They did not know the temper in which this man had long been accustomed to meet suffering.

The Emperor's first order was to drive towards Donchery where Bismarck had passed the night. The road climbs up the shoulder of hill between the little châteaux of Fresnoy and Bellevue, and then again meets the Meuse, which has made a long detour round the Presqu'ile d'Iges. As one comes in sight again of the river and Donchery, one finds an almost English landscape, such as often meets the eye between Wallingford and Reading. On the left, the mellowing woods vested the steep ascent from the Croix Piot: on the right, the calm brown river curved round towards Donchery and, beyond, the ground rose and lost itself in the outskirts of the Forest of Arden, which hides the Belgian frontier. It was a gracious scene. As Napoleon looked at it, however, one thought dominated his mind: it was that he did not want to meet the German staff in Donchery.[2] He saw on the left, on the hill-side, below the woods a weaver's cottage, a cottage not so different in style from that in which he had conferred with the Austrian Emperor at Villafranca. Near it he decided to wait in his carriage till General Reille returned with the German representative, and there in a short time he was greeted with every appearance of respect by the man to whom, above all, he owed the torment he was enduring, the man whose host he had so often been, by whom he had been once again outwitted, and who described him therefore " as stricken down by God's Almighty hand ".

Bismarck was still in bed in Donchery when he

---

[1] Verly : *Etapes Douloureuses*.
[2] Napoléon III : *Œuvres Posthumes*.

heard from General Reille that Napoleon had left Sedan, but fearful lest his captive should escape to the King who was so much less astute and so much more chivalrous than himself, the Chancellor, without washing or shaving, hurried on his dusty uniform and drove off to offer his courtesies to the defeated Sovereign.[1]

Bismarck, finding himself alone with a half-dozen enemy officers, had a sudden qualm and looked inadvertently at his revolver. The Emperor noticed the glance, and his expression altered.[2] Whether he thought that Bismarck was afraid, or was about to menace his victim, we do not know. But though the manner of the diplomat was deferential, he vetoed the proposal of an interview with his King. They were told that the weaver's cottage was poor and dirty. "*N'importe!*" was the Emperor's answer. He and the Chancellor climbed the creaking stairway of the cottage and seated themselves on two rush chairs in a little whitewashed room ten feet square, before a plain deal table.[3] But then the Emperor found the place too dirty, and came back finally into the open air.[4]

Bismarck was afterwards to boast of the criminal manœuvre by which he had presented the Ems telegram as an insult to France. But, at that moment, he told Napoleon a different story. It was France alone who had wanted war, he insisted: it was for France to end it. We have already drawn attention to the moderation of Bismarck in his victories. This great quality did not desert him when he had the

[1] Bismarck : *Letters to his Wife*, No. 27.
[2] Bismarck : *Memoirs*, i, 98.
[3] Bismarck : loc. cit.
[4] Letter of Colonel Beauchamp Walker to Lord Augustus Paget, 3rd September, 1870, in the possession of Sir Victor Wellesley.

CHÂTEAU DE M. AMOUR—BELLEVUE, NEAR SEDAN
By the courtesy of M. Philippe Ninnin, of Sedan.

"In a charming quiet country house, he awaited the signing of the capitulation."

Emperor of the French a prisoner in his hand. Unlike Moltke, he appeared at that moment to want to stop the war . and it was in that sense that he pursued his hour of audience with Napoleon. He was shrewd enough to see that France would not surrender easily, and that he must adopt every possible guarantee against revenge.

While Emperor and Chancellor were still conferring, and they were together over two hours,[1] Moltke came up. The Emperor rose and held out his hand, hoping to win the Chief of Staff to soften his conditions. Moltke was neither less respectful than Bismarck nor less firm. He demanded that he should have the whole army as prisoners in Germany.

" Those are very hard terms," said the Emperor brokenly, " very hard terms."

" If they are not accepted," said Moltke, " I shall reopen fire within two hours." [2]

2

The Emperor had taken farewell neither of the troops around him, of the battalion of grenadiers whose uniform his son was wearing, nor of the *Cent Gardes*. Perhaps he had thought of returning. But when Bismarck suggested his turning back and resting in a charming quiet country house, the recently built Château de Bellevue, which the Germans had already requisitioned from a citizen of Sedan (of the name of Amour), he agreed, and there he awaited Wimpffen, his suite, and the signing of the capitulation. Exhausted once again, though it was still early in the morning, he had once more lain down on a sofa. When Wimpffen came to tell him that the convention was signed, he rose, his eyes full of tears,

[1] Ibid. [2] P. Guériot : *Captivité de Napoléon III*, p. 43.

stretched out his hands to the general, and drew him to his heart.

It was a little after two that the King, and the Crown Prince, arrived at Bellevue. As Napoleon waited at the foot of the Château steps to receive the King, to whom but three years before he had so sumptuously done the honours of his capital, his face was ashen. The King, who in his kindness and his courtesy was far more typical of all that was noble in his country than his intriguing Chancellor, greeted the fallen Emperor with a gesture of compassion, almost brotherly. For long he held Napoleon's hand in his.

" Sire," he said, " the fortune of war has decided between us. It is very painful for me to meet Your Majesty again in such circumstances as these." The words were the more chivalrous because he who spoke them really believed that the man he saw before him was to blame for all his troubles, and William could have known little of what physical torment added to Napoleon's exhaustion. The demeanour of the Emperor was quiet and calm. He was master of himself and full of dignity. But, at times, when he spoke his eyes were wet with tears. " I believe I really comforted him," wrote King William to his Queen. The Crown Prince regretted that the war had been so costly and so terrible. " And so much more," answered the Emperor, " when we never wanted it." [1] The two Sovereigns spent half an hour together, exchanging words of courtesy as to the valour of each other's armies, and as they spoke, the King's own eyes were wet. Like his people, he had a warm and tender heart, and he was too little of a democrat to have forgotten chivalry. It is perhaps unnecessary to add that, when the

[1] Kaiser Friedrich's *Tagebuch*, p. 112.

journalists of Paris wrote of this interview, they represented King William as an ogre, menacing the very life of the Emperor.[1]

Napoleon's thoughts in all his tortures were not centred on himself. That day he wrote to Eugénie, who with communications cut, still knew nothing. "It is impossible," wrote the unhappy man, "to tell you what I have endured and am enduring. We made a march contrary to all the principles, and to common sense. It could not but lead to a catastrophe. The catastrophe has been complete. I would have chosen death before a surrender so disastrous, and yet in the circumstances in which I found myself it was the only way to avoid a butchery of sixty thousand men.

"Still, if all my torments were only centred here! I think of you, of our wretched country, of our boy. God protect them. What is going to happen at Paris?

"I have just seen the King who has been very much the gentleman, and even cordial. Tears were in his eyes as he spoke to me of the pain which I must be feeling. He has placed at my disposal one of his castles, close to Hesse Cassel. But what does it matter where I go? I feel that my career is smashed, that my name has lost its brightness. I am in despair."[2]

As the night of that sad Friday fell, he asked to be left alone in his room, without a lamp. And seating himself at the window, which looked up the valley of the Meuse towards Carignan and Beaumont, he revolved his fears and his solicitudes, while over the rich valley, the houses, the clumps of woods, the sky darkened, and from the lowering clouds rain fell upon the torches of the vast bivouac of the conquering and captured armies in the Presqu'ile d'Iges, on

[1] Giraudeau: *Napoléon III Intime*, p. 419.
[2] *Revue des Deux Mondes*, 1st October, 1929.

the shattered walls of Sedan and on the still smouldering village of Bazeilles. In front of his window were ranged the Prussian batteries which at a word could still overwhelm all in destruction and death.

As the hours wore on, the dark and the reflections could be endured no more, and the Emperor asked for books. He tried to read a novel, written by his old friend, Lytton—it was *The Last of the Barons*—but nothing could fix his wounded thoughts. At last his servant helped him to undress; but exhaustion had robbed him even of the power to rest. The sleepless hours dragged on in pain and fever. Such was the last night in France of the last Emperor of the French.

On the next morning, 3rd September, at half-past eight, he started for the Belgian frontier on his way to Germany. Ashen-grey, and shivering with fever, he came out of the little Château into drenching rain. Over his uniform he wore a long black cloak with a heavy hood, and, drawing his slow steps in pain, he at last took his seat in the closed carriage, and with General Reille beside him, and a troop of the Death's Head Hussars for escort, he drove into the storm.

It was another day of wretchedness. He dared not pass through Sedan, though it was on his road. Perhaps he guessed that his own soldiers realized his presence and greeted him with menace and insult. "The people," so the first Napoleon had written in the bitterness of his heart, "are glad to avenge on us the respect they pay us." Once or twice during the day this Emperor had shown himself—to be greeted, for the first time, with hisses and execration.[1] So he reached the forest of the Belgian frontier, and drove down the long wooded hill which brought

[1] So Zola : *La Debâcle*. Denied by Bismarck : Busch, i, 161.

him to the little River Semois and the old home of Godefroy de Bouillon. It was a quiet village buried in the hills, not more than fifteen miles from Bellevue. There he turned again to the pen for a relief from the agonizing thoughts which in the intervals of his physical throes pressed so heavy on his heart. For he knew that what he had seen was not worse than what he had yet to bear. For ten days he had heard nothing from either his wife or his son.[1] " After the irreparable misfortunes of which I have been the witness," he wrote to her, " I think of the dangers which you are running, and I am much disquieted as to the news I shall receive from Paris . . . In my present position, I should, it seems to me, give you full powers as Regent since I am a prisoner. The march to-day amidst the Prussian troops has been torture."

It was that very afternoon that the heroic Empress, who for six weeks had faced as Regent the tumult and recoils of Paris, left, as the British Ambassador wrote, " with pluck but not hope," knowing that for herself all was lost and yet fighting as best she could to throw every soldier available into the defence of France, and seeking every road which could lead to foreign intervention and honourable peace— it was that afternoon that she heard the news of Sedan. Then for a time even her self-control gave way, worn down as she was by all those sleepless weeks and the news of disaster upon disaster. For hours she remained alone in the Tuileries, dazed, repeating the words : " The army captured ! The Emperor a prisoner ! " Next day she was to face revolution, and to be advised that only by flight could she save France from civil war in the face of the enemy.[2] For there were not a few in Paris who

[1] Kaiser Friedrich's *Tagebuch*, loc. cit.
[2] See R. Sencourt : *Empress Eugénie*, chs. xiii, xiv.

preferred to take up arms against this heroic woman than to strengthen their motherland against the invader. The statues and the names of their leaders are to be seen to-day, still undefaced, in many cities of France. Those of the Empress Eugénie have been everywhere removed.

The news of the revolution reached the Emperor at Verviers, at the end of the Sunday when the Empress, leaving the Tuileries, and thrust with her reader into a common cab, had driven through the Parisian mob which was screaming for her blood, and found refuge with her dentist, the American, Dr. Evans. During that day the Emperor had driven during the long hours of the morning over the high and lonely road which leads over the hills and woods of the Belgian Ardennes from Bouillon to the tiny village of Recogne. There he had stopped to lunch in the old grey posting house, a mile away from Libramont, where he had taken the train to Namur and Liège. The weather, after the mist and rain of the days before, had given him a blue unclouded day, one of those bright September days which in their golden freshness breathe a charm and peace denied to the gaudiness of summer, days which are freshest of all in the cleanness of an air which has poured down with rain its weight of dust and thunder, and which are singularly refreshing in the high air of the Forest of Arden. But the Emperor knew that such weather, on a Sunday, in Paris, was more dangerous than a tempest. With the first vague news of Eugénie's flight in his mind, he was brought the following evening to the Castle of Wilhelmshöhe.[1] To that castle he was not a stranger. As a little boy of four or five, when his uncle was King of Westphalia, of which Cassel was the capital, he had come there.

[1] P. Guériot : *Captivité de Napoléon III.*

And the memorials of the Bonapartes had not all disappeared. Indeed, as the Emperor wandered through the rooms, he found himself face to face with a picture which spoke to the depths of his being. There on the wall was the portrait of Hortense.[1]

He had first to wait in anxiety to know that the Empress was safe, and then in dread at hearing nothing from her, at the thought she had perhaps condemned him as a coward. At last in the middle of the month, the reassuring words of comfort and affection came. "Those tender expressions which your letters breathe have done me great good," he wrote in answer, "for I was much hurt by your silence. Indeed, the misfortune which falls upon us is very great, but what makes it worse is the state into which France is falling, a prey to invasion and to anarchy." Had those twenty years of building, had those lives of all his soldiers, been given uselessly? "When I think," he wrote, "of all the brave men I have seen die, and die in vain, it breaks my heart."[2]

3

The King and Queen of Prussia, nobly free from the pettiness which disfigured the English in their relations with the prisoner of St. Helena, did all they could to ensure both the comfort and the dignity of their prisoner at Wilhelmshöhe; and in the quiet life of the Schloss, as he breathed the resinous air of the woods around it, Napoleon's nerves grew calmer, and he had some respite from the physical agonies which had been so violently accentuated by his excitement and his movement. But there could be little relief to his inward trials, when he had to receive, one after another, his generals as they were

[1] F. Giraudeau: *Napoléon III Intime*, p. 425.
[2] *Revue des Deux Mondes*, 1st October, 1929.

taken prisoner, and listen to their endless disputes and mutual recriminations. Hardly less painful was the evidence, not to be disguised, of the internal discord in France, and of the violent attacks upon himself. Neither Thiers, nor the Radicals knew mercy. The calumnies, which were never to cease, beat down on him like hailstones driven by winter wind. " To be slandered," he said, echoing Marcus Aurelius, " is part of my business as a Prince." [1]

Then it was that the man showed his inner greatness which, behind his sensualities and intrigues, he had somehow managed to preserve. He neither threatened, nor made recriminations. An unruffled patience, a readiness to suffer, a sense of what was due from fallen majesty, these sustained his judgment and raised it to the heights ; no word of uncharitableness or unwisdom came from his lips or from his pen. " Better a thousand times," he rather wrote, " to rest in oblivion and wretchedness than to owe one's rise to a surrender of one's dignity, or of the interests of one's country." " They write to me from the provinces," so he confided to Eugénie, " that the reaction in my favour is making progress, but I confess that I follow the flow of events without forming any very ardent wishes that they should turn to our advantage. The sight of France laid waste, and laid low, is not made to arouse ambitions." [2]

" I shall say nothing to you," he wrote to La Valette, " of the things which are happening, for there is too much to say of them, and you must guess all the feelings which rend my heart. I lean on this last word, for one may really say that the heart is rent and torn when it is the prey of so many impressions and so many contradictory impulses.

[1] P. Guériot : *Captivité de Napoléon III.*
[2] *Revue des Deux Mondes*, 1st October, 1929.

Love of my country, hatred of those who govern it, horror of being in a foreign land, longing for peace, scorn of grandeur, regret for the soil of one's birth, the wish for rest and ardour to struggle anew, such are the preoccupations which fight together daily in my soul." [1]

It was torture to be able to do nothing, but no matter what his sufferings, he could in the most trying experience, keep an equal mind. "As long as the country lacks its due experience of a government which has no strength, is unable to guarantee order, and compromises prosperity, it will not come back to us; to appreciate one must compare," he wrote. "I receive the most absurd proposals. Someone advised me to ask him who is the master to-day to intervene to give me back my properties. I answered that, if it must be, I would humiliate myself to obtain better conditions for France: but for me personally, I would rather eat black bread than ask anything for my own personal interest. I cannot understand how people can fail to conceive the dignity which one should maintain in misfortune." [2]

4

Both the King and the Queen of Prussia went far out of their way to show every kind of courtesy and attention to their Imperial captive, nor was there lacking at Wilhelmshöhe the company of faithful women. Lady Cowley was the first to come, bringing into His Majesty's presence once more with her joyousness, her good nature, and her little corkscrew curls,[3] a score of faithful messages. Contessa Castiglione appeared again, but not for long. The

[1] F. Wellesley: *The Paris Embassy*, app.
[2] *Revue des Deux Mondes*, 1st October, 1929.
[3] Maxwell: *Lord Clarendon*, ii, 285.

Countess of Montijo offered to come and console him. "My dear Countess," he answered, "I have just received your letter and I am most deeply touched by the generous offer you make me to come to Cassel to look after me with a mother's care. Indeed, I should be very pleased to see you; nevertheless, in my present position, I prefer to remain alone with those who have followed me here. I have even asked the Empress who wanted to come here to do nothing for the present. So I must beg you not to put yourself out, but I am not the less grateful for your kind attention. *Je vous renouvelle l'assurance de mon tendre dévouement, Napoleon.*"[1] Then came Madame de Mercy-Argenteau, who was summoned from her home at Chimay to carry an important message to Bismarck at Versailles. The Emperor's first concern was for the soldiers for whom he had capitulated at Sedan. He believed that they were cold and hungry, and what he had most at heart was that they should share the good treatment he was himself receiving from his enemy. And this his bewitching Ambassadress succeeded in gaining. But he had two other messages: one was that his son might be accepted in his place as the sovereign of France; the other that Belfort should be preserved to France lest enemies should make it a loaded revolver aimed at her heart, and that neither the French battleships nor Algeria should be forfeited. But for these Bismarck, with the English already aroused, was too shrewd to ask. Madame de Mercy-Argenteau came back to Wilhelmshöhe with the answer; she seated herself at the spinet and played Boccherini's minuet, and Martini's *Plaisirs d'Amour*. She offered to remain with him. But that he vetoed, and so, with a present of pearls that had been the possession of Hortense, this lady was sent back to her husband.

[1] Doctrines of the Duke of Alba; for facsimile see opposite illustration.

FACSIMILE OF LETTER OF THE EMPEROR TO THE COUNTESS OF MONTIJO
By courtesy of His Grace The Duke of Alba.

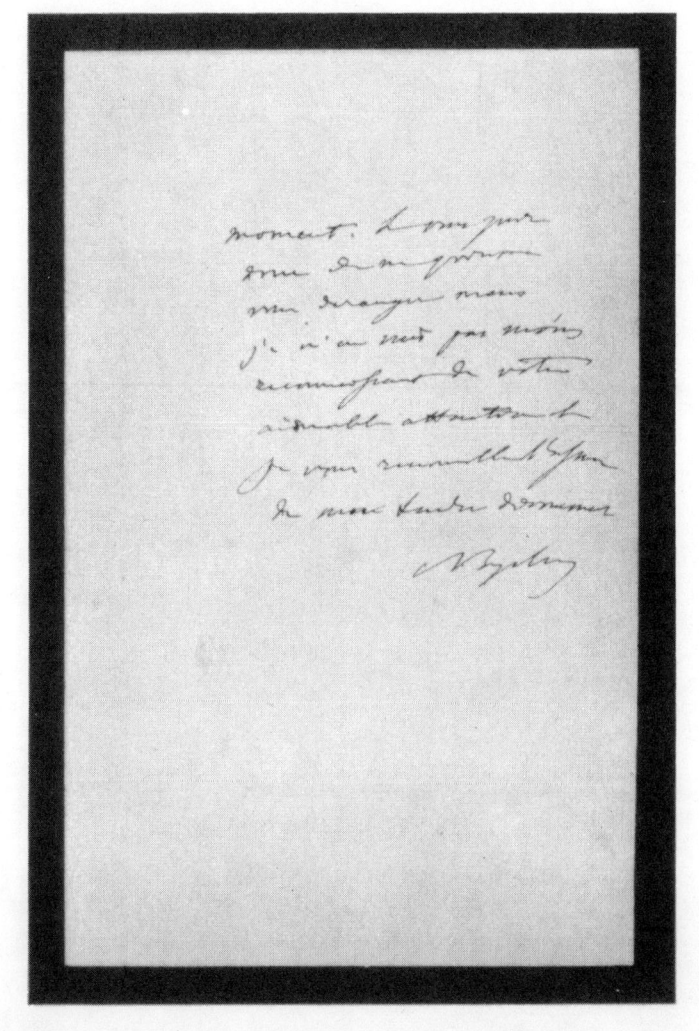

FACSIMILE OF LETTER, CONTINUED, OF THE EMPEROR TO THE COUNTESS
OF MONTIGO

By courtesy of His Grace The Duke of Alba.

When the door closed, she had remained beside it motionless till his valet led her away.[1]

It was on a November morning, after the fall of Metz, that Napoleon received the amazing news that Eugénie had arrived. Seeing that the Prussians had refused to treat with her, and that she could do no more, she determined to elude Bismarck, and to see him who, through all, was still her husband, and to whom she now felt a tenderness that she had forgotten for many years. He was ill, he was a prisoner, he was dethroned. Those were the facts that arose above all memories and melted her heart. She expected no effusive greeting, but as the Emperor received her at the door of the castle, the words he spoke were conventional in the extreme. She was abashed. It was not until they found themselves alone that he could trust himself to speak otherwise. His manner could not have been called formal then.[2]

In the afternoon the German General called, and greeted her with the courtesy he was wont to show to sovereigns. But, fearing interference from Bismarck, she dared not remain long. She said to the Germans no word of her departure. Instead, that evening she took her carriage and, with Count Clary, dismissed it before she reached the station. Still alone with Clary, she took the first train passing through Cassel. She went to Hanover, and then The Hague.

5

The prisoner of Wilhelmshöhe had no Montholon or Las Cases in his suite to write his memorial. He was better served by the witness of his enemies. General von Monts, who was in command at Cassel,

[1] Mercy-Argenteau : *Last Love of an Emperor*, chs. xv, xviii.
[2] A. Filon : *Souvenirs sur l'Impératrice Eugénie*.

felt like almost every German that Napoleon was to blame, and his bitterness had been increased by the death of his son in the war. When the Emperor had first arrived at the station, Monts had refused to lend him his carriage. But in a short time, his prisoner had captured him. The Emperor, for example, said quite frankly that, even at the risk of losing his crown, he should have resisted the current of opinion which made the war practicably inevitable. But it was less in the generosity of his opinions as an enemy than in his courtesies and his humanity that Napoleon III impressed the German general. It was the tenderness in his expression when the Empress or the Prince Imperial was mentioned, it was the warmth with which he interceded for the life of a stray dog which had followed him in the park, offering all sorts of sums to keep it fed; it was his thoughtfulness for the German servants; it was above all his insistence that the sentinels should have warm underclothes and cloaks.

The other German witness, Mels, was a journalist, a contributor to *The Times*, and a Jew. To this man, who rapidly won his confidence, Napoleon did speak of the weakness of the French in their disloyalty to the centre of unity, the throne; and of the treachery of Trochu, who had betrayed the Empress at the last. Such animadversions were part of the statesman's consciousness which leaves us in the records of this man so many memorable sayings, those sayings which recall his big part in European history. His defence of his own reign was sound. His remarks on Germany are highly significant. He pointed out that up to the time of Bismarck the French view of Germany had been always affectionate, at times enthusiastic. And this was Napoleon's own impression. " It was a fine country, a country of which I was very fond, and where one could be very happy. In the course of a life full of adventures, joys and sorrows, I have often felt homesick for Germany. I was far from suspecting that my wishes to get back to your country were to be fulfilled in such a way as this!"

Napoleon already doubted, as all Frenchmen doubt, whether Bismarckian Germany was as hale and strong as the winning Germany of Goethe. "Do you know," he asked, with one of those curious anticipations of the future which give him such significance to-day. "Do you know what the dream of a united Germany will cost you? A price which I hope will cure once for all those who let themselves be carried away by fancies of sovereign power. In spite of herself, yes, I really believe it will be in spite of herself, Prussia in twenty or thirty years will be forced to become aggressive. And then, all her clever turns of diplomacy, all the valour of her troops will avail her nothing. Europe will crush her. Then it will be seen what Bismarck's dreams have cost her."

"But there, we cannot agree," he said with a smile to his German journalist, taking hold of both his hands. "You will forgive me if I have rubbed your patriotism the wrong way." [1]

Such distinctness of vision, combining with such manners, give Napoleon III a quality surely not short of greatness. Perhaps we shall better appreciate it if we contrast with it the bearing of his adversary during those winter months.

For at this very time that the Emperor was thinking of how he could avoid hurting the feelings of a German writer, improve the lot of German soldiers, and save the life of a German dog, Bismarck was noting with

[1] Mels: *Wilhelmshöhe*.

triumphant scorn the starvation and the illness of poor children in France. " His insistence on the bombardment of Paris, his scorn at ' the English catchwords of humanity and civilization ', his jeers at the sufferings of the civil population and the children in Paris, the dinner-table ridicule of the appeals and tears of Favre and Thiers—by these and fifty other similar self-revealing acts, recorded and gloated over by Busch, and the jackals of the backstairs, he proved that he neither wished, nor intended to be generous . . . Behind the impressive record of achievements lies an unforgettable chronicle of envenomed pettiness and coarse brutality." [1] Such are the words of an admirer, and for the most part they are founded irrefutably, not on French, but on German evidence. But Napoleon III did not speak in such terms. When in conversation with Count Benckendorff a few months later the name of Bismarck was mentioned, the Emperor paused. Then " C'est un homme fort remarquable " he said —no more.[2]

6

When the Emperor arrived at Cassel, the crowd were hostile to him : and it was with a singular mingling of resentment and curiosity that the citizens of Cassel would gather to see the fallen enemy of Germany go by. But as that short ungainly figure approached, with his slow step—as they saw his large head bending to the right, the waxed moustache, the little pointed beard, the heavy curve of the nose —the mysterious power of the man would gather in his eyes, and with a gesture of extreme courtesy

[1] G. Grant Robertson : *Bismarck*, p. 278.
[2] Baron A. Mayendorff's *Papers*.

he would acknowledge the presence of the crowd.[1] And then as he passed on, among his staff, those simple Germans would find that an uninvited idea was being welcomed in their minds. Their reverence of kingship as kingship had overcome their antipathy to the enemy, and allowed his magnetism to persuade them that here was indeed a heart of kindness and goodness, a man they could revere and trust.

And towards the close of his imprisonment a suggestive incident gave new confirmation to this growing conviction. On the 2nd March an A.D.C. arrived with a telegram from the Queen of England, warning him to prepare for a weight of bad news. What the news was the German journalist knew, and taking it in his hand, he went to meet the Emperor in the garden of the castle. But, when the Emperor saw Mels with the telegram, he did not look at it. He remembered that the journalist had just lost his little daughter. Taking the message with one hand, he held with the other the hand of the sorrowing father. He thought only of the words he owed to the man in mourning. " What Napoleon said to me I do not know," wrote Mels, " but his words came from the heart, for I felt that they touched mine."

" And now," said the Emperor, " don't bother any more about me. Your place is with your own people." [2]

As Mels turned, the Emperor's staff came up to open the telegram. But His Majesty waited till the little Jew had disappeared at a bend of the path. Catching his eye, Napoleon raised his hat. Only then did he open the telegram. It told him that the vote of France had turned finally against him.

[1] Mels : *Wilhelmshöhe*.
[2] Mels : *Wilhelmshöhe*, p. 188.

XVIII

DEATH WAYLAYS

> Why, just at first
> I was quite simply, credulously glad
> To think the old life stood again for me,
> Like a fond woman's unforgetting heart,
> But now that death waylays me—now I know
> This isle is the circumference of my days,
> And I shall die here in a little while.
> So also best, Fallopius,
>   For I see
> The gods may give again but not restore.
> And though I think that, in my chair again,
> I might have argued my supplanters wrong
> In this or that. . . .
>   Yet other ways
> It may be that this dying serves the turn.
>   EDITH WHARTON : *Vesalius in Zante.*

I

"WHEN I am free, it is in England that I would wish to go and live with you and Louis in a little cottage with bow windows and climbing plants." So a fortnight after his arrival at Cassel, Napoleon had written to Eugénie,[1] and in the strength of this hope, he had courteously declined a pressing offer of hospitality from that tiny but captivating island of Elba which, seven miles long and two miles broad, had been for several months the whole of the empire and kingdom of His Majesty Napoleon I.[2] On 19th March he had landed at Dover, and greeted wife and son with warm embrace. It had grieved him not to arrive in time for the

[1] *Revue des Deux Mondes*, 1st October, 1929.
[2] Montgomery Carmichael : *In Tuscany*, pp. 216, 217.

birthday of the Prince Imperial.[1] The English, remembering at last that he had always been a friend of England, welcomed him ; in a few hours he was at Camden Place, near Chislehurst, the old home of a woman he had loved, or thought he loved, after his escape from Ham. Through all those years a sort of link had been kept up, and even before the war had commenced, the owner had written to say that once again the house was ready.

There again his old courtiers gathered around him, and planned for his return. There they watched the ghastly adventure of the Paris Commune : there they learned that the mob had burned the palace of the Tuileries and the Château of St. Cloud. The riot and arson showed that Napoleon's reign had not been a sinecure. " All the Powers of Europe," he himself observed to Count Benckendorff, " will recognize to-day how difficult my task was when during my reign, I tried to take every possible measure to ensure order and stability." [2] Napoleon had realized that if a task remained to him, it was not for him to return to France : that he who passed so many years in exile must die in it. But he cherished the idea that with the return from captivity of the army of Bazaine, and the soldiers of the guard, a coup to restore the Empire was not unthinkable.[3] He listened to the Empress and her interminable reflections on the treachery of Trochu. He walked up and down with his arm in the arm of his son. He went for little changes to the Isle of Wight, and to Torquay where he found the hotel too dear. He was greeted by the Prince of Wales on whom, had he but guessed it, his mantle was to fall, for Edward VII never forgot either the politics or the

[1] F. Giraudeau : *Napoléon III Intime*, p. 446.
[2] Baron A. Mayendorff's *Papers*.   [3] Ibid.

tastes of the Tuileries. He received the Queen at Camden House, and thanked her for her innumerable kindnesses : with her he arranged that the Prince Imperial might go to Woolwich (not to Sandhurst, for the Prince of the Asturias was there already). His whole heart centred on this boy on whom he looked not only with a father's love, but with a sort of worship. When his pangs returned and warned him that the end could not be far away, his order was still that the Prince's work must not be disturbed.

"I found him," wrote Lord Malmesbury, "much more affected by the calamities of Paris and by the anarchy reigning in France than by his own misfortunes. The fact that the Communists were capable of such atrocities in the presence of the Prussian armies seemed to him the acme of humiliation." [1] At Chislehurst, in the autumn of 1872, he felt his strength finally failing, but one idea still hung upon his mind. It was that old idea which he had commended to Palmerston and the Queen in 1863 : the idea of a Congress, or rather of a League of Nations : "an International Council to watch over the affairs of Europe, to follow and study the various phases which the Relation of State to State might assume, and to interpret and explain treaties." He suggested that in connection with this Council, a code of International law should be gradually prepared. He even dreamed of an international parliament, charged with the formation of general laws to govern the relations of sovereign states.[2]

On this subject he wanted to write his last book, but something told him that his strength would fail before it could be done. The pain and illness were worse again in December ; Sir William Gull

[1] *Memoirs of an Ex-Minister*, p. 375.
[2] *Œuvres Posthumes*, p. 138.

and Sir Henry Thompson were called in to consult with Conneau and Corvisart. They diagnosed the presence of a large stone in the bladder, and decided that it must be removed.[1] Thompson operated on 2nd January, 1873, and again two days later. " One cannot tell you what he has suffered," wrote the Empress that week to Madame Cornu. " He has undergone, I think, the greater part of the miseries of mind and body which it is given to man to endure. Will not a cry of justice at last arise in this France which he has loved so much and which he loves enough still to silence these frightful calumnies which have caused him so much pain ? "[2]

A third operation was to take place at noon on 9th January. But when the English surgeon came in at half-past ten, and felt the patient's wrist, he could hardly detect the pulse, and realized that it was the end. Eugénie returned, but Napoleon did not recognize her. At any moment his breath and heart might fail. Some stimulants were given, and the priest was called : and then the Church prepared him for the final change. As the Roman athlete was prepared for his race in the *Circo Agonale*, so according to the ancient rite was the dying man strengthened for his ordeal. The sacred oil was pressed upon his eyes, his ears, his lips, his hands. The words of pardon were spoken. If indeed he repented of his intrigues and excesses, we are not told. He had already written in his will that he regretted the pain that any of his actions might have caused his Empress. At the last, and almost without knowing it, the old conspirator was borne up by the everlasting arms of the Church. The long file of mistresses had vanished : the stainless wife remained, and she was

[1] F. Schlagintweit ; *Krankheit und Tod des Kaisers Napoleon III.*
[2] *Lettres Intimes à Madame Cornu,* quoted in *Empress Eugénie,* p. 308.

leaning over him, with tears of sympathy and love. And then as his brain grew dark, one memory struggled forward. He turned to Conneau, and was heard to speak the name of Scdan. And then the breath ceased, and calm fell upon his livid features. When his son came in from Woolwich an hour later, and knelt to say " Our Father ", it seemed as though the Emperor were asleep.

2

Sedan ! But surely there was more than Sedan. Had the dying man looked back on the twenty-two years of his dictatorship, what scenes he could evoke ! He who had wandered so far in Italy as an insurgent, and who had languished so long in prison and in exile could recall experiences as brilliant as those of Malmaison and the Conqueror. He could hear again the great shouts which greeted his first progress in the South ; he could see the old veterans crowding back to worship him, he could hear the chisp-chasp of the trodden leaves as, with the young Countess de Teba on horseback beside him, he rode over them in the Forest of Fontainebleau ; he could see the Queen of England bending at Windsor to fix the Garter to his knee ; the King of Sardinia riding at his side through the streets of Milan that his aid had won ; the christening of his heir in Notre-Dame, with a Pope and a King as godfathers ; the Lake of Annecy surrounded by its mountains which he had made French, and himself with Eugénie in her gold burnous, moving over its waters in a barge of triumph—like Antony with an immaculate Cleopatra on the waters of a lovelier Cydnus ; the blue mirror of the African port, and the Arabs in turban and jewels gathered at Bab Azoun to do him homage ; the thick lips of Princess Metternich, after she had made one of those audacious sallies which for forty years after his fall were still to be the wonder of Vienna, and which for ten years were the highest salacity of his court ; he could see the ice on the lake of the Bois de Boulogne, while his slow legs skated stubbornly forward ; he could hear the rich soprano of Mrs. Moulton in the Court Chapel as she sang the *Agnus Dei* at High Mass. He could see his boy grow up the Son of France, and see his collection of the wonders of the world admired by sovereign after sovereign, and each of them his guests in the Tuileries and on the Champ de Mars. He could see the great of Europe gathered at his dinners, and his jewelled Empress, as she turned, throw down the table the sparkle of her glance.

He could see other scenes : Donna Virginia Castiglione in her cambric nightgown at Compiègne, the sweet eyes, the blooming presence of Lady Mary Craven, the curls and bosom of Madame de Mercy-Argenteau as, at the end of the underground passage into the Elysée, she sank into his arms.

He might have thought of solider things—of the order he had given to France, the railways completed, the production and commerce increased, the well-being of the people, the disappearance of unemployment, the free trade with England which had fed the people, the clearing, beautifying, rebuilding of Paris, the reservation of the Bois, the trees in the Champs Elysées, the sward of the Parc Monceau, the central arteries of traffic. He might have thought of the changes in Italy which he had made, and the Alpine frontier which he had secured against the great new country ; of the steadfast alliance that he had maintained with England ; of the new independence of Rumania which he had encouraged. Even the rise of Prussia and the unification of Germany he had championed, though they brought his fall.

He might have looked into the future, and seen that fall avenged, and his Empress there to see ; he might have seen an older fancy realized : the Austrian dominions broken up : the Ottoman Empire shrinking out of Europe. Poland and Rumania emerging as strong nations ; the Vatican making her settlement with Italy almost on the precise lines that he had so insistently commended ; Russia, crashing as he had foreseen, because there was nothing of his own ideals in her system. All that was to come. He was to be the Modern Napoleon—the man who by his work made, and prepared for, the Europe of which the founder of his dynasty had dreamed. For this we see to have been his fate : to have been the man of a time two generations later than his own : of a time which alike in its love of comfort, in its loose conscience as to the relations of men and women, in its taste for tobacco, for diversion, for careless spending, and international congresses, in its mingling of light pleasures with humanitarian generosities, in its ever present sense of the problems of unemployment, of communism, of the well-being of the workman : a time which in these things has trended back from a belief in parliamentary government to a dependence on dictators like himself. That is his significance : not to be recognized, not to be comprehensible, but in the light of what was done by the men who were young when he, more than any was the guiding, the prophetic mind of France and Europe. If we are to pluck out the heart of his mystery, we must look to ourselves for his explanation, as we shall find in his grotesque, his clumsy, and his generous figure, the type of ourselves. Disease gradually robbed him of the power hidden in the reactions of his temperament—the power which Lytton diagnosed and which Victoria understood—

but even in his weakness and his mistakes, he, as a Bonaparte, proved that there was in him, as in his more famous predecessor, an elasticity, a resilience, which make him a power when he seemed to have left the world branded as a failure. He completed the career of Napoleon I. Who has completed his own?

Even in the age which fulfils so many of his prophecies, and brings into the world of fact so many of his dreams, his memorable sayings have a cogency that is far from being exhausted. Even when his Empress saw his cause triumph, she might have noted that victorious France and victorious England seemed to have forgotten what Napoleon III never forgot, to be generous to his enemies, and to seek the welfare of their people. During the Crimean War he had Russian products at his Exhibition; at the end of the Austrian War, he had fallen in love with the Austrian Emperor. But, at Versailles in 1919, it was Bismarck's psychology which ruled, not that of Napoleon III. Clémenceau and English Conservatives were still insisting that the screw of starvation should be put on women and children rather than negotiate for a sane and enduring peace. Was France still to find her example in Bismarck? Had Germany nothing to learn from Napoleon III?

Let us remember still that he never tried to disturb the economic unity, the *Zollverein*, of Germany: still less did he ever dream of disturbing that of Austria-Hungary. In all his ambition for Poland, he never spoke of anything so ancient and provocative as giving her a corridor through Prussia. Though a partisan of nationality for Germany, for Italy, for Rumania, for Hungary, he maintained the ideal of concord, of peace, of unity among all nations. " It is civil war to fight in Europe," he loved to repeat. "The time for conquests is over," he said again. "I long for the time when the great questions which divide Governments and peoples can be settled peacefully by European arbitration . . . Let our only thought of obstacles be to overcome them, and of incredulity to confound it."

And his European ideal is no less cogent to-day than the social one which he was already promulgating a hundred years ago:

To admit any saving that without disorganizing the public service will allow the reduction of the taxes that press the hardest on the people, to encourage undertakings, which, by developing agriculture give work to those that want it; to provide for the old age of working-men by establishing benefit societies: to introduce into our legislation modifications tending not to ruin the rich for the benefit of the poor, but to base the prosperity of each in that of all: to restrain within proper limits the employment which depends on the State: to avoid the shameful tendency which leads the State to undertake works which private enterprise can do better.

" His ideal was peace within and among all nations —a peace founded on conciliation between men, on undeviating principles of authority, of moral duty, of love for the men who toil and endure, and on the dignity of the people as a whole."

Nor was it his habit to trust to any mechanical scheme either political or economic. He tried to remove the restrictions which hinder private enterprise. And to strengthen the same motive which gives the man with power and privilege a sense of his responsibilities, and to the poor their patience and their hope, he consistently encouraged religion, supporting the Church which was the most powerful spiritual instrument in France and in Europe, but also showing every courtesy and consideration to other denominations. He was not a theologian, probably not even a believer, but he looked towards heaven for a charity which men without the graces of an interior life too often allow their selfishness to stifle.

There are some men to whom one can look for theories and ideals more valuable than they attained in practice. So it is with this mixed man whose weaknesses are too gross to extenuate : but in France, as in Germany, such weaknesses are common ones, never regarded as monstrous. Looking indeed at Napoleon III—

> You
> Shall find there a man, who is the abstracts of all faults
> That all men follow.

For at least five and forty years it was his habit " to fill his vacancy with his voluptuousness ". But if he had the fault of Mark Antony, he had also much of the generosity, some of the grandeur. One—

> must not thinke
> There are evils enow to darken all his goodnesse.
> His faults in him seeme as the spots of Heaven,
> More fierie by night's blacknesse. Hereditarie
> Rather than purchaste. What he cannot change
> Than what he chooses.

That is the truer word to say of him, because it is the more sympathetic. And if his political importance was rather in the sense that he was a Rabbi ben Ezra, with projects nobler than his accomplishments, and also another Hernani, an agent of the forces round him, rather than their master, yet it must be remembered that his significance for the future was always bound up with definite principles actively exerted, with a dictatorial power maintained for more than twenty years and singularly fruitful, and with a gift to win and hold the hearts of men. " As long as I live I must regret him," wrote the Queen of Holland when she heard of his death. "It was impossible to know him in his intimacy without admiring and loving his patience, gentleness, unselfishness." [1]

He was far from being a hero. He was still further from being a saint. He was one of those whose taste for intrigue convinces them that the end justifies the means. We must not forget that, at the instigation of Cavour, he, for Italy, played many of the tricks which in the case of Bismarck were afterwards turned against him. But he remained for those among whom he lived both solicitous and lovable. It was not only his mistresses who were his admirers. Both his mother and his son adored him, and his wife, at the end, wrote that there was something in his gentleness which made her think of Christ. There is much in his story which can be explained only by his personal magnetism. Behind that magnetism nevertheless was also a warm and deep benevolence: a regard not only for his people, and his country, but also for Europe, if not for the world. There, it was said, was a man who was really good to everyone.[2] He was generous to his enemies: he was always faithful to those who had befriended him. Among his courtiers, there was not one but loved him; long after his death the peasants remembered his reign as a golden age, and the veterans of his defeated army, when they heard his name, felt a straining at their hearts, and the tears started to their eyes, so warm was their devotion to him who, with all his oddness, all his failings, all his contrasts, and all his surprises, was not quite unworthy to be the last, for he was also, both in will and deed, the kindest of their Sovereigns.

[1] *Lady Burghclere's Papers.*
[2] A. Carey: *Empress Eugénie in Exile*, p. 560.

SOURCES

THE Sources of the Earlier Part of the Life of Napoleon III and indeed up to 1858 have been dealt with so elaborately by Mr. Simpson in his two volumes, *The Rise of Louis Napoleon* and *Louis Napoleon and the Recovery of France* and *Cambridge Modern History* that it is better to refer my readers back to them. My notes show my dependence on the *Mémoires de la Reine Hortense*, and the *Mémoires* of Valérie Masuyer published in 1914, and 1915 in the *Revue des Deux Mondes*. To these must be added those of Princess Mathilde, and of the Duc de Morny published in the same review. The classic source for the period is *The Life of Napoleon III* by Blanchard Jerrold.

I do not touch unpublished sources before Chapter V. There I have availed myself of the report of Maupas in the *Papiers de Cerçey*, and the dispatches of Hübner, now in the national archives at Vienna. *The Secret of the Coup d'Etat* by the Earl of Kerry and Professor Allison's *Monsieur Thiers* are also new material. I am the first to make references to the *Morning Post* for the period : that paper was then in very close relations with the French Embassy, and performed in England a function similar to that of the *Moniteur*.

In Chapter VI, I again make use of the *Morning Post* and Hübner's dispatches, especially of his intimate and vivid relation of the Emperor's courtship. I continue to make use of the Masuyer reminiscences, in the *Revue des Deux Mondes*, and begin to draw on the thirty volumes of the 1st Earl Cowley, from whose papers Colonel Fred. Wellesley has already drawn the materials of his valuable and fascinating book, *The Paris Embassy*. I find more fresh material in the Life of the Countess of Montijo (*La Condesa de Montijo*) by Señor Klanos y Torriglia, the *Entretiens avec l'Impératrice Eugénie* by M. Paléologue, and my own *Empress Eugénie*. For private information I draw on Miss Amy Paget who remembers that given by her kinsman, Lord Cowley. I owe one detail to Major Oakley, whose mother, Lady Oakley, was at school with the Empress.

In Chapter VII, I am able to give an entirely new account of the Emperor's activities in the Crimean War from his *Conversations* with Cowley. Other valuable sources of information are the MS. in the Archives of the Quai d'Orsay, and the unpublished letter of Merimée placed at my disposal by Dr. Lepelletier. Newly published sources for this chapter are Merimée's *Letters to the Countess of Montijo*, and Mr. Hector Bolitho's *Albert the Good*.

For Chapter VIII my new sources are again the Cowley Papers. The later part of this chapter is based on a leading article written by myself on Paris in *The Times Literary Supplement*, 15th May, 1929. To this I have added a few details from the new book of M. André Bellesort : *La Société du Second Empire*.

For Chapter IX, I have, as unpublished sources again, the Morny Papers, the Cowley Papers, and the archives of Paris and Vienna, and the unpublished letters of Merimée : and as new published sources the first volume of the *Carteggio Cavour Nigra*, the *Cavour* of M. Paléologue, and the important paper of Monsieur A. Pingaud, *Un Projet d'Alliance Franco-Russe*, and again Colonel Wellesley's *Paris Embassy*.

For Chapter X my unpublished sources are again the Merimée letters of Dr. Lepelletier, the archives of the Quai d'Orsay and Vienna, and the Cowley Papers. Of newly published sources, the *Carteggio Cavour Nigra*, and A. L. Dunham's *Anglo-French Treaty of Commerce* are the more important, as well as the *Cavour* of M. Paléologue. I have also made particular use of *The Times*. The War Correspondent of the *Morning Post* was at this time George Meredith.

The classic sources for the episode are :—

General Fleury : *Mémoires*.
Randon : *Mémoires*.
Macmahon : *Mémoires*.
Marquis de Massa : *Souvenirs*.
G. Panzini : *Il 1859*.

XI. In this chapter, my unpublished sources are again the Vienna archives and the Cowley Papers.

The latest books on the period are :—

J. Maurain : *Politique Ecclésiastique du Second Empire*.
Mollat : *La Question Romaine*
Paléologue : *Cavour*.

The classics are :—

The Pamphlets of M. de la Gueronnière.
Marquis de Ségur : *Recits d'un Frère*.
General de Lamoricère : *Mémoires*.
General du Barail : *Souvenirs*.

Thouvenel's *Secret de l'Empereur* and Pierre de la Gorce, vol. iv, are both particularly valuable. Most French books on this subject are biased by anti-clerical feeling. Of this *Rome et Napoléon III* by E. Bourgeois and Claremont, though masterly, is not free.

XII. The unpublished sources are again the Cowley Papers, and the archives of Paris and Vienna.

New published works are :—

Dr. Engels-Janosi : *Rechberg*.
Archives Diplomatiques relatives à la Guerre de 1870.
L. D. Steefel : *The Schleswig-Holstein Question*.
Riker : *The Rise of Roumania*.
W. Oncken : *Die Rheinpolitik des Kaisers Napoleon III*, which, though free from errors, must be read with caution on account of its omissions.

XIII. The unpublished sources are the Record Office, the Vienna archives, the Cowley Papers, the Quai d'Orsay, the Duke of Alba's archives ; I have also used certain numbers of American newspapers.

Of published sources in recent years are the monumental and exhaustive volumes of Count Egon Cæsar Corti, *Maximilian and Charlotte in Mexico*. On Napoleon's relation to the American States very little has been printed : and this chapter incorporates, therefore, new material except where it follows Count Corti.

Chapter XIV. The unpublished sources are Merimée's letters, the Cowley Papers, Lady Burghclere's papers, the Vienna archives, and the Record Office.

Of published material the new sources are :—

Empress Frederick's Letters.
Oncken : *Rheinpolitik*.
R. Sencourt : *Empress Eugénie*.
Baroche : *Souvenirs*.
Salomon : *Ambassade de R. Metternich*.

XV. The unpublished sources are the Record Office (which is particularly valuable in its letters from Lord Lyons), Lady Burghclere's letters, and the Vienna archives.

The Last Love of an Emperor, by the Countess de Mercy-Argenteau, provides very valuable details, but is not always reliable. Much new information as to this period is to be found in Dr. Oncken's *Rheinpolitik*. Book VI of the *Second Empire* by M. de la Gorce is very illuminating, and Vitzthum's *Denkwurdigkeiten*, as well as, of course, *L'Empire Libéral* of Emile Ollivier. M. R. Salomon's *Ambassade de Richard Metternich* is the most important of the new books.

XVI. The long controversy on the origin of the war is best

discussed in Professor R. H. Lord's *Origin of the War of 1870* with several newly published documents, and M. Salomon's new book *L'Incident Hohenzollern*. M. Paléologue's *Entretiens* adds details. All the protagonists wrote their memoirs, but few indeed are reliable on either side.

As for the part the Emperor played in the War, the following are the authorities :—

Comte de la Chapelle : *Œuvres Posthumes de Napoléon III*.
Baron A. Verly : *Les Étapes Douloureuses*.
General A. Lebrun : *Mémoires*.
Wimpffen : *Mémoires*.
Trochu : *Mémoires*.

There is much new information in the Emperor's own letters, *Revue des Deux Mondes*, 1st October, 1929, of which a part was originally published by F. Giraudeau : *Napoléon III Intime*.

XVII. Unpublished information from Lady Burghclere's papers.

The other new information is in the *Paris Embassy* and the Emperor's Letters, *Revue des Deux Mondes*, 1st October, 1929. *La Captivité de Napoléon III*, by P. Guériot, is a new book, and admirable.

The sources are :—

General von Mont : *Captivite de Napoleon III*.
Melhiel's : *Wilhelmshöhe*.
Mercy-Argenteau : *Last Love of an Emperor*, but again not always reliable.

XVIII. Unpublished sources, Lady Burghclere's papers.

Newly published, *Revue des Deux Mondes*, 1st October, 1929, for the Emperor's letters ; *Le Correspondant*, 25th August, 1920, for *Lettres Intimes à Madame Cornu* from the Empress Eugénie. *Krankheit und Tod des Kaisers Napoleon III*, by F. Schlagintweit.

The classic sources are :—

Filon : *Souvenirs sur l'Impératrice Eugénie*.
W. Jerrold : *Life of Napoleon III*, vol. iv.
F. Giraudeau : *Napoléon III Intime*.

This list would be incomplete without a reference to the light thrown on the whole period by Baron Beyens in his *Second Empire* and M. Paléoloque in his *Entretiens avec l'Imperatrice Eugénie*.

No student of the period can be ignorant of the work of M. Seignobos or the classic volumes of M. Pierre de la Gorce.

INDEX

A

About, 125
Aladénize, 76
Alba, Duke of, 135
Alba, Duchess of, 183
Albert, Prince Consort, 149, 152–3, 155, 156, 158–9, 163, 225
Alexander I, Emperor of Russia, 24, 25
Alexander II, Emperor of Russia, 168, 187–9, 194–5, 197, 200, 219, 252, 292–3
Alexandre de Beauharnais, 14
Alphand, 180
Anne of Austria, 178
Antoine Bonaparte, 67, 301
Antonelli, Cardinal, 237–8
Azeglio, Massimo d', 217

B

Barail, General du, 129
Baroche, Madame (quoted), 305
Bassano, Duke de, 21, 127
Baudelaire, 183
Bayard family, 57
Bazaine, 274, 275, 326, 332, 333, 363
Béchavet, 93
Bellanger, 265
Belgrave, 180
Benckendorff, 189, 360, 362
Benedetti, 315, 320
Berezowski, 292, 294
Bernard, 201, 202
Berthaud, 89
Bertrand, Abbé, 30
Beust, 259, 318
Bismarck, 166, 256–9, 261, 280–291, 295, 297, 299, 313–320, 345, 347, 358–9
Bixio, 190
Blanc, Louis, 83
Blessington, Countess of, 70, 79, 90, 91
Boulay de la Meurthe, 119
Bourquenay, 165

Bugeaud, 98
Bulwer Lytton, afterwards Lord Lytton. See Lytton
Buol Schauenstein, Count, 193, 205

C

Cambridge, Duke of, 153, 156, 165, 193, 205
Camp, Maxime du, 108
Canrobert, 325
Capua, Prince of, 70
Caroline Murat, Queen of Naples, 23
Castellane, Maréchal de, 8
Castiglione, Countess, 191, 195, 196, 303, 355, 367
Cavaignac, 98, 99, 105
Cavour, 166, 190, 192, 196, 198, 205, 206, 207, 217, 218, 226, 227, 239, 241, 261, 288, 372
Changarnier, 326
Charles V, King, 38
Charlotte, Empress of Mexico, 274, 286
Charrière, 118
Châteaubriand, 231
Chevalier, Michel, 223
Clarendon, 4th Earl of, 127, 147, 148, 166, 168, 312
Clothilde, Princess, 197
Cobden, 223
Colonna, Prince, 183
Col-Puygellier, 76
Conneau, 79, 88–9, 190, 265, 365, 366
Cornu, Madame, 85, 97, 191 n., 193, 265
Corvisart, 365
Coutts, Thomas, 57
Cowley, 1st Earl, 120, 126, 129, 133, 136, 143, 144, 150, 154–5, 159, 165, 166, 167, 171, 187, 191, 192, 205, 206, 207, 208, 226, 242, 244, 255, 259, 273, 277, 282, 297
Cowley, Countess, 355
Craven, Lady Mary, née Yorke, 367
Cuza, Prince, 251

378

INDEX

D

Decazes, 20
Dellessert, 65
Diderot, 235
Disraeli, 70
Doudeauville, Duke de, 135
Drouyn de Lhuys, 124, 136, 167
Ducrôt, General, 336
Dufraisse, Maret, 123
Duhamel, M. Georges, 277
Dumanoir, 323

E

Edward, Prince of Wales, afterwards Edward VII, 163, 258, 363
Eglinton, Earl of, 71
Elizabeth, Empress, 294
Ely, Marchioness of, 183
Essling, Princesse d', 127
Eugène de Beauharnais, 14, 15, 21, 23, 24, 31
Eugénie de Guzman, Empress of the French : Sees Louis Napoleon prisoner, 65 ; repels his advances, 113, 135 ; captivates him anew, 136-8 ; her character, 139-143 ; shows alarm, 150 ; talks to Cowley, 154 ; visits Windsor, 155 ; has no great trust of ministers, 167 ; writes to Cowley about Bernard, 201-2 ; welcomes Emperor home, 222 ; loyal to the Pope, 242, 245-8 ; opposes Moslems, 251 ; and supports Emperor's foreign policy, 252-3 ; impressive and able, 265-6 ; encourages Mexican royalists, 273, 275 ; weeps at Maximilian's death, 293 ; goes to Constantinople, 303 ; and Egypt, 305-6 ; dangerously patriotic in crisis, 314 ; but not more responsible for war than others, 319-320 ; has misgivings, 321 ; sees Emperor go, 323 ; her lost regency, 331-2 ; receives letter from fallen Emperor, 349 ; abdicates, 351-2 ; comes to Wilhelmshöhe, 356-7 ; sees Emperor die, 365.
Evans, 352

F

Favre, Jules, 95, 196
Flahault, Charles de, 103, 107, 292
Flaubert, 183, 184
Fleury, General, 211
Fleury, Louise, 23,
Fortoul, Madame, 138
Fould, Achille, 120, 245-6
Franz Josef, Emperor, 121, 196, 206-7, 215, 219-222, 294
Frederick, Prince of Prussia, 218, 288, 348
Frederick, Princess of Prussia, 283, 285, 257
Frederick VII, King of Denmark, 257
Froehner, 264
Fry, Miss Joan, 82

G

Garibaldi, 293
Gautier, 172
Gerbner, 27, 46
Gioberti, Lorenzo, 221
Gladstone, 221, 318
Godefroy de Bouillon, 351
Gordon, Madame, 65
Gortschakoff, 188
Gramont, 315, 316, 320
Granville, 2nd Earl, 36, 121, 122, 189
Gricourt, 67
Guizot, 80, 104, 308
Gull, Sir William, 364

H

Haussmann, 124
Henry IV, 182
Holland, Lord, 57
Hortense, Queen, 13-29, 34, 37, 38, 42-50, 55-6, 58, 62, 68-9, 103, 353
Houdetot, Count, 55, 56
Howard, Miss, 90, 91-2, 101, 113, 138
Hübner, Baron (afterwards Count), 100, 102, 126, 136, 143, 196, 204
Hugo, Victor, 125, 130, 173

I

Isabel, Queen of Spain, 189

INDEX

J

Jérome Bonaparte, King of Westphalia, Prince of Montfort, 41, 63, 175, 352
Johnson, President of U.S.A., 275, 276
Johnson, Samuel, quoted, 270
Joseph Bonaparte, King of Spain, 22, 28
Josephine, Empress, 13, 14, 132
Juarez, 271, 276, 293
Julius Cæsar, 244
Jurien de la Gravière, 274

K

Klindworth, 298

L

Lacordaire, 231
La Guerronnière, 240
Lamennais, 130
Lamoricière, 235
Lansdowne, Marquis of, 183
Las Cases, 357
La Vallette, 354
Le Bas, Philippe, 30–32
Le Boeuf, 320
Lenoir, Richard, 119
Lennox, Lord William, 71
Léon, Count, 71
Leopold I, King of Belgium, 208, 277, 299
Leopold II, King of Belgium, 144
Lesseps, F. de, 185, 304
Letitia, Bonaparte, Madame Mère, 28, 40–41
Leuchtenberg, Duke of, 45
Lieven, Princess, 57, 187
Lincoln, Abraham, 275
Lindsay, Mrs., 55
Locock, Sir C., 171
Logan, 276
Louis Bonaparte, King of Holland, 13, 22, 25, 36, 39, 40, 41, 66
Louis XVIII, King of France, 25
Louis Philippe, King of France, 38, 43, 80, 84, 106, 130, 146, 160, 303
Ludwig, King of Bavaria, 295
Lyons, Lord, 310, 317, 351
Lytton, Lord, 70, 73, 83, 199, 318

M

Macmahon, Marshal, Duke of Magenta, 210–11, 216, 325, 330, 332–3, 335, 336, 337, 338, 339, 341
Magne, 173
Malmesbury, 3rd Earl of, 200
Mansart, 178, 179
Marie Amélie, Queen, 70
Marie Antoinette, Queen, 140
Marie Louise, Empress, 22, 121
Marguérite, General, 343
Marx, Karl, 99
Mastai-Ferretti, Count. *See* Pius IX
Masuyer, Valérie, 38, 39, 43, 44, 48, 63, 84, 125
Mathilde Bonaparte, Princess, 41, 63, 66, 113, 125, 304, 322
Maupas, M. de, 108, 109, 112
Maximilian, Emperor, 190, 272, 274
Mels, 358–361
Mentschikoff, 147
Mercy-Argenteau, Countess, 246, 302–3, 356, 367
Metternich, Prince Clement, 297
Metternich, Prince Richard, 228, 242, 244, 247–8, 252, 261, 289, 366
Millet, 183
Mocquard, 108
Monckton Milnes, 158
Montalembert, 117, 231
Montholon, Count, 357
Montijo, Countess of, 135, 138, 356
Monts, General von, 357, 358
Morny, Duke de, 23, 102–5, 107–110, 118, 127, 173, 174, 175, 186, 200, 243, 279
Mouchy, Duchess de, 304
Moulton, Mrs., 367
Murat, Prince Achille, 57, 127

N

Napoleon I, 13, 14, 17, 21, 26, 32, 33, 75, 162, 163, 179, 209, 362, 369
Napoleon II, Duke of Reichstadt, 22, 51, 121
Napoleon III: born, 18; paternity doubted, 20; an expansive child, 23; affectionate and frank, 24; sensitive, 29; at first badly

INDEX

taught, then better, 30; grows vigorous, 32; hears of death of Napoleon I, 32; has high ideals, 34; generous impulses, 35; dreamy and sensuous, 35; has curious eyes, 36; is a good sportsman with unstable temperament, 36; an amorous male type, 37; writes on defence of Switzerland, 38; joins his brother, 39; thought a carbonaro, 40; irreverent in Church, 41; arrested in Rome, 42; joins insurgents, 42; implores help of Mastai-Ferretti, afterwards Pope, 45; catches measles, 46; hidden from Austrians, 46; escapes to France, 47-52; loves conspiracy, 53; meets French officers, 55; enters Paris, 55; flees to England, 57; refuses to give up name of Bonaparte, 58; returns to Switzerland, 59; writes *Revue Politique*, 59, 60; has prophetic ideas, 61; considers marriage with cousin Mathilde, 63; Strasbourg adventure, 63-5; captured and exiled to America, 66; criticizes America, 67; sees his mother die, 68, 69; returns to London, 70; keeps a mistress, 71; his sport, 71; studies industrial life, 72; writes *Idées Napoléoniennes*, 72; impresses Lytton, 73; invades France, 75; captured, tried, and imprisoned in a fortress, 76, 77; grows rheumatic, 79; begins to write, 80; interest in unemployment, 81; and in the lives of the poor, 82; becomes more reserved, 83; takes advantage of his disabilities, 84; is reconciled to the Church, 85; becomes conscious of a life deliberately planned, 86; and waits new opportunities, 87; escape from prison, 88-9; and settles in London, 90; renews friendship with Lady Blessington, 91; and with Miss Howard, 92

Elected deputy in France in 1848, 94, 95; and claims his seat, 96; speaks in the Chamber, 98; defeats Cavaignac at the polls, 99; speaks at Lyons, 100; disliked by Thiery, 101; takes tone of authority, 102; meets Morny, 103; has control of army and police, 106-7; brings off *coup d'Etat*, 108; rides through Paris and is exhausted, 109; instals Miss Howard in Paris, 113; meets Eugenia de Guzman, 113; tours the South, 114; speaks at Lyons, 115; at Bordeaux, 116; mingles doggedness with tact, 117, 118; assumes title of Emperor Napoleon III, 120-122; proud of plebiscite, 122; reforms administration, 123; assists the poor, 124; brings his family around him, 125-6; and also old imperialists, 127; character analysed, 128-133; in love with Eugenia, 136-7; proposes to her, 138; anticipates Entente Cordiale, 144

Orders fleet to Dardanelles, 148; works hard for peace, 149; involved in complications, 150; declares war with Russia, 151; meets Prince Albert, 152; thinks of visiting Crimea, 153; visits Windsor, 155-6; Victoria depicts his character, 157; Pianori shoots at him, 159; receives Queen Victoria, 160-164; plans lines of peace, 165; annoyed with Palmerston, 166-7; impressed Clarendon, 168; intrigues with Cavour, 169; has an heir, 172; interest in commercial matters, 175; introduces building societies and irrigation, 176; improves Paris, 180-184; his conflicting motives, 185.

Doubts Morny's flatteries, 188; reserved with Russia, 189; intrigues with Sardinia, 191; doubts England, 193; joins Russia against Austria, 194; bombed by Orsini, 196; receives Cavour at Plombières, 197; his policy, 198; and deceptive bonhomie, 199; makes treaty with Russia, 200; feels English alliance endangered, 202; tours

Brittany, 203 ; integrity undermined by adultery, 204 ; conspires war against Austria, 208 ; wins battle of Magenta, 211 ; enters Milan, 213 ; wins battle of Solferino, 215 ; stops war, 219 ; confers with Franz Josef, 220–221 ; triumphal entry into Paris, 222 ; makes commercial treaty with England, 224 ; takes Savoy and Nice, 226–8 ; appears innocent, 229

Worships at Mass, 231, 233 ; supports the Church, 232 ; question of coronation, 238 ; plans diminution of temporal power, 240 ; protects Pope, 243, 246 ; dances with Empress, 248 ; plays with the map, 250 ; loses sympathy with Turkey, 251 ; and Russia, 252 ; cultivates Rumania and Poland, 252 ; desires international Congress, 253 ; becomes democratic owing to disease, 255 ; desires to avoid war over Schleswig-Holstein, 259 ; not always responsible for mistakes, 261 ; under-estimates Bismarck, 261 ; writes life of Cæsar, 264 ; faithful to old friends, 265 ; dominated by Empress, 206 ; listens to Mexican royalists, 270, 272 ; distrusts United States, 277

Interviews Bismarck at Biarritz, 281, 282 ; encourages Austro-Prussian war, 283 ; recognizes mistake, 287 ; reason of his policy, 288–290 ; popular in the country, 292 ; becomes Knight of the Order of Christ, 293 ; receives Franz Josef, 294 ; involved in Luxemburg affair, 296 ; devoted to Prince Imperial, 298 ; not eager for war, 289, 298 ; affair with Mercy-Argenteau, 302–3 ; party at Compiègne, 305 ; surrenders to Ollivier, 307–9 ; obtains great majority in plebiscite, 309 ; health weaker, 305, 310

Believes he can score off Hohenzollern candidature, 314 ; supports Gramont's foolish claims, 316 ; believes peace possible, 316 ; votes for war, 321 ; apprehensive, 322 ; ill, 322 ; leaves Paris, 323 ; under fire, 324 ; in torment, 325 ; resigns command, 326 ; leaves Metz for Châlons, 327–330 ; controlled by Empress, 331, 332 ; accompanies Macmahon, 333 ; in misery, 335 ; arrives at Sedan, 336 ; in battle, 338–343 ; surrenders, 345 ; meets King William, 348 ; goes through Belgium, 350, 351 ; to Cassel, 352 ; magnanimous in adversity, 354–5 ; writes Countess of Montijo, 356 ; impresses Germans, 358–361 ; comes to England, 362 ; plans international Congress, 364 ; dies, 365–6 ; his career, 367–371.

His modernness, 61–2, 82, 98, 116, 124, 125, 144, 156, 170, 173, 177, 184, 185, 190, 200, 224, 229, 246, 254, 277–8, 290, 357, 364, 367–8, 370

Napoleon Jérome, Prince, 41, 153, 165, 200, 267, 280, 300
Napoleon Louis, Prince, 15, 26, 29, 39–40, 42, 44, 45, 49
Napoleon Louis, Prince Imperial, 172, 222, 308, 328, 362, 364, 366
Nicholas, Emperor of Russia, 120, 121, 146, 147, 148, 149, 189
Normanby, 3rd Marquis of, 144

O

Offenbach, 183
Ollivier, Emile, 307, 308, 311, 314, 315–16, 321
Orloff, Count, 280
Orsay, Count d', 70, 92, 113
Orsini, 196, 222

P

Palmerston, Viscount, 66, 150, 166, 172, 184, 187, 223, 240, 258, 279
Paris, 124, 177–184
Parquin, 64
Peel, 223
Persigny, Fialin, Duke de, 63, 65, 127, 159, 302
Philippe Auguste, King, 178
Pianori, 159

INDEX

Pierre Bonaparte, 301
Pillé, Mlle, 305
Pius IX, Pope, 45, 145, 197, 227, 236–246, 293
Poniatowski, Prince, 183
Pourtalès, Countess, 304

R

Raglan, Lord, 158, 159
Rechberg, Count, 260, 285
Reille, General, 342, 345, 350
Reuss, Prince, 286
Roccaserra, 45
Rochefort, 300
Rothschild, James de, 169
Rouher, 173, 174, 262–3, 299, 306, 333
Rousseau, 275
Russell, Lord John, afterwards Earl, 187, 260
Russell, Lady Emily, 312, 313

S

Salamanca, 243
Sandeau, 183
Schuyler family, 67
Schwarzenberg, Prince, 121
Ségur, Marquis de, 239
Seward, 295
Seymour, 43, 48
Smith, Adam, 223
Somerset, Duke of, 70
Sophia, Queen of Holland, 260–1, 266, 295, 300, 372
Sophie, Archduchess, 145
Souza, Madame de, 23
Stendhal, 139, 184
Stéphanie, Grand Duchess of Baden, 23, 38, 56
St. Albans, Duchess of, 57, 70
St. Arnaud, 108, 112, 151
Ste. Beuve, 130–1, 264

Stratford de Redcliffe, Lord, 146, 148, 150, 168, 187
Sultan, 251

T

Taillandier, 65
Talleyrand, 22, 105
Talleyrand, Count, 228
Tascher de la Pagerie, Countess, 130
Thélin, 79, 88 89, 127, 265
Thiers, 20, 101, 102, 111, 123, 173, 190, 299, 320, 351
Thompson, Sir William, 365
Thouvenel, 193, 227, 245
Tirmache, 85, 127
Trochu, General, 330, 363
Troubetskoi, Princess, 189

V

Vaudrey, 64, 65
Veuillot, 231
Victor Emmanuel I, King of Italy, 166, 212–14, 216, 227, 241, 332, 366
Victoria, Queen, 134, 147, 153–4, 156–9, 160–4, 171, 195, 202, 208, 258, 364, 366

W

Wagner, 153
Walewski, 126, 137, 147, 148, 170, 175, 188, 198, 207, 218, 227, 280
Wellington, Duke of, 70
William, King of Prussia, 24
William I, German Emperor, 219, 258, 315, 348–9, 353
Wimpffen, General de, 339, 341, 347
Winterhalter, 183

Z

Zappi, Carlo, 43, 48, 54